Adobe Photoshop CS3 Extended

for 3D and Video

Chad Perkins

Adobe Photoshop CS3 Extended for 3D and Video
Chad Perkins

Copyright © 2008 by Chad Perkins

This Adobe Press book is published by Peachpit.

Peachpit
1249 Eighth Street
Berkeley, CA 94710
510/524-2178
510/524-2221 (fax)

For the latest on Adobe Press books, go to www.adobepress.com
To report errors, please send a note to errata@peachpit.com

Peachpit is a division of Pearson Education

Development Editor: Anne Marie Walker
Editors: Becca Freed, Nancy Peterson
Proofer: Eric Schumacher-Rasmussen
Production Coordinator: Myrna Vladic
Technical Editor: Wayne R. Palmer
Compositor: David Van Ness
Indexer: Valerie Perry
Cover Design: Mimi Heft
Cover Art Direction: Charlene Charles-Will
Cover Illustration: Jonathan Caponi
Cover Production: Mike Tanamachi

Notice of Rights

Notice of Liability

Trademarks

ISBN 13: 978-0-321-51434-9

ISBN 10:   0-321-51434-3

9 8 7 6 5 4 3 2 1

Printed and bound in the United States of America

To Heefee, Mikey, Natty, wedgekase,
and the First Wives Club.

Acknowledgments

Some amazing people have either directly or indirectly helped me with this book or in my career.

Hands down, the most important influence in my life is my wife, who has taken on the role of honorary single parent since I started writing this book.

Thanks to my beautiful kids. You amaze me every day with your wisdom, your humor, your ability to memorize lyrics, and your mad art skills.

My parents. Thank you both for all the lessons you taught me. I would never have attempted such a big task if it weren't for the passion for life and learning that you inspired in me.

Thanks to the Davies. You're the best! We love you to pieces.

Thank you to the phenomenal team that helped make this book possible. Thanks to Deke for referring me to my agent, Matt Wagner. Matt, thanks for all of your trust and help, and for connecting me with Pam Pfiffner. Pam thanks for getting the ball rolling. Becca Freed, thanks for your patience and direction. It was great working with you. And a mega super huge thanks to my editors, Anne Marie Walker and Wayne Palmer. You both offered such amazing insight and help. The book has greatly benefited by your wisdom and experience. Your feedback was never condescending or irritating, and your insights were always valuable. Without you, this book would have sold two copies, one to each of my parents. And then they probably would have sold them on eBay after reading them. Thanks also to all of the others at Peachpit who helped with screenshots, layout, and other tasks.

I must give credit to Ashley Still, John Nack, Zorana Gee, Michael Clifton, Pete Falco, and the rest of the Photoshop team. Your talents and ideas are inspiring. Photoshop is such a joy to use for so many different tasks, including the new 3D and video features covered in this book.

Special thanks to Lynda and Bruce for your incomparable kindness and down-to-earthness. You are truly great people and deserve all of your success. Lynda.com is one of the best sites on the Internet. Also thanks to Max, my right-hand man at lynda.com. And I must thank all the wonderful editors at lynda.com, particularly Paavo, Brian, Murphy, and Dustin for all of your help early on.

Thanks also to all of the people who have supported me. People from all over the world have offered kind words or purchased my training. In my line of work, I couldn't do what I do if it weren't for you.

Contents

Introduction

I am well aware that many readers skip right over the introduction. But I invite you to defy tradition and read this one, because it provides you with some very important information that you'll need to get the most out of this book. The new features in the Extended edition of Photoshop CS3 are very particular, and this intro may prevent you from banging your head against the wall because something won't work.

About Photoshop CS3 Extended

Photoshop CS3 introduced two new "flavors," or versions, of Photoshop: Photoshop (the standard version) and Photoshop Extended. We've all known and loved the standard version for years. Some standard versions, such as Adobe Flash or the previous versions of After Effects, are essentially just limited versions of their Professional editions. Such is not the case in Photoshop: You don't miss out on any features by sticking with the standard edition.

By using Photoshop Extended, you get all sorts of cool *new* features. You can now import and manipulate 3D files, moving and rotating them in their native 3D space. You can also see cross sections of 3D models and change their textures, camera angle, and lighting. You can rotoscope, bring in video, animate layers, interpret alpha channels, and more. You'll learn about all of these features and a whole host of other valuable features throughout this book.

You can even import video files that have audio, preview that audio in Photoshop, and export to a video file with audio output. But as you'll see in Chapter 6, "Video Basics," the audio capabilities of Photoshop CS3 Extended were a last-minute addition to the feature set, so they are difficult to figure out on your own. Photoshop's audio capabilities aren't even listed in the Help Viewer! I'll show you the secret of audio later on in Chapter 6.

Photoshop Extended also introduces several other new features for engineers, medical professionals, and other people that aren't me. Since engineering and biology aren't nearly as fun to study as a 3D sorceress who shoots out magic from her enchanted staff, I'll leave the more technical features for another book to cover. You'll have your hands full with just the 3D and video features of Photoshop Extended.

How Can I Tell Which Version of Photoshop I'm Using?

If you want to quickly discern whether or not you are using the Extended version of Photoshop, you can simply glance at the menu bar at the top of the interface. If you see an Analysis menu (in between the Filter and View menus), you are using the Extended version.

To take the world's most impressive and popular image editing software and add all of these new features is nothing short of revolutionary. Because Photoshop is used extensively in the postproduction workflow of many professionals, it will be exciting to see what creative professionals worldwide will do with these new tools. The mere existence of these new tools is a wonderful thing, but the real surprise is how complete they are right off the bat. If Adobe had just allowed the importing and moving of 3D files, I would have been happy. Very happy, actually. Fortunately, Photoshop's first attempt in these new arenas is a grand slam. I hope you enjoy using these new tools as much as I do.

Who Should Use This Book?

It is perfectly natural to question what benefit the new features in Photoshop Extended offer you. Maybe you're already a Photoshop user, or a 3D user, or a video user who is comfortable with your high-end workflow. Photoshop doesn't do 3D modeling or high-quality 3D rendering, and it doesn't do high-end video editing. So what's in it for you? The answer, of course, is "plenty." Let's take a brief look at what the Extended version of Photoshop offers each of these demographics.

Photoshop Users

Under the moniker "Photoshop users," I include all users of Photoshop, even if your workflow is print based. I'm addressing Photoshop professionals first because you might be tempted to think that there's nothing in this book for you. On the contrary!

Entering the complex 3D world

Maybe you've been intimidated in times past by professional-grade 3D and video software packages. If so, the Extended features discussed in this book will be right up your alley. What could be better than experimenting with these crazy new concepts inside the safe, familiar, and comfortable world of Photoshop? I've been working in 3D programs for years, and there's no better transition to the complicated world of 3D than Photoshop CS3 Extended.

Product mock-ups

How many times have you wanted to mock up a realistic DVD case, book cover, CD label, or soda can in Photoshop? It's actually not hard to create from scratch in Photoshop, because it's an amazing application. However, if you decide to edit those objects once they're created, you're in trouble. If you decide later that you'd like to change the "camera" view of the 3D object, it's probably easier to just start all over again than to try to manipulate and reposition what you've already made. Such is the plight of those operating in a 2D world trying to mimic a 3D world.

So, in the words of Led Zeppelin, it is to you I give this tune. The new 3D features of Photoshop allow you to bring in 3D objects and manipulate them in 3D dimensions. If your client or boss wants to view your DVD cover mock-up from the top instead of from the front, it's essentially a one-click fix. Or, if you want to swap out the musician on the cover of your CD mock-up, it's a simple cut and paste.

I've always loved the way a 3D wireframe mesh looks when used artistically and appropriately in designs. I'll show you how to do that in this book as well. Typically, to get access to a 3D wireframe, you need to go back to your high-end 3D program and change a bunch of settings there, then render out a still image of the wireframe. Not only is it much faster and more user friendly in Photoshop, but the image also maintains its original 3D attributes! You can move and rotate around the wireframe in 3D space as you please, and then quickly switch back to the regular textured version if you want to.

Removing unwanted objects with Image Stack modes

In Chapter 9, "Creative Video Techniques," I'll introduce you to a new feature of Photoshop Extended that allows you to take a series of photos and instantly remove any elements that change in the photo. This an invaluable tool for fixing, for example, photos of a city in which people walk in front of the camera, or a series of images with noise in them, or other such issues.

Using video in a print environment

And as far as video goes, you might take a still shot from a movie trailer to create a mock-up to woo a big name client. Or you might have a video you need to play at a big presentation that needs editing. No need to outsource that anymore! You can easily handle that task right from good old Photoshop. And even if you don't have video footage to use, you can create some from scratch in Photoshop Extended. You may have no clue how to do any of this, but you'll have these abilities down pat after completing this book.

3D Users

It is perhaps 3D users who benefit most from the new features in Photoshop CS3 Extended. Included in this demographic are architects, video game designers, graphic designers, those who create previsualizations for film and broadcast, engineers, motion graphics artists, scientists—the list goes on. No matter what your background might be, you can greatly benefit from the 3D features in Photoshop Extended.

Changing textures

Most likely, you already use Photoshop to alter textures applied to 3D objects. Photoshop now saves you a step by allowing you to adjust the textures of 3D objects within Photoshop CS3 Extended. You can then see the updated textures instantly applied to your model while you're still working on changes. For example, if you're creating a scar on the texture of a character's face, it's a tremendous benefit to see that mark show up on your 3D object immediately. If it's too large, or too small, or too gory, or whatever, you can change it then and there, all without leaving Photoshop.

Creating 3D worlds from a photo

In "Vanishing Point and 3D" (on the CD that accompanies this book), I'll show you how to use the enhanced Vanishing Point filter to create 3D worlds from any image. You'll convert a photo of a hotel hallway into a 3D scene and take a digital "walk" down the hall. You can also export these 3D scenes to 3D applications from the Vanishing Point filter.

Sending 3D objects for review

How many times have you wanted to show clients or friends a video game character, an invention, or a piece of real estate, only to be frustrated by the inability of a static image to show off your design? Imagine how easy it would be to just send them a PSD file with the entire 3D object and all its textures embedded in it. Others could then quickly and easily move and rotate it in 3D space to examine it from every angle. In Chapter 10, I'll share with you a third-party plug-in from Strata that allows you to embed 3D objects from Photoshop into a PDF file that can show 3D objects to all computer users, not just those with Photoshop.

Cross sections

Photoshop also has a very complete cross-section feature. The cross section that Photoshop creates won't display the backside of surface normals as transparent, so your cross section will look good from any angle. The cross-section feature in Photoshop works better than any comparable feature in any 3D program that I've used.

Video Users

Although Photoshop is not a full-featured video editing or animation application by any means, it does have many beneficial features that video users probably won't find anywhere else.

Painting on video

Of all the video programs I've ever used (or even heard of), none come close to Photoshop Extended's video painting capabilities. And painting on video is often needed in a video workflow. For example, you might need to paint over an actor's blemish, remove technical video hardware that accidentally made its way into the shot, and so forth. You can use Photoshop's wide array of Painting, Cloning, and Healing tools to get the job done.

Photoshop filters and video

You now have the ability to use Photoshop filters on video. In Chapter 9, you'll learn how to warp video using the Liquify filter and add postproduction lighting using the Lighting Effects filter, among others. The best part is that all effects and adjustments applied to video in Photoshop CS3 Extended are nondestructive and do not harm (or even alter) your source footage in any way.

Animated Layer Styles

Not only can Photoshop's huge collection of various Layer Styles effects be applied to video layers in Photoshop, but the various properties of the effects can be animated as well. For example, you can animate the size of an Outer Glow or animate its color to change over time. In Chapter 8, "Editing Video," you'll animate Global Lighting to simulate a time lapse shot.

Powerful color correction

Most professional video applications have a comprehensive set of tools for adjusting luminance and color in video. But few, if any, have the large suite of image altering tools that Photoshop has. In Photoshop CS3 Extended, you can apply any type of adjustment layer to video, use Blend modes, and perform many other image alterations.

Layer mask animation

With Photoshop's powerful brushes, you can create 8-bit grayscale layer masks. In Photoshop Extended you can also animate the position of those layer masks to reveal objects or to create other visually appealing effects.

Creating cel animation

You can also use Photoshop's rich brushes and drawing tools to create traditional cel animation. In Chapter 9, you'll look at features that are available to help you do this, including onion skinning.

Instant slide shows

Photoshop CS3 Extended includes a feature called Make Frames from Layers that creates an animation using your layers as frames. If you have a multilayer PSD file, you can slow the frame rate of your document and create a slide show using this command.

Using This Book

Your computer hardware and your prior knowledge of the aforementioned disciplines are very important issues to address up front. So let's review those topics, as well as how to use this book, its accompanying CD of exercise files, and bonus chapter.

Hardware Requirements

If you're like me, you completely ignore hardware requirements when installing a program. I always have a fairly solid computer that's never more than two years old with several upgrades in between. And when I do take the time to look at system requirements, they seem so rudimentary; for example, "make sure you're working on an Apple IIe or higher" or "you must have at least 16k of RAM." My computer usually has far more than enough power to run my applications.

Photoshop CS3 Extended is a *very* different story. It's not that Photoshop Extended requires a very hefty system, but it does have a lot of specific requirements. If your computer does not meet these requirements, you will not be successful when working with Photoshop's Extended features, particularly 3D. These requirements can be found either on the purchased software box or on www.adobe.com.

Prerequisite Knowledge

Because of the specific nature of this book, it is not a fundamental, start-from-scratch Photoshop book. I assume you know the most basic concepts, such as how to use the interface, what palettes are, what tools are, what layers are, and so forth. I don't explain them here.

That being said, I do my best in this book to remind you of and teach you many concepts that are very simple but essential. Even if you are new to Photoshop, you'll be able to follow along just fine. I'll also introduce you to new concepts pertaining to 3D and video. So, if you are new to these areas of study, I'll explain the basics, or at least the basics that pertain to Photoshop. It will be a great learning experience for you, no matter your background.

Reading the Book

The first six chapters in this book explore 3D using Photoshop Extended, and Chapters 7 through 10 cover video. I often build on concepts as you move from chapter to chapter, but feel free to skip ahead to any chapter that you'd like. Just keep in mind that I might reference 3D Object mode in Chapter 3 without stating what that is or how to get there because I covered that in Chapter 1.

Using the exercise files on the CD

On the CD that accompanies this book, you'll find a folder called Exercise Files that contains all the files referred to during the exercises in the book. The exercise files are organized by the chapter in which they are used. So, for example, all of the files needed to perform the exercises in Chapter 3 are in the Chapter 3 folder. I will refer to each folder throughout the book.

The bonus chapter

On the disc that accompanies this book, you'll also find a folder called Bonus Chapter. In that folder is a PDF file that contains an additional chapter, "Vanishing Point and 3D." Here you'll find all the ins and outs of what Vanishing Point offers 3D users, as well as 2D designers. In this chapter, I'll show you how to take an ordinary photo of a hallway, and turn it into a complete 3D environment, using nothing but Photoshop. Exercise files for the Vanishing Point and 3D chapter are also included on the disc.

Which Platform Should I Use?

Even though the screen shots in the book are Windows screens, Photoshop CS3 Extended works almost identically on both the Windows and Mac platforms. I'll provide keyboard shortcuts for both platforms each time they are mentioned in the book.

1

Photoshop's New 3D Abilities:

The Basics

Let's start out by looking at Photoshop Extended's new 3D capabilities. If you're a 3D user, you're probably already using Photoshop in your work, to either create textures or to touch up still renders. A little later on in the book, I'll show you a few additional new features in Photoshop CS3 (in both Standard and Extended editions) that are not specifically intended for 3D users but can be useful nonetheless.

Importing 3D Files

To bring 3D files into Photoshop, you can just open them as you would any other file. Choose File > Open, press Ctrl/Cmd+O, or if you're using Windows, you can use my favorite way to open files by simply double-clicking anywhere in the blank gray areas. If you'd like to follow along with the example in this chapter, you can go to the Chapter 1 folder (in the Exercise Files folder on this book's companion disc) and open the wizard lady.3ds file in the wizard lady folder (**FIGURE 1.1**) in Photoshop.

FIGURE 1.1 Use the wizard lady.3ds file to follow along with me. Pay no attention to the other files for now.

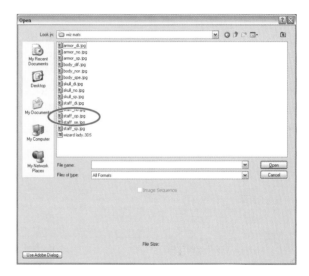

Vector-based 3D Technology

When importing a 3D file, a dialog pops up before the 3D file is actually imported, because Photoshop stores the 3D object in a new document. Any time you create a new document, Photoshop asks what dimensions it should be, and 3D files are no exception. So now the question to ask is "What size should I make my 3D file?"

The good news is that 3D technology is essentially vector-based. This means that you can scale images up as big as you'd like, and as often as you'd like, without losing any quality whatsoever. Such is not the case with Photoshop's usual fodder: pixel-based images.

While you can create a very large document to house your 3D file, you might also want to consider the impact on the size of your Photoshop document. As is the case with standard (non-3D) Photoshop documents, creating a larger document results in a larger file size.

The caveat is that many times your vector 3D objects will have raster (aka pixel-based) textures applied to them. When such objects are made larger, the quality of the textures decreases, but the quality of the 3D mesh remains crisp. Keep in mind that these same rules apply to 3D objects that you manipulate in Photoshop as well.

Consider this information when specifying the size of your file. If you have a 3D model without textures applied to it, you can create a document as large as you'd like. If you have raster texture maps applied to it (such is the case with our wizard lady here), you need to keep in mind the resolution of the texture maps when creating the file dimensions and when increasing the size of the object.

Finding 3D Files

I know from experience that sometimes it's a pain to use exercise files that come with a book, so if you'd like to, you can use one of your own 3D files. Alternatively, you can use one of the many 3D files that ship with Photoshop CS3. They're really sweet 3D models, but they can be hard to find. Be sure to install all of Photoshop's content as well as the program itself when you've downloaded the software.

If you've purchased Photoshop on a disc, you'll need to load the content discs and look for the Goodies folder in the Photoshop content. You can then place the files wherever you'd like.

If you've had Photoshop do the installation for you, go to the application's folder. On Windows, this will be in Program Files > Adobe > Adobe Photoshop CS3 by default. On a Mac, this will be in the Adobe Photoshop CS3 folder in your Applications folder by default. On both platforms, provided you've installed the content, you'll see a folder in the Photoshop CS3 directory called Goodies. Inside the Goodies folder is another folder called 3D models. All the folders inside this folder represent different 3D models (**FIGURE 1.2**). Some of these files are very useful (like the model of a DVD case), and some of them are just cool (like the Crude Robot). If you're new to the world of 3D, know that these 3D files are in Maya's .obj format. The other files in these folders (such as .mtl and .jpeg files) are just there to make the .obj files look better when opened in Photoshop. Think of them as good clothes and bronzer for your pale, naked 3D model.

FIGURE 1.2 Inside each folder is a 3D model in .obj format for you to play with. I'll be opening up one of my favorites, Crude Robot, a little later on in this chapter.

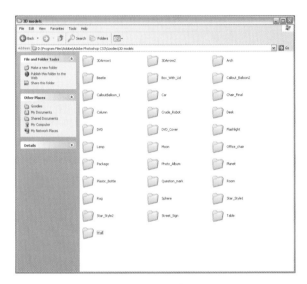

3D File Formats Recognized by Photoshop

This looks like a great time to cover the 3D file formats that Photoshop recognizes. I've already mentioned the file format .obj, which is from the 3D powerhouse Maya. Photoshop also opens the files from another great Autodesk application, 3DS Max, and recognizes its .3ds file format. As a fan of 3DS Max, I can tell you that this is among the most powerful of the file formats that Photoshop can import.

NOTE Maya is a product of Autodesk, which is a major player in the 3D software world. Autodesk creates the most popular software packages used in the film, video game, architectural, and engineering industries. This includes Maya, 3DS Max, and AutoCAD.

But the most powerful 3D format that Photoshop can understand is the .u3d (Universal 3D) format. This format can store camera, lighting, animation, and other types of data that can be read and utilized by Photoshop. This format is also recognized by Acrobat and Acrobat 3D, which makes sense because Acrobat and Photoshop share a common 3D engine. Even though the .u3d format is meant to be a universal standard 3D format, and even though it's the most powerful file format Photoshop can recognize, there isn't much support for it among the big, professional 3D software applications. At the time of this writing, there are also no free file format converters available. So, at the end of the day, as cool as .u3d is, it isn't that practical just yet.

Although it is even less popular than the .u3d format, Photoshop can also recognize the Collada format (.uae). Like .u3d files, the Collada format was created by a group of collaborating companies to become a standard 3D file format as well.

It's just the wackiest thing that even though there are so many file formats out there that were intended to be the standard, no one can figure out which one to use! Perhaps all the head honchos in the world of 3D just need to get together for one final, definitive round of Paper, Rock, Scissors to determine which file format is the actual universal format.

Additionally, Photoshop opens the Google format, .kmz. Officially, this is the file format of Google Earth 4, but it also can be seen in Google's entry-level architectural modeling program, Sketchup. There are some exciting things happening between Photoshop and Google, and I'll discuss another one of them later in Chapter 10, "Plug-ins and Resources."

Exporting a 3D File

Right about now you're probably wondering which 3D file formats Photoshop can export to. Unfortunately, there is no way to export a 3D file as such from Photoshop. The good news is that 3D files are embedded into your .psd (PhotoShopDocument) file once imported. When reopening .psd files with 3D files in them, the 3D layers retain their 3D behavior and nothing is lost. In other words, the .psd format is the only "3D format" that Photoshop can export to. I know, kind of a bummer, eh? But again, remember that this is Photoshop's first attempt at 3D. You can't expect a 1.0 release to include 3D, video, and masterful file conversion tools as well.

Transforming 3D Objects

Now that you know the basics about how Photoshop treats 3D files, you're ready to start manipulating them. I realize that this "manipulation" sounds cruel, but trust me, 3D models feel no pain. All we're talking about here is moving, rotating, and scaling 3D objects.

The New (and Hidden) Object Tool

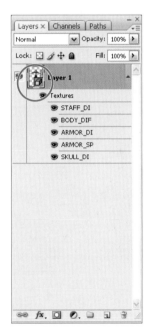

The first thing you need to know about using 3D in Photoshop is that you access almost all 3D features by using the new Object tool. Unlike other Photoshop tools, though, the Object tool is not available in the Tools panel. To access the Object tool, you need to double-click the layer thumbnail in the Layers panel of a 3D layer. A 3D layer is denoted by a little gray 3D box icon (**FIGURE 1.3**). Be sure to double-click the thumbnail (i.e., Preview) area, not the area where the name of the layer resides.

NOTE   You can also access these tools from the menus by choosing Layers > 3d Layers > Transform 3d Model.

TIP   So what exactly does the Object tool/mode do? For all intents and purposes, you'll do almost all of your 3D editing in the Object tool mode. If you want to move, scale, rotate, change cameras, change lights, see a cross section, and so on, you'll want to be in this mode.

FIGURE 1.3 This little gray cube on the layer thumbnail icon indicates that this is a 3D layer.

To avoid frustration of biblical proportions, you need to be aware that this "tool" acts more like a mode. With a regular tool you can select it, use it, and go on about your business. Not so with the Object tool. Using it is much like using Free Transform or creating text: Photoshop expects you to either accept or cancel any adjustments you make before moving on to something else. You can accept transformations made to 3D layers by clicking the check mark in the options bar at the top-right area of the interface (**FIGURE 1.4**). You can also press Enter/Return to accept changes. To cancel changes, click the circle with the slash through the middle (like the familiar "no smoking" signs) located on the options bar, or press the Escape key.

FIGURE 1.4 Use these icons to cancel or accept transformations, respectively.

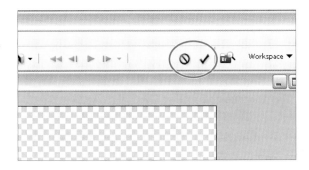

While you're adapting to the way this tool works, you'll probably forget about this little accept or cancel rule once or twice, so go ahead and just practice messing up so you know what to do. Double-click the layer thumbnail of your 3D layer to access the Object tool. Next, pretend to forget that you're in Object tool "mode," and try to do something else. Click a tool in the regular Tools palette on the left side of the interface. Of course, you know you can't do that until you accept or cancel out of Object tool mode. Violating the laws of man and nature by attempting to do something else while in Object tool mode opens a pop-up giving you three options: Apply, Cancel, or Don't Transform (**FIGURE 1.5**). Choosing Apply will apply all changes made since entering Object tool mode. Don't Transform will discard all changes made in the current session of the Object tool mode. Selecting either option will also exit the mode and take you back to Photoshop's standard tools. Cancel will close the dialog and return you to Object tool mode as if you had never tried to leave, effectively just canceling your cancellation.

FIGURE 1.5 You must pick one of these options before moving on. You can't leave 3D "mode" to use other Photoshop features until you do.

Using the Transformation Tools

When you first bring 3D objects into Photoshop, there is something inherent in your being that wants to spin it around in three dimensions. Or maybe it's just me. To be honest, the first time I rotated a character in 3D space in Photoshop, I think I might have cried just a little. I've never been so happy to see the backside of something. To manipulate the object in 3D space, make sure the Edit the 3D Object button is selected (**FIGURE 1.6**). Selecting that button ensures that you're using the same tools for transforming 3D objects that I'll be using in the following figures. We'll talk about its neighbor, Edit the 3D Camera, a few pages down the road.

FIGURE 1.6 The Edit the 3D Object button. Photoshop users the world over have been waiting to see that button in Photoshop for a long, long time.

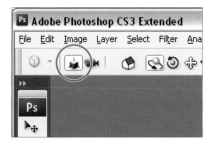

When you are in Edit in 3D Object mode, there are essentially six tools you use for navigation (**FIGURE 1.7**).

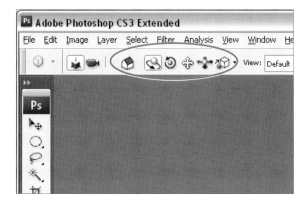

FIGURE 1.7 The six 3D navigation tools while in the Edit the 3D Object mode.

Return Object to Initial Position tool. The first tool looks like a little house. This little icon is the stuff nightmares are made of because, like the Haunted Mansion at Disneyland, there are no windows and no doors. Use this button to reset the view of your 3D object back to its initial position. This button is a total lifesaver. It's very easy (especially when new to the world of three dimensions) to move, zoom, or twist a 3D object to an undesirable extreme by accident. Click this button and you're back to square one. Just remember that once you've moved your object around and accepted the transformation, you've effectively created a new initial position. Clicking the house takes you back to the last accepted position, not the real initial position when you first imported the 3D file. To step back in time to previous accepted states, simply press Ctrl/Cmd+Z to undo.

NOTE Even though the top of the document window refers to your original 3D file when it is first imported, Photoshop doesn't ever change your original model. When you save the PSD file that stores the 3D model, a copy of the model is stored in the PSD. Photoshop is not a 3D modeling program and doesn't even have the capability to alter your source 3D files.

Notice that this button does not have a default keyboard shortcut associated with it unlike the other 3D tools. No matter how much you use this tool, I highly recommend leaving this tool shortcutless. You can imagine how long it might take you to orient your object in 3D space. Being able to destroy all of that work with an accidental press of a shortcut key is a power you probably don't want.

Rotate the 3D Object tool. The second 3D tool from the left is used to rotate 3D objects. Simply select this tool, and then click and drag your 3D object; you can rotate in every dimension. As previously mentioned, when you first start exploring and experimenting with all three dimensions, there's a lot of freedom there. That freedom can easily lead to an undesirable disorientation of your object, or it might even cause your 3D object to disappear completely.

To constrain this tool to rotate only in the standard clockwise/counterclockwise fashion that you might be more familiar with in 2D applications, hold down the Ctrl/Cmd key while dragging left and right with your mouse. This rotates the object around the imaginary Z axis. To constrain the rotation to occur around only one axis (either around the X axis or the Y axis), press the Shift key while dragging.

There's a slight trick to this. If you're dragging in more of a left-to-right fashion when you hold the Shift key down, Photoshop assumes that you want to constrain rotation around the Y axis (moving the object side-to-side, or pinned in place vertically). If you are moving the mouse in more of an up and down motion, Photoshop assumes that you want to rotate the object around the X axis (moving the object from front to back). It's also important to note that once you've pressed the Shift key to constrain the rotation to a given axis, you do not have to keep the key pressed to maintain the constraint. So, if you want to rotate your object freely or constrain the object to rotate around a different axis, you'll need to let go of the mouse and click to rotate again. These keyboard shortcuts really add a great deal of functionality to this tool, as well as the other 3D tools in Photoshop. Don't forget that if you rotate your 3D object without restraint and it gets completely discombobulated eight ways from Sunday, you can always click the Return Object to Initial Position button discussed previously (the little house icon).

Roll the 3D Object tool. This tool mimics a camera "roll," wherein the camera is rotated in a clockwise/counterclockwise manner. This looks similar to the rotation of 2D objects. If you were trying to assemble a clock with 3D hands, you might use the 3D Roll tool to rotate the hands to point at the correct numbers. When this tool is selected and you click and drag left or right, your object will rotate around the Z axis, which is similar to using the Rotate the 3D Object tool with the Ctrl/Cmd key held down.

Hey! Speaking of holding down the Ctrl/Cmd key, if you hold that key down while using the Roll the 3D Object tool, you'll be able to rotate your 3D object in all dimensions. Interestingly enough, this modifier does *not* behave in the same way as the modifier keys for the Rotate the 3D Object tool. When you let go of the Ctrl/Cmd key while using the Roll the 3D Object tool, you are automatically brought back to the regular roll mode.

Inasmuch as the last two tools dealt with rotation, the next two tools deal with the movement of 3D objects.

Drag the 3D Object tool. Think of this tool like the Move tool in Photoshop, only for 3D objects. Click and drag to move your object anywhere you want. Now I can hear some of you already asking why this only moves in two dimensions (X and Y). You probably saw this coming, but if you want to move an object along the Z axis using this tool, simply hold down the Ctrl/Cmd key while dragging. Notice that while you have this modifier key held down, dragging left and right behaves in the same way. However, if you now drag up and down, you'll be able to zoom closer to and farther away from your object along the Z axis. Let go of the key, and dragging up and down restores the default behavior of actually moving the object up and down (along the Y axis).

Using the Shift key, you can constrain movements made using this tool to either the X axis or the Y axis. Like using the modifier keys with the Rotate the 3D Object tool, pressing the Shift key once locks the constraint. Let go of the mouse button to release the constraint.

Slide the 3D Object tool. You might have noticed that when I talked about the two 3D rotate tools they were essentially interchangeable as long as you knew the shortcut keys for both. The same holds true for the 3D movement tools. The Slide the 3D Object tool behaves exactly like the Drag tool did when you held down the Ctrl/Cmd key. In other words, if you select this tool and then click on your 3D object, dragging left and right moves the object left and right. Dragging up and down brings the object closer to the viewer or farther away.

Like the inverse of the Drag tool, holding the Ctrl/Cmd key toggles the Drag tool. This allows you to move the object up and down when your mouse moves likewise. And again, like the Drag tool, pressing Shift enters a constrain "mode," except that it constrains the movement along the X or Z axis instead of the X or Y axis. As before, release the mouse button to unlock the constraint.

Scale the 3D Object tool. This final tool on the hit list of 3D transform tools allows you to make your 3D object larger or smaller. Simply select this tool, click on your 3D object with it, and drag upward to make the object larger or downward to make the object smaller. Hold down the Ctrl/Cmd key to scale an object in only the Y axis (up and down).

Scaling vs. Zooming

Scaling is making an object larger, whereas zooming is getting closer to it. You might be wondering about the difference between scaling an object and zooming into an object in Photoshop Extended, because they both appear to have similar results. If Photoshop were a full-fledged 3D modeling environment, the differences would be more obvious. And actually, when using .3ds files, there isn't much of a difference, truth be told. The difference comes when using 3D lights. As I'll discuss a little later on, .3ds files don't store lighting information so zooming and scaling have essentially the same result.

Since we're traveling from left to right through the 3D tools while in Object tool mode, it might seem that the View drop-down list is next. However, immediately to the right of the Scale the 3D Object tool is an unassuming little down arrow that hides a powerful secret. Click it to learn how in the world Paris Hilton got famous. Just kidding. The secret isn't quite that powerful, but it's still really cool. Clicking this arrow reveals what Photoshop calls the Object Position box. Personally, I think this is not a very descriptive name for this area because it does so much more than just allow you to move an object.

You can use this one drop-down list to adjust position (location), orientation (rotation, for all intents and purposes), and scale (size). At first glance it might appear that you need to know what precise numbers to type in to take advantage of this drop-down list. This is fortunately not the case. If you place your cursor precisely over any of the X, Y, or Z characters in this window, you'll get the old After Effects scrub icon (**FIGURE 1.8**). Be sure that your mouse pointer is over the actual letter (not the adjacent numeric field) in order to get this icon. When you see this icon, simply click and drag left or right to alter a property and watch it change in the document window. If you'd like to move, rotate, and scale a 3D object, and you have the end result in mind , this method might be the most efficient way to get the job done.

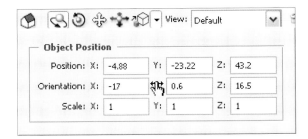

FIGURE 1.8 Ah, yes. The good old scrub icon from After Effects. Whenever you see this icon (it's actually all over the place in Photoshop), just do as the arrows indicate. Click and drag to the left or right to scrub the values.

Making View Adjustments with the Arrow Keys

One of the coolest things you can do with all of the 3D transform tools is use the arrow keys on your keyboard to make view adjustments. You'll first need to select one of the 3D transformation tools (such as the Rotate the 3D Object tool or the Slide the 3D Object tool) to make this work, but all of them can take advantage of these sweet arrow-key shortcuts. This applies to the camera editing tools as well. Using the arrows on your keyboard to "nudge" your view around will yield wildly different results, depending on the tool you have selected. For example, if you had a tool selected (such as the Drag the 3D Object tool) that panned your view (or your camera), using the left and right arrow tools will move the viewer from left to right. But if you select an orbit tool, (such as the 3D Rotate or Roll tools), the same arrows would rotate the view from left to right around your object. Using the arrows to navigate around your object doesn't give you much control, but it is much faster and easier than dragging with your mouse. It's also much easier to get back to where you started from using the arrow keys. If you're new to the world of 3D, you might consider using the arrow keys while you're getting used to using another dimension.

The Standard Photoshop Move Tool

While we're talking about moving 3D objects around, this is as good a place as any to interject the difference between moving 3D objects with the 3D move tools and moving 3D objects with Photoshop's standard Move tool. You can move 3D objects around along X and Y axes with both, but there is a very significant difference between the two methods.

Let's look at an example. Using 3D tools, drag a 3D object past the top of the document window, so that some of the object is hidden (**FIGURE 1.9**). If you move the object with one of the 3D tools and drag it back down, it behaves as you would expect. The once-hidden top of the 3D object is now plainly visible (**FIGURE 1.10**). While still in 3D Object mode, I'll put the model up again until the character's head is out of the screen.

FIGURE 1.9 My wizard lady with her head in the clouds.

FIGURE 1.10 When we bring the model back down with 3D tools, her head returns as expected.

Next, make sure that you're out of Object tool mode so that you can use the standard Photoshop tools. Watch the difference when you perform the same movement with the standard Move tool. My wizard queen has been decapitated by that Move tool! (See **FIGURE 1.11**.) The point is 2D tools don't treat 3D objects as such. They only see the actual pixels in the document, not the 3D information stored behind the scenes. Perhaps it seems like a minute detail, but this concept will really help you grasp how Photoshop generally works with 3D objects.

FIGURE 1.11 When bringing the model back down with the Move tool, the object is treated like a regular old 2D layer.

Bringing Multiple 3D Files into the Same File

After fiddling around with a 3D object for a while, you'll probably want to bring in other 3D objects to play with as well. However, you'll notice that as you use the traditional methods to open a 3D file, Photoshop creates a new, separate document every time you do so. This is the same way it works with 2D art. And, as with 2D art, to combine 3D elements you can select the Move tool and just drag and drop one 3D file from the image window of one document to the image window of another (**FIGURE 1.12A** and **FIGURE 1.12B**). Also, as with 2D images, hold down the Shift key while dragging to center the newly placed object inside the document. You can also drag and drop from the Layers panel to the image window. If you'd prefer to combine 3D files using menus, you can go to the Layer menu and select Layer > 3D Layers > New Layer from 3D File. This opens a dialog that allows you to import a new 3D file that automatically becomes another 3D layer in the current Photoshop document.

FIGURE 1.12A Two separate and lonely 3D files.

FIGURE 1.12B "May I have this dance?" By dragging and dropping, the two files become one.

Using Preset Views

To the right of the six transformation tools and the down arrow with the power-ful secret is the View drop-down list. Click the arrow to see a list of preset views to choose from. These views are supposed to mimic viewports in a 3D program. You'll see all the basics here: Top, Bottom, Left, Right, and so on. Selecting one of these from the drop-down list changes the view of your 3D object to that view (from the top, from the bottom, etc.).

Note that these preset views are primarily utilitarian in purpose. Rarely (if ever) will you want to position a 3D object in a scene with the object directly facing the camera, perfectly perpendicular to your view, or turned to its side exactly 90 degrees.

These preset views can be of benefit for showing an architectural or engineering work. Or, when used to composite a 3D object into a scene, they can also be used as a jumping off point.

For example, if you wanted to put a 3D character in a scene that was from the point of view of a lamppost, looking down onto the city street below, you might start out in Top view and tweak and adjust the view as necessary.

Using the 3D Camera Tools

Before we wrap up this chapter, let's talk about using the 3D Camera tools. The behavior of the 3D Camera tools is much like the 3D Object tools.

To access the camera tools, you first need to change the mode from Edit the 3D Object to Edit the 3D Camera (**FIGURE 1.13**). So, click the Edit the 3D Camera button. Notice that the transform tools you've see so far convert to their camera-editing equivalents. Note that the icons for these tools update to display little cameras on them. If you have 3D camera information in your 3D file, those cameras (or the names of them anyway) will show up in the View drop-down list. You can select them here for quick access or to make further angle changes using Photoshop's camera-editing tools.

The camera tools, as you've probably noticed, are extremely similar to the tools you've already looked at. For that very reason, I won't take the time to discuss each one here. But I will point out a few important concepts about working with cameras in Photoshop.

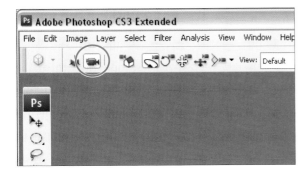

FIGURE 1.13 Companion to Edit the 3D Object; when this button is clicked, you are in Edit the 3D Camera mode. The tool set that these buttons access are very similar to those in the Edit the 3D Object mode.

I should also point out that if your 3D files don't have camera information embedded in them, the Edit Object tools and the Edit Camera tools are essentially identical. This is because you can only edit one 3D layer at a time. But the Edit Camera tools can be useful even if your file doesn't have camera information, as you'll see.

NOTE If in future versions of Photoshop we are able edit multiple objects at once, we could speculate that the camera tools would perform significantly different roles. Think of a movie set. Moving the actors individually and moving the camera would have markedly different results. But again, because the "actors" (aka 3D objects) and the cameras are on the same track, transforming one is akin to transforming the other in the current version of Photoshop.

Save custom views. One handy advantage of using cameras instead of the object-editing tools is that you can save custom views in Camera mode. (See the section "Using custom views" next.) To do this, simply click the little disk icon to the right of the View drop-down list (**FIGURE 1.14**). Another cool little secret is that once you've saved a custom view, you can access it from either the Edit Object tools or the Edit Camera tools. Just remember that these custom views can only be created using the camera-editing tools, not the standard Edit Object tools.

FIGURE 1.14 Click that little disk icon to save a custom view.

Delete custom views. Also accessible using either toolset is the ability to delete custom views. To delete custom views, just select the view from the View drop-down list and click the trash can icon to the right. Note that standard views like Top and Right cannot be deleted, only views that you have created.

Using custom views

Let's look at an example of custom views. Open the file Herbie Cam.3ds from the Chapter 1 folder. This is a robot I created named Herbie. When I was creating this robot in 3DS Max, I created a few different cameras and named them. In this example, you'll see that you can use these camera views in the .3ds file when it is imported into Photoshop.

1. With the file open, enter the 3D Object mode and click the View drop-down list to reveal the various view presets. At the bottom of the list you will see the two custom views that correspond to the cameras I created in 3DS Max (**FIGURE 1.15A**).

FIGURE 1.15A The custom views at the bottom of this list correspond to the custom camera angles I created in 3DS Max.

2. Select either conquering (which is the default view in this file) (**FIGURE 1.15B**) or diminishing (**FIGURE 1.15C**) from the list to choose that view.

FIGURE 1.15B The "conquering" view. Notice how powerful and noble Herbie looks because of the camera angle.

FIGURE 1.15C The "diminishing" view. Notice how weak and frail poor Herbie looks with this camera angle.

NOTE Most of the high-quality models I'll be using in this book come from my colleague, David Gibbons, who has a great talent in the 3D arts. Herbie the Robot is something I created in the style of cheesy 1950s-era science fiction movies. Please do not blame David for my poor character modeling skills displayed here.

The Power of Camera Angles

Even though the camera tools are simple, never underestimate the power that camera angles have to set an emotional tone for a scene.

Look again at Figures 1.15c and 1.15d. In the "conquering" view, the camera looks up at the character from the bottom. This makes Herbie look extremely tall and heroic.

In contrast, the "diminishing" view shows Herbie at a distance and considerably smaller. But it's the angle of the placement of the camera that makes the largest contribution here. It's pointing down at Herbie, which conveys the idea that Herbie is weak and helpless.

As you become more aware of these concepts, you will notice camera angles such as these in many movies, from independent films to Hollywood blockbusters.

2

Playing with Lighting and Appearance Settings

As mentioned in Chapter 1, "Photoshop's New 3D Abilities: The Basics," there are multiple ways to perform 3D transformations in Photoshop. However, from this point on, I'll be covering 3D tools that don't have an equivalent. In this chapter, you'll look at tools to light, cut up, and change the appearance of 3D objects. Remember that these tools, like the tools you've already seen, must be accessed in the Object tool mode.

Lighting in Photoshop

Let's delve into the Lighting and Appearance Settings area. If you're an experienced 3D user (which you don't need to be to benefit from these tools), you understand the power of lights in the world of 3D. Lighting not only sets an emotional tone, but it can also make objects appear more realistic. And as in real life, well-placed lights can also conceal flaws and blemishes. This is probably why photo studios spend three or four hours lighting my face for a portrait. Unfortunately for me, lights can only do so much.

Photoshop also gives you the power to play with lights a little. You can bring in lights from your 3D scenes (depending on the file format), or you can override that lighting by creating light effects from scratch inside Photoshop.

To access the lighting and appearance settings, click the Lighting and Appearance Settings button. The icon for this button looks like a cube with a paintbrush on it (**FIGURE 2.1**). If you remember from a few pages back when I talked about the Scale the 3D Object tool, I mentioned that the down arrow to the right of that icon held a magic secret. Well, to the right of the Lighting and Appearance Settings cube-and-paintbrush icon, there is a similar down arrow, but there's no magic secret with this one. Clicking the down arrow next to the icon does the same thing as clicking the icon. The same holds true for the Cross Section Settings button to its right, which we'll look at in just a bit.

FIGURE 2.1 The Lighting and Appearance Settings button.

As you might expect, there are two sections here—one for lighting and the other for appearance. I'll talk about lighting first.

Right away you'll see that you have lots of choices. In a move of great convenience, Photoshop makes Lights From File the top choice. This option uses the lighting information built into your 3D file, *provided* that the 3D file format you're using supports lights.

You'll have to be a little careful about using this preset. Sometimes the lighting info from your 3D application doesn't quite come over correctly into Photoshop, and it may cause your layer to be hopelessly black. In such cases, even changing lighting from inside Photoshop or lightening the textures won't fix this problem. You'll need to go back to your 3D application and either change the lighting setup or delete the lights altogether in some instances. I'll discuss troubleshooting in much greater detail in Chapter 4, "Editing Textures of 3D Objects." If there are no lights in your 3D file, or if you want to change the existing lights, you can select a preset from the Light Settings drop-down menu (**FIGURE 2.2A**). Here's a list of the various light settings and what they do. I'll use the file Werewolf.psd from the Chapter 2 folder to show what each setting does (**FIGURE 2.2B**). Know that these light settings work similarly regardless of the file you're using. Feel free to use whatever 3D object you have available to explore these options.

FIGURE 2.2A Select your lighting from this drop-down menu.

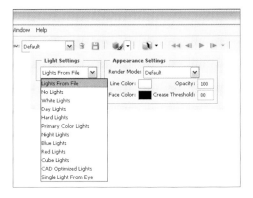

FIGURE 2.2B This is the file I'll use to show the various light settings.

- **Lights From File.** The default light setting. Photoshop will use the existing lights in your 3D file, if they're there. If there are no lights in the original 3D file, or if Photoshop cannot detect them, the White Lights setting is used. The results are fairly uneventful, as you might expect from a default setting (**FIGURE 2.2C**).

FIGURE 2.2C The default Lights From File setting.

- **No Lights.** The darkness created from this preset resides somewhere between "had a bad day" dark and "end of the world" dark (**FIGURE 2.2D**). No Lights definitely darkens a layer, but typically not enough so that the textures applied to the object are indiscernible. The thing to know about No Lights is that this effect *can* be restored at any time by going back to the light settings

FIGURE 2.2D The No Lights setting. Sometimes, this doesn't act as it should. In this case, it actually returned brighter results than White Lights! In the next chapter, you'll see an example of this setting working as you might expect it would.

and selecting a different lighting preset. This is great because No Lights creates such a powerful darkness sometimes that it's difficult (if not impossible) to get all of that luminance data back with standard Photoshop adjustments like Levels, Curves, and so on.

NOTE The No Lights lighting preset can sometimes produce unexpected results. In the case of the werewolf, it actually made it brighter! There really isn't a way to predict when these unexpected results will make their presence known, because this is a glitch.

- **White Lights.** Similar to the default light setting (**FIGURE 2.2E**). This setting is bright, but not too bright, and it doesn't have a color tint, so, it's a very average bright. Goldilocks would approve.

FIGURE 2.2E The White Lights setting.

- **Day Lights.** Attempts to simulate daylight by having a large light source shine down onto your object from the top of the image (**FIGURE 2.2F**). It's slightly brighter than White Lights but still has no color tint. This also lightens shadow areas a little, but thankfully it leaves pure black alone. What it's really trying to do is simulate something in daylight. So, just as in real life, it generally lightens all areas and reduces overall contrast.

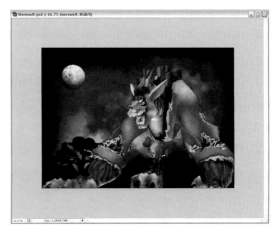

FIGURE 2.2F The Day Lights setting.

■ **Hard Lights.** Creates the effect that your 3D object is being "blasted" by a great deal of light from all directions (**FIGURE 2.2G**). This is usually the brightest of all the light presets. It also has no color tint. And even though it joins Day Lights in preserving pure black, it really blows out shadows quite a bit. I guess that's what you might expect from "hard" lights.

FIGURE 2.2G The Hard Lights setting.

■ **Primary Color Lights.** This setting adds a smattering of red, blue, and green light (**FIGURE 2.2H**). It's almost like putting gels on theater lights. And like theater lights, the color tint tends to darken the light output a bit. The red light shines from above and behind the object, the green light shines out from the perspective of the viewer, and the blue light shines up from the bottom. Keep in mind that these are general directions, so the colors blend quite a bit over most of the surfaces of the object.

FIGURE 2.2H The Primary Color Lights setting.

- **Night Lights.** This setting seems to be the most dramatic lighting preset of the bunch, and I really like this one. It tends to darken everything as the name implies, but it also adds these really interesting bursts of color (**FIGURE 2.2I**). A cool blue light comes up from the bottom and a warm pale-orange light comes down from the top.

FIGURE 2.2I The Night Lights setting.

- **Blue Lights.** Adds a blue tint and tends to darken a little (**FIGURE 2.2J**).

FIGURE 2.2J The Blue Lights setting.

- **Red Lights.** Similar to Blue Lights but with red (**FIGURE 2.2K**).

FIGURE 2.2K The Red Lights setting.

- **Cube Lights.** Simulates four precise lights being placed around the object, as if in the corners of an imaginary cube around the object. Cube Lights have a brightening effect that brightens all areas of the object in a more uniform way (**FIGURE 2.2L**). The brightness is a little brighter than Day Lights, but it also applies lights from every direction, which tends to greatly reduce shadow areas. So, whereas White Lights or Day Lights would probably work better when compositing a 3D object into a scene, Cube Lights would probably be better for showing off all the intricacies of a new product or building.

FIGURE 2.2L The Cube Lights setting.

- **CAD Optimized Lights.** Creates bright lights with strong contrast (**FIGURE 2.2M**). The large light source emanates from the viewer, as if the viewer were shining a large, diffused light at it from his or her perspective.

FIGURE 2.2M The CAD Optimized Lights setting.

- **Single Light from Eye.** Points a light at the 3D scene from your point of view. Imagine that your view of the 3D object is like a video camera with a light attached to it. Objects that point directly at that "camera" will be brightest. The results are very similar to CAD Optimized Lights except they are not as bright here (**FIGURE 2.2N**).

FIGURE 2.2N The Single Light from Eye setting.

In a New York minute, that's a rundown on what these settings do. As you'll quickly figure out, this isn't professional-quality lighting. Photoshop's 3D lighting is not meant to be an alternative to the really high-end lighting that you'll find in dedicated 3D applications. You don't have control of light placement, shadows, and other parameters that make lights as important as they are. As a matter of fact, you can't change anything about these lights at all!

That being said, these lighting effects can pull off some impressive feats when used creatively. We'll revisit a few of these settings a little later in the book. Don't forget that you can also use Photoshop's good old, industry-standard, amazingly powerful, existing toolset of image correcting effects. Levels, Curves, Hue/Saturation, and all their buddies work on 3D layers, just like they do on 2D layers. We'll look more closely at these later in the book as well.

3D Lighting in Photoshop

While the lighting presets are nowhere near as powerful as the standard color and luminance tools in Photoshop, and there is no way to adjust them, they still can be very helpful. Lighting in 3D space can really bring out or diminish cracks and crevasses, or give interesting back lighting to your 3D object. Back lighting can increase or decrease the apparent volume of a 3D object.

Remember that volume is like the 3D thickness of an object. Volume is the only difference between a square and a cube. Because objects in the real world have volume, it's imperative to convey 3D depth (aka volume) in your layers. The lighting presets in Photoshop can add those subtle lighting effects to the edges of your objects, which emphasize their volume.

Lighting a 3D object from the back, or lighting folds and creases in a 3D model, can be faked with Photoshop's standard 2D image editing tools, but it's much more difficult. Also, keep in mind that when 3D lights are "faked" with 2D tools, those image adjustments are useless if the object is moved, scaled, or rotated in 3D space.

I prefer to add a lighting preset that gives me the general idea of what I'm going for and gives me the 3D effects that are hard to imitate, like shadows and backlighting. Then I might use standard effects like Levels, Curves, Hue/Saturation, and so on to complete the desired effect. So, even though the 3D lights discussed here aren't extremely powerful or even adjustable, they do serve as a great foundation to the final look of the object and should not be neglected.

Displaying 3D Wireframes

Lights are but one side of the Lighting and Appearance Settings coin, so to speak. The other half of this dialog box deals with Appearance Settings. That nomenclature is quite a big umbrella. Doesn't everything technically count as the object's appearance?

This area actually changes the render settings for 3D objects, which allows you to display their wireframes and meshes in a variety of ways. If used creatively, this drop-down menu of options gives you the capability to create some very engaging and interesting art. To see the wireframe of a 3D object, click the render mode drop-down menu on the right side of the Lighting and Appearance Settings area. As you can see from this list, there are several different choices here (**FIGURE 2.3**). As you randomly select from these render modes, many appear to be very similar, or they appear to do nothing. But I assure you, there are many hidden gems among this list.

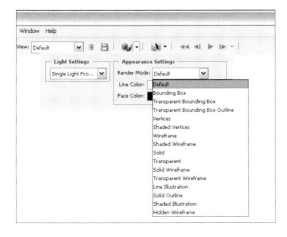

FIGURE 2.3 The various render modes.

To get a better sense of these modes and how they can be used in a real-world setting, I'll use the file Commercial_Property.psd from the Chapter 2 folder (**FIGURE 2.4** on the next page). This model is from an actual project produced by my architectural rendering studio, Aveconta, although the background has been altered for this project. There's a fair amount of geometry here, so changing the render mode will significantly change its appearance. If you're changing render modes with a 3D object that is very simple (say, for example, a flat playing card), you won't get a good sense of what effect these modes are having on your object.

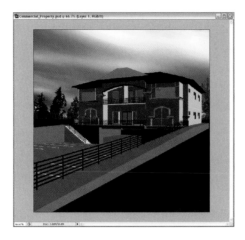

FIGURE 2.4 The file I'll use for exploring render modes.

Soon we'll look at some interesting and creative art that can be created using render modes. But before you can make these render modes jump up and dance, you need to understand the four options in this area. They are the keys to getting the most out of the render modes. Conversely, certain properties—Line Color, Face Color, Opacity, and Crease Threshold—only make visible changes when you are using a render mode that supports them. For example, if you are using the Wireframe render mode, the Opacity property in this area will do nothing.

Even though these four properties won't make complete sense until I've discussed the render modes associated with them, I'll quickly go over what these four properties do. It will be good preparation for when I explain the render mode list.

- **Line Color** refers to the color of the wireframe.

- **Face Color** refers to the color of the faces (i.e., polygons) visible in some render modes.

- **Opacity** seems self-explanatory, but it pays to note that it operates on a per-polygon basis, which is different than the way opacity works in the good old Photoshop Layers palette. The Opacity slider in the Layers palette universally lowers the opacity of everything on the layer. Because the Opacity slider in the Light and Appearance Settings drop-down menu affects the opacity of individual polygons (i.e., faces), you get some interesting transparency effects as semitransparent areas pile on top of one another (**FIGURE 2.5**). I mentioned this earlier, but remember that all of these parameters (including opacity) only work with certain render modes.

FIGURE 2.5 Notice the interesting effect from reducing the Opacity value in the Appearance Settings area. This is caused by overlapping semitransparent polygons. This is much different than reducing the Opacity value in the Layers palette, which uniformly reduces the opacity of the entire layer.

■ **Crease Threshold** is the most abstract of the group. The "crease" is the line formed by the connecting of two faces. In some render modes, you might want to display fewer lines (aka creases) for complex models. Thus, Crease Threshold allows you a way to reduce these lines by specifying a minimum angle that the polygons must be in relation to one another for their crease to show. In other words, if I have two faces that meet at a 90 degree angle, and my Crease Threshold is set to 91 degrees or more, the line at the junction where the two faces meet will not be visible. Behold these examples of Crease Threshold: **FIGURE 2.6** shows the image with an extreme value of 0, and **FIGURE 2.7** shows the image with the opposite extreme value of 180.

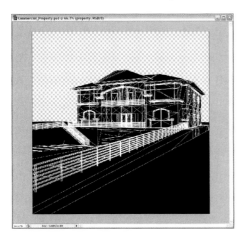

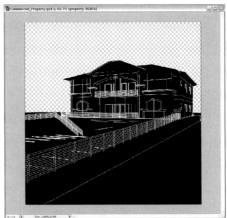

FIGURE 2.6 Crease Threshold with a value of 0.

FIGURE 2.7 Crease Threshold with a value of 180.

Even though math is typically the bane of the digital artist's existence, Crease Threshold is worth the brain sweat in my opinion.

NOTE You might get odd and unexpected results using the Commercial_ Property.psd file and other 3D files in Photoshop Extended. It is absolutely imperative that your computer meet the minimum hardware requirements in order to run Photoshop Extended correctly. Also, if you're experiencing problems with the render modes, try canceling out of 3D Object mode and then reentering it.

The Wireframe Render Modes

The render modes are described in the following list, as is the basic idea behind what they're doing. Just be aware that what some of these modes do may not be readily apparent at first (Shaded Vertices, I'm looking in your direction). Also, if you're not using the exercise files provided with this book, you may want to create a new blank layer, fill it with a solid color, and place it beneath your 3D object while experimenting with these modes. Sometimes it can be difficult to see a wireframe when it's on top of the default gray and white checkerboard background (**FIGURE 2.8**).

TIP   To fill a layer with a solid color, first select the desired color as your foreground color in the Tools palette. Then, with the layer selected, use the keyboard shortcut Alt+Backspace (Windows) or Opt+Delete (Mac).

FIGURE 2.8 What the heck is this? It's Exhibit A for the case against using a transparent background while you're working with wireframes. For better results, put a layer of solid color beneath the 3D layer.

- **Bounding Box.** A bounding box is used throughout all Adobe programs, from Illustrator to InDesign to After Effects. Essentially, a bounding box is an imaginary box drawn around the extremities of an object. For an example of this in everyday Photoshop, see **FIGURE 2.9A**. This render mode creates a bounding box around every element of your 3D object, not around the entire whole (**FIGURE 2.9B**). Bounding Box uses Line Color to determine the color of the box.

FIGURE 2.9A The rectangular outline around this heart is called a "bounding box."

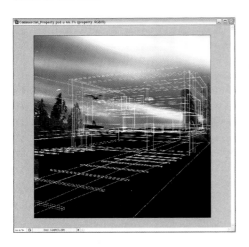

FIGURE 2.9B The Bounding Box render mode creates bounding boxes around every element of a 3D object.

- **Transparent Bounding Box.** This mode also creates bounding boxes around all elements, but instead of only making an outline, it actually makes semi-transparent boxes. The color of the box is determined by the Face Color (**FIGURE 2.9C**).

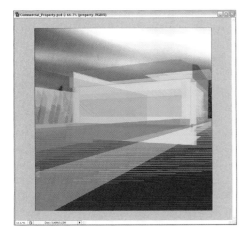

FIGURE 2.9C Transparent Bounding Box mode. I changed the Face Color here to blue to help it stand out against the background a little more than it would with the default black.

- **Transparent Bounding Box Outline.** This mode is a combination of Bounding Box and Transparent Bounding Box. It makes semitransparent boxes with outlines. Face Color controls the color of the boxes, whereas Line Color controls the color of the edges (**FIGURE 2.9D**).

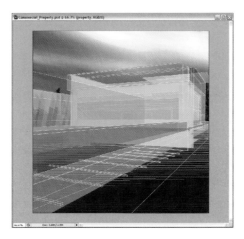

FIGURE 2.9D Transparent Bounding Box Outline mode, again with blue as the Face Color.

- **Vertices.** This mode uses Line Color to display every vertex of the mesh. I don't use this mode very often because those little vertices are so difficult to see, even with extra image adjustments (**FIGURE 2.9E**). It could serve a more utilitarian purpose if you're trying to hunt down a vertex that is causing problems with your mesh. But for visual design, unless you're creating constellations, you probably won't find this mode very helpful.

FIGURE 2.9E The Vertices mode is usually difficult to see, even after using other Photoshop tools to improve the appearance. Having a large number of vertices like this can help a little.

- **Shaded Vertices.** This mode also displays the vertices, but the color of the vertex is determined by the regular color of the object's original mesh, before textures are applied (**FIGURE 2.9F**).

FIGURE 2.9F Shaded Vertices mode. Depending on the color of your original object, this can be the most difficult render mode to see.

- **Wireframe.** This mode simply creates a wireframe of the 3D object. Wireframe uses Line Color to determine the color of the wireframe (**FIGURE 2.9G**). This is a great feature of Photoshop Extended that can be really useful to many Photoshop users. Designers, for example, can take advantage of wireframe mesh objects for use as design elements in standard 2D layout projects.

FIGURE 2.9G Wireframe mode.

- **Shaded Wireframe.** Like Shaded Vertices, this mode creates a wireframe that is colored according to the original color of the object (**FIGURE 2.9H**).

FIGURE 2.9H Notice how Shaded Wireframe mode creates a wireframe that gets its color from the original object. Sometimes, as is the case here, the result is visually interesting.

- **Solid.** This is similar to the default setting (**FIGURE 2.9I**). None of the other options have any effect in Solid mode.

FIGURE 2.9I The Solid render mode is the equivalent of the default render mode.

- **Transparent.** This mode is the same as the Solid mode except that the Opacity parameter in the Lighting and Appearance Settings can be used to adjust its opacity (**FIGURE 2.9J**). This might seem useless because of the Opacity slider in the Layers palette. However, the transparency here compounds in

3D, which creates interesting effects as semitransparent polygons in front interact with semitransparent polygons on the back side of the object. Also, this is one of the modes that you can use in conjunction with Lighting settings as well.

NOTE Generally, render modes that allow you to see the original object can also be used with the Lighting settings.

FIGURE 2.9J Transparent mode. It looks like Solid until you lower the Opacity. Now you can see inside the building, as it were. The Opacity here is at about 40%. That's just enough to allow you to see who's working overtime. Joking aside, I just love the way this looks.

■ **Solid Wireframe.** A combination of both Solid and Wireframe modes, it displays the model and the wireframe using the Line Color (**FIGURE 2.9K**).

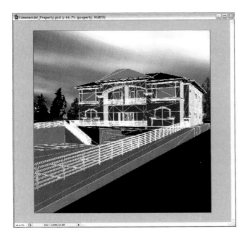

FIGURE 2.9K Solid Wireframe mode. This is like a combination of Solid and Wireframe modes.

- **Transparent Wireframe.** This mode is much like Wireframe mode. The difference is that it also displays a semitransparent version of the object, as well as the wireframe (**FIGURE 2.9L**). The Opacity slider can be used to reduce the opacity of the mesh further.

FIGURE 2.9L Transparent Wireframe mode. This is like a combination of Transparent and Wireframe mode. Here the Opacity is reduced to 50%.

- **Line Illustration.** Now this mode is really interesting. It attempts to give the 3D object the appearance of a hand-drawn illustration (**FIGURE 2.9M**). It does this by applying a wireframe (using the Line Color) and changing the color of the entire mesh to the Face Color. And finally, you get to use Crease Threshold! As discussed earlier, a low value will create a wireframe with more edges (**FIGURE 2.9N**), and a higher value will create a more basic outline (**FIGURE 2.9O**). What I love about this mode is that there are so many choices.

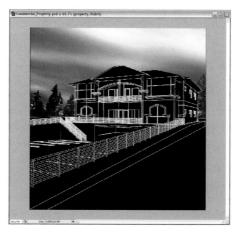

This is a great way to create the very popular "toon shader" look, which makes 3D objects look like hand-drawn cartoons. If you look closely at many modern hand-drawn cartoons, you'll notice many objects that are actually composited 3D

FIGURE 2.9M With Line Illustration mode. This is probably my favorite effect for creating interesting art with 3D objects.

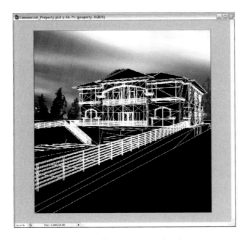

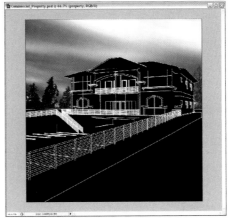

FIGURE 2.9N Line Illustration with a low Crease Threshold setting.

FIGURE 2.9O Line Illustration with a high Crease Threshold setting.

elements that are made to look like hand-drawn cartoons. You obviously have much more control over toon shader type effects in a full-fledged 3D application. But for a quick-and-dirty cartoon effect, you can't beat the Line Illustration render mode. It offers some amazing creative possibilities.

- **Solid Outline.** This mode is like Solid Wireframe except that the density of the wireframe can be controlled by Crease Threshold.

- **Shaded Illustration.** This mode creates a wireframe using the Line Color, and the wireframe is composited on top of a lightened version of the 3D object (**FIGURE 2.9P**). Crease Threshold can also be used to adjust the density of the mesh.

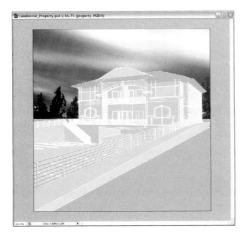

FIGURE 2.9P With Shaded Illustration mode.

- **Hidden Wireframe.** This mode has a similar effect to Line Illustration but without all the control. It is called Hidden Wireframe mode because it shows all of the wireframe. Therefore, Crease Threshold has no effect. And, as with Line Illustration, Line Color controls the outline color, and Face Color controls the color of the solid color applied to the mesh.

And that is what Photoshop calls the render modes. We'll explore some fun and creative techniques with these later on in the book.

NOTE Those of you with a 3D background will recognize instantly the buzzword "render" and will probably take this opportunity to ask about Photoshop's render capabilities. Unfortunately, this is a limitation with the current version. At this time, Photoshop does not allow you to output with a really high-end rendering engine. There are some third-party solutions currently in development that we'll talk about in Chapter 10, "Plug-ins and Resources."

Creating Cross Sections of 3D Objects

Continuing on our linear trajectory through the 3D tools, the next area is the Cross Section Settings. The icon looks like the aftermath of a fight between Pac-man and a ninja, and Pac-man didn't fare so well (**FIGURE 2.10**). Click the Cross Section Settings drop-down menu to see all the available options. And as with the Lighting and Appearance Settings, the button and the drop-down arrow do the same thing.

FIGURE 2.10 The Cross Section Settings icon— it looks like Pac-man split in half.

If you're not familiar with the concept of a cross section, it is like viewing a slice of your 3D object. Think of dissecting that frog in high school biology but without the icky goo. Being able to slice open a 3D model and peek inside it can be useful for several reasons.

For one, it's very helpful when dealing with architectural buildings. Take for example the file Boring_House.psd from the exercise files in the Chapter 2 folder (**FIGURE 2.11**). It looks like a plain old boring house on the outside. But using the Cross Section feature in Photoshop allows you to see the plain old boring inside as well (**FIGURE 2.12**).

FIGURE 2.11 The house model from the exercise files that I'll be using.

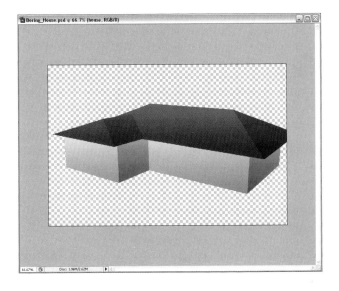

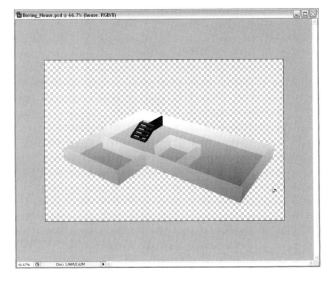

FIGURE 2.12 Creating a cross section allows you to see what's inside.

You can also use the Cross Section feature to create interesting objects based on other objects. If 3D modeling is a new arena for you, this feature might open the door to more possibilities. Take, for example, the planet image from the sample files that ship with Photoshop (**FIGURE 2.13**). After some extremely brief fiddling with Cross Section features, you can convert that planet to a nice wooden bowl (**FIGURE 2.14**). You can perform a similar operation to convert a character to just a pair of pants, or take a cross section from an American football to make a canoe, or take a cross section of a couch to make… uh, … half a couch? Whatever. You get the idea.

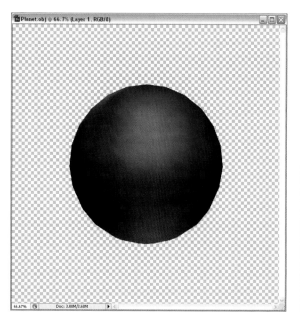

FIGURE 2.13 A 3D model of a planet that ships in the Goodies with Photoshop. You'll find it in the Planet folder in the 3D models folder.

FIGURE 2.14 With the help of Photoshop's Cross Section features, you can convert the planet into a wooden bowl.

Let's take a closer look at the options when creating cross sections. I'll use the house file I mentioned earlier, Boring_House.psd, from the exercise files included with the book.

Cross Section Settings. Click the Cross Section Settings drop-down menu to see loads of options, all of which deal exclusively with creating a cross section. These settings are pretty exciting, because they allow more customization than anything else you've seen so far.

To slice away a chunk of your object, select the Enable Cross Section check box to create the cross section (**FIGURE 2.15**). Without this box selected, all the other options are grayed out, so click this first.

FIGURE 2.15 Click this check box to turn on the cross section.

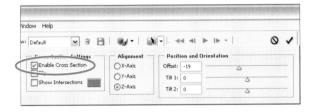

Let's talk briefly about the other options in this area.

- **Flip.** This option inverts the portion that is cut away and the portion that remains. So Flip would work great if, for example, you wanted to turn the wooden bowl into a simple helmet (**FIGURE 2.16**).

FIGURE 2.16 Selecting Flip in the Cross Section Settings can convert the bowl into a helmet. I actually learned this trick from watching my kids.

- **Show Intersections.** When you first apply a cross section, you'll notice that there's a little red stroke around the edge of the model that was cut away. That is because Show Intersections is on by default. To turn off the line, deselect the Show Intersections check box. If you want to see your intersections but don't like the default color, you can change it by clicking on the color swatch to the right of Show Intersections. This opens the Adobe Color Picker and allows you to select a new color for the intersection lines. You can see the Show Intersections lines in the next figures of the house cross section.

Alignment. The next area is the Alignment area. It is here that you choose around which axis you want the cross section to occur. In other words, the plane that is created to make a cross section moves along the selected axis. This might seem contradictory at first because the slice plane is actually perpendicular to the axis, but just remember that the axis refers to how it *moves*, not how it *slices*. **FIGURE 2.17** shows the Boring_House.psd file sliced using the X axis, **FIGURE 2.18** shows it sliced using the Y axis, and **FIGURE 2.19** shows it sliced using the Z axis. This may take some practice to get down, or you can always just play around with it until you get it right.

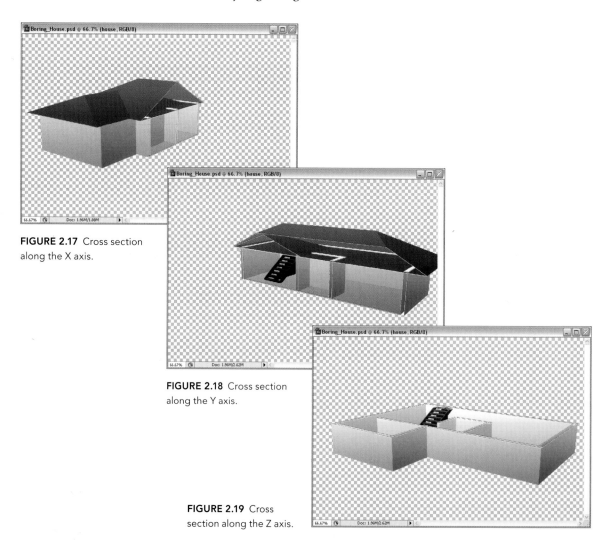

FIGURE 2.17 Cross section along the X axis.

FIGURE 2.18 Cross section along the Y axis.

FIGURE 2.19 Cross section along the Z axis.

Position and Orientation. The Position and Orientation area is last, but certainly not least. This area is where you really get some great control over how your mesh gets sliced up. The Offset slider allows you to control just how much of the model is hidden by the cross section. A negative value eats away more of the object (**FIGURE 2.20**); a positive value restores more of it (**FIGURE 2.21**). Of course, if Flip is selected, the Offset slider will behave in the opposite way.

FIGURE 2.20 Offset with a negative value hides more of the house.

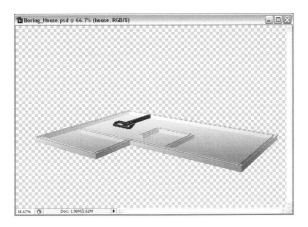

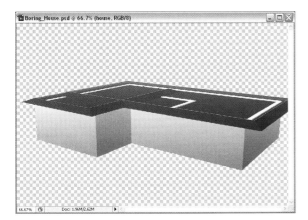

FIGURE 2.21 With a positive value, the Offset property reveals more of the house.

Underneath the Offset slider, you'll find Tilt 1 and Tilt 2. While these sliders sound like the Cat in the Hat's mischievous little henchmen, they're actually used to rotate the cross section. Tilt 1 rotates the cross section from front to back (**FIGURE 2.22**), and Tilt 2 rotates it from left to right (**FIGURE 2.23**). But this is relative to the model, not to your view of it. So if you rotate the object, Tilt 1 may appear to you to rotate the cross section from your left to your right.

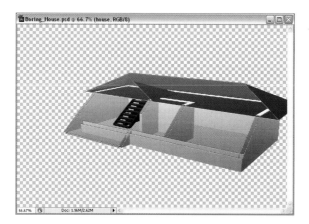

FIGURE 2.22 After adjusting Tilt 1.

FIGURE 2.23 After adjusting Tilt 2.

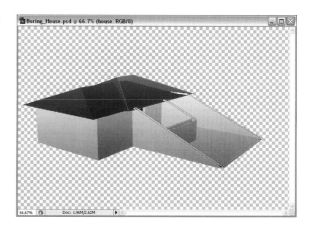

After you accept the session of transformations by exiting 3D Object mode, Photoshop retains the cross section information, including tilt values. So, when you return to transform your 3D object, you'll see that the values don't reset to zero; they are as you left them when you last accepted the transformations. I love that. This behavior makes it so much easier to adjust and tweak your cross section later on if you need to.

A Cool Rendering Trick

Once you've learned about and are comfortable using cross sections and render modes, there's a cool trick you can do. If you want to display a 3D model with two different render modes in different places, follow these steps. For this example, I'll use Herbie the Robot. You'll find him hanging out in a PSD file called Herbie in the Chapter 2 folder.

1. Put your object in the desired render mode. I'll just use the default mode (**FIGURE 2.24**).

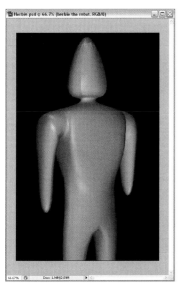

FIGURE 2.24 To create the appearance that one object is simultaneously displaying two different render modes, first select a render mode on a 3D object.

FIGURE 2.25 Next, create a cross section.

2. Create a cross section (**FIGURE 2.25**). I'll create mine along the X axis and turn off Show Intersections, but you can choose to set up your cross section as you'd like.

3. Accept the transformation by clicking Enter/Return.

4. Duplicate the layer by dragging it to the Create a new layer icon at the bottom of the Layers palette, or use the keyboard shortcut Ctrl/Cmd+J.

5. Flip the cross section of the original layer (**FIGURE 2.26**).

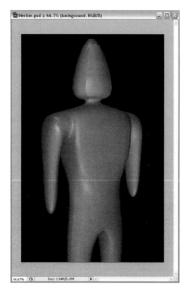

FIGURE 2.26 On the original layer, enable Flip in the Cross Section Settings.

6. Change the render mode of one of the layers and bask in the glory of your new trick (**FIGURE 2.27**).

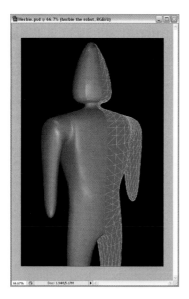

FIGURE 2.27 Change the render mode of the duplicate, and look at that! Two different render modes on the same object, or so it would appear.

7. (Optional) If you performed these tasks on the duplicate layer, you may need to drag and drop the duplicate below the original layer in the Layers palette if you're getting some visual ugliness (**FIGURES 2.28** and **2.29**).

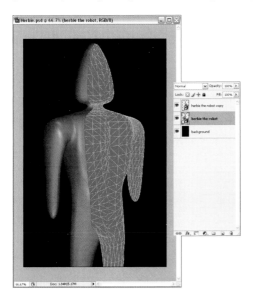

FIGURE 2.28 Depending on which layer you have on top, you might get undesirable results like these.

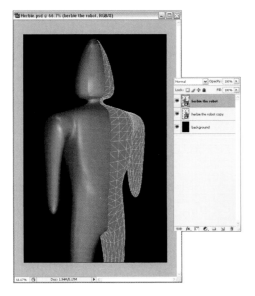

FIGURE 2.29 Change the stacking order to remedy the situation.

3

Even Cooler
3D Tricks

In this chapter, we'll start experimenting and getting creative with all the tools you've been learning about. And now that you know what 3D tools are available, you can start using them with standard Photoshop features.

Using Layer Styles on 3D Objects

Let's begin by checking out the Layer Styles in Photoshop. A layer "style" in Photoshop lingo is a series of effects applied to a layer. Each effect that can be applied as a Layer Style (such as Outer Glow, Drop Shadow, etc.) has many parameters and options to adjust. You can control how these effects blend with each other, manipulate the direction of the synthetic light source, and much more. That's why Layer Styles are so powerful.

The best feature about Layer Styles is that they are nondestructive. Nondestructive is an editing term that basically just means nonpermanent. So, if at any time you decide to remove the effects or alter them, you can do so quickly and easily. And since 3D objects exist as a self-contained layer, you can use Layer Styles to add 2D effects to 3D objects.

Here are some mini-lessons of a few creative ideas using Layer Styles on 3D objects. This is by no means an exhaustive list, but it is sure to inspire. Feel free to follow along with the examples, or just get ideas from the images here.

Creating a Glowing Silhouette

Using our beloved wizard sorceress, we'll add an Outer Glow effect. Here are the steps for achieving this effect.

1. Open wizard lady.3ds from the wizard lady folder in the Chapter 3 exercise files folder (**FIGURE 3.1**). Use the default resolution of 1024 x 1024.

   FIGURE 3.1 The wizard lady image.

2. This step is optional, but you can enter 3D object mode so that you can adjust the lighting. You want the image to be very dark and be barely able to discern the character, so the glow you apply to her will seem more dramatic. With another file, you might want to use No Lights, but in this case use the Default lights, which are actually pretty dark. You might also want to zoom in just a little (**FIGURE 3.2**). Accept the changes and exit 3D Object mode when you're happy with the way she looks.

FIGURE 3.2 Zoomed in on the wizard lady with the Default lighting mode.

3. Create a new blank layer by clicking the New Layer button at the bottom of the Layers palette (**FIGURE 3.3**). Technically, this isn't really part of the trick, but the silhouette and glow will look much better on top of a background.

TIP   When you create a new layer by clicking the Create a new layer button at the bottom of the Layers palette, it places a blank new layer on top of the currently selected layer. To save a couple of steps, you can have Photoshop create the blank new layer below the currently selected layer by clicking the Create a new layer button while holding the Ctrl/Cmd key.

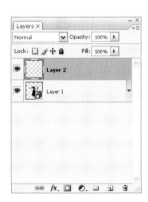

FIGURE 3.3 Click the New Layer button to add a new, blank layer.

4. Select a color from the Adobe Color Picker by double-clicking on the foreground color swatch in the Tools palette (**FIGURE 3.4A** and **FIGURE 3.4B** on the next page). Typically, at least with this example, black looks best. However, select a shade of red for the background so you can see the silhouette and glow more clearly. While a dark character looks intense and powerful

against a black background, it doesn't make for great screenshots for a book. The Outer Glow effect uses the Screen Blend mode by default. In plain English, this means that unless the background color is darker than the glow, you won't see it unless you change the Blend mode. So even if you follow along and select a shade of red, be sure it's a dark red so that the glow you apply to it will be visible.

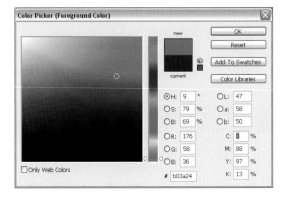

FIGURE 3.4B Double-clicking the foreground swatch opens the Adobe Color Picker.

FIGURE 3.4A Double-click the foreground color swatch, which is the swatch on the upper left.

5. Fill the new blank layer by using the keyboard shortcut Alt+Backspace (Win) or Opt+Delete (Mac). Make sure that the new blank layer is selected, not your 3D layer!

6. Drag the new layer of solid color below the 3D layer in the Layers palette. (**FIGURE 3.5**).

FIGURE 3.5 Be sure to put the solid color layer below the 3D object in the Layers palette.

7. Open the Layer Style dialog by double-clicking in the blank area of the 3D layer to the right of the layer's name in the Layers palette (**FIGURE 3.6A**). The dialog opens, displaying the Blending Options area. Alternatively, you can open the Layer Style dialog by selecting an effect from the fx drop-down list at the very bottom of the Layers palette (**FIGURE 3.6B**). For this exercise, double-click the blank area of the 3D layer.

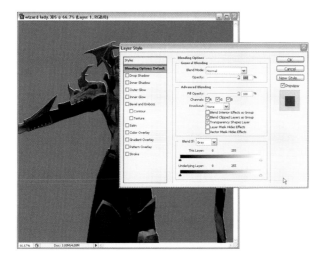

FIGURE 3.6A
Double-click in this area to the right of a layer's name to open the Layer Style dialog.

FIGURE 3.6B You can also jump right to a desired effect by using this drop-down list.

8. In the Layer Style dialog, make sure the Preview check box (on the right side of the dialog) is selected (**FIGURE 3.7**). You'll then be able to see the results of your changes on the 3D object while you make adjustments in the Layer Style dialog.

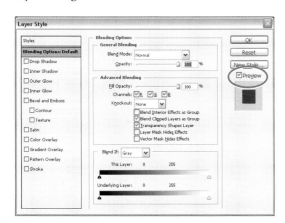

FIGURE 3.7 Select the Preview check box so you can see the results of the effects that you apply.

9. Turn on Outer Glow by selecting the check box next to its name on the left side of the dialog (**FIGURE 3.8**). Enabling that box only turns the effect on and off. The real power of this effect is in the next step.

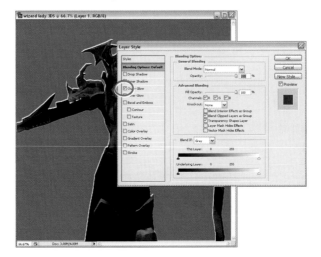

FIGURE 3.8 Click the check box to turn the effect on and off.

10. Click the words Outer Glow next to the check box. This changes the main area of the dialog to show the options for Outer Glow (**FIGURE 3.9**). Here's where it gets juicy. See the sidebar "Outer Glow Parameters" (page 61) for some info on mastering these settings.

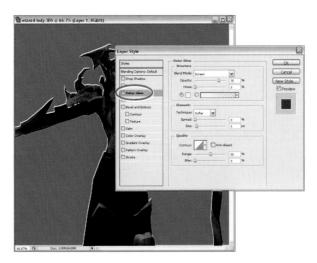

FIGURE 3.9 Click on the name of the effect to see its options.

11. We'll use most of the default settings. But this glow is a little too subtle, so change the Spread value to 8% and the Size value to 30 px (pixels). These changes make the glow a little more substantial (**FIGURE 3.10**). Feel free to go wild and crazy here! Having a really interesting and nonstandard glow won't negatively affect your results in the slightest.

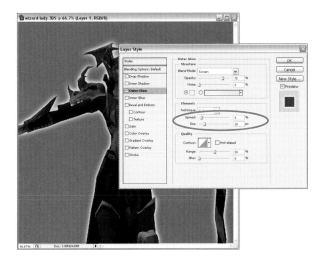

FIGURE 3.10
Adjusting the Spread and Size settings makes the glow more prominent.

12. Click the OK button or press Enter/Return to accept the changes and apply the Layer Style.

Now take a look at what you created. Pretty sweet, in my humble opinion. But the best part is that these effects are nondestructive. At any point, even after you've saved, closed, and reopened the file, you can double-click the fx icon that now shows up on your layer in the Layers palette (**FIGURE 3.11**). The Layer Style dialog reopens with all of your settings intact, and you can make changes as you please—add new effects, or remove all effects entirely.

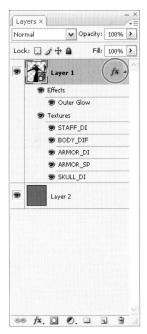

FIGURE 3.11 This fx icon indicates that Layer Styles have been applied to this layer.

TIP   To quickly get rid of Layer Styles applied to a layer, just drag and drop the word Effects (immediately below the name of the layer you've applied styles to) from the Layers palette to the trash. If you do it correctly, the icon that you drag to the trash will be a big "fx."

In addition to being able to change effects at any point, you can also toggle the visibility of individual effects, or the entire style. Simply click the arrow to the right of the fx icon that appears on the layer after you've applied a Layer Style

to it (**FIGURE 3.12**). The Layer Style expands, and you'll be able to see all of its components. You'll see an eye icon next to the word Effects, as well as each effect applied. In this case, Outer Glow is the only effect you've applied, so there are only two eyes. If you want to temporarily remove just an effect, click the eye icon next to it. I always feel so guilty poking those things in the eye. Nevertheless, once you click the eye, the effect will be disabled. Click that same spot again to bring back the effect. Clicking the eye icon next to Effects temporarily hides all effects.

TIP If you want to quickly copy Layer Styles from one layer to another layer, click and drag the fx icon on the layer to another layer while holding the Alt/Opt key.

Another great thing about Layer Styles is that they are live effects. If you change the content of the layer, the style will automatically update. So now, if you were to take the 3D layer back into its editing mode and then rotate it, the glow you applied to it updates (**FIGURE 3.13**). If your computer is powerful enough, this update even happens in real time while you rotate!

FIGURE 3.12 Click the arrow to the right of the fx icon to expand and collapse the list of effects applied to the layer.

FIGURE 3.13 These Layer Styles are so dynamic! If you make any changes (such as rotation here), the Layer Style automatically updates to glow around the new shape outline created by the angle change.

Here is just a brief summary of what the Outer Glow parameters do. I find that the Photoshop Help on this stuff can be hard to figure out.

- **Blend Mode.** Specifies the Blend mode of the glow only.

- **Opacity.** A "master" opacity control for the entire effect.

- **Noise.** Introduces random noise in the glow, but the noise isn't extra colored pixels like you might expect. The noise is actually like little holes in the glow, and the higher the Noise value, the more holes there will be. Think of this as "opacity noise."

- **Solid Color/Gradient.** You can select the swatch on the left to use a solid color for the glow or click the radio button on the right to use a gradient for the glow instead. Note that the default gradient (which just takes the default color and fades it to transparent) doesn't do much. Click the gradient to open the Gradient Editor to select a more interesting series of colors.

- **Technique.** To understand this option (and those that follow), you need to understand how Outer Glow works behind the scenes. Basically, it makes a blurred, slightly larger copy of the layer and fills that layer according to the choices you make here. Technique determines how closely that copy (the glow) matches your original. You have two choices: Softer and Precise. Softer is the default and smoothes the edges so that the glow looks more ethereal and organic. But use Precise for those times when the glow needs to follow the contours of the original object more closely.

- **Spread.** Increases the size of the "copy" of the layer I just mentioned. Another way to look at this is that Photoshop is uniformly increasing the size of the layer's transparency and blurring that. A larger Spread value creates a bigger glow that is thick where it touches the object.

- **Size.** This should probably be called "blur" because that is more descriptive of what it does. Increasing the Size value adds more blur.

- **Contour.** Click the down arrow next to the Contour swatch (the default contour looks like a ramp) to see the default library of contours. This is a tough parameter to describe, but it's worth the strain on your brain to learn it. Contour controls the glow falloff. Think of the 3D wizard lady lying on a table (like Frankenstein's monster), and imagine that you could take a

(continued on next page)

cross section of the glow at that angle. That is what the contour would look like. The right side of each contour preset represents the glow closest to the object, whereas the left side represents the glow at the farthest visible point away from the object. The height of the contour represents the brightness of the glow, with areas at the top being the brightest and areas at the bottom being darkest. As a result, if you choose a contour that looks like mountains, the end result would be rings of glow around your object.

- **Anti-aliased.** Softens edges of the glow for a slightly smoother effect. I typically only use this option if I'm getting undesirable dots (called "noise").

- **Range.** Determines how much of the glow is affected by the contour. Let's say you used a "mountainy" contour to create glowy rings as mentioned previously. Increasing the Range value tells Photoshop that you want the rings of glow to encompass more of the glow, so the rings will be both bigger and closer to the object. Reducing the Range value tells Photoshop that you want less of the glow to be taken up by the contour, which makes the rings of glow much smaller and farther away from the object.

- **Jitter.** This parameter only works when using a gradient glow. Jitter randomizes where the colors in the gradient go. Let's say you want to create a sparkly aura around a character, and you want many colors in the sparkles. Simply select a gradient with many colors and increase the Jitter value. Instead of having waves of color, it will take the colors of the gradient and scramble them around randomly.

Creating a Glowing Wireframe

I remember as a young lad watching all those sweet futuristic 1980s kid movies like *War Games, Cloak and Dagger,* and so on. And if there's one thing I learned from that genre of films, it's that cool, green wireframes indicate spy secrets and government plots. So, in this next mini-lesson, you'll use the same Outer Glow effect you just looked at to create a more intense wireframe—a wireframe that screams of conspiracies and hacking government computers running DOS.

Open the Herbie Cam.3ds file at the default resolution (1024 x 1024) from the Chapter 3 folder, put Herbie in the Wireframe render mode, adjust the position of the robot as desired, and accept your changes to exit 3D Object mode. Next, create a new blank layer, fill it with black, drag it underneath the layer with Herbie on it, and apply some Outer Glow to Herbie as you did to the wizard lady earlier.

This time, go to the Outer Glow options and click once on the glow color swatch (**FIGURE 3.14A**) to open the Adobe Color Picker. From here, select a circa 1980s computer wireframe green (**FIGURE 3.14B**). Choose the RGB values 93, 243, 11. You might also want to fiddle with the Spread and Size values to make this glow look a little better (**FIGURE 3.14C**).

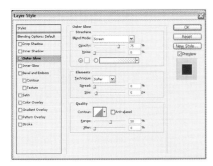

FIGURE 3.14A Click the swatch in the Outer Glow options to change its color using the Adobe Color Picker

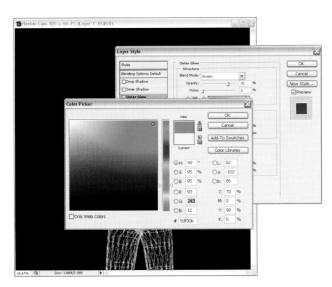

FIGURE 3.14B Let's use this techy green.

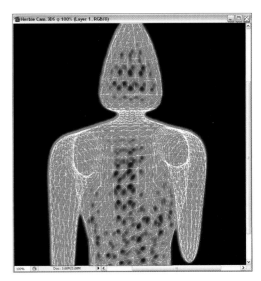

FIGURE 3.14C This is the glow after making it more substantial by adjusting Spread and Size.

This short lesson shows you a very important fact about the way Photoshop creates wireframes from 3D objects. That is, Photoshop actually displays the wireframe mesh with transparency. It might seem like an insignificant detail, but this is what allows you to add effects like this to all the individual "wires" instead of the entire object.

It is very important to note that the different render modes produce these variations in transparent areas. You've just looked at two examples using the exact same Outer Glow effect with wildly different results, all due to the differences of transparency in their respective render modes. And if you were to change the wireframe mode of the robot back to its default render mode, you would have a very similar result to the previous example with the wizard lady.

The Spacebar Shortcuts

Here are some *great* navigational shortcuts to toggle the tools used to zoom in, zoom out, and pan around your documents in Photoshop. To zoom in, hold the spacebar and Ctrl/Cmd and then click on the area you want to zoom in on. To zoom out, hold the spacebar and Alt/Opt-click. As with zooming in, Photoshop attempts to center the area you click on as you zoom out. To pan around an image, simply hold the spacebar and click and drag around with the mouse. The nice thing about these keyboard shortcuts is that they just temporarily toggle these functions. So, while you're selecting or painting, for example, you can use these shortcuts to reposition your document. As soon as you release the keys on the keyboard, the tools you were using before become active again. These keyboard shortcuts also work in some other Adobe programs (like Illustrator), although to zoom out you'll need to hold the Ctrl/Cmd key in addition to the others. Note that these shortcuts will also work in the document window *while* you have the Layer Style dialog open!

Using Multiple Layer Styles and Render Modes

Thanks to the variations in transparency that the render modes produce, you can also combine Layer Styles in interesting ways by duplicating 3D layers and adjusting the render mode and Layer Styles of the duplicates.

For example, you can combine the render modes of two different copies of a wireframe to create an outer glow around the entire object and also around the individual wires of the wireframe.

Reopen the Herbie Cam.3ds file from the Chapter 3 folder. Using Herbie and a black background layer for this example, follow these steps:

1. Enter 3D Object mode. Create a silhouette effect by applying the No Lights render mode and applying a green Outer Glow effect. Adjust as desired.

2. Duplicate the layer.

3. On the duplicate layer (the one on top), change the light settings back to Lights from File, or something else more standard.

4. Also on the duplicate layer, change the render mode to Wireframe. And that's it! (See **FIGURE 3.15A**.) Simply changing the render mode to Wireframe causes the Layer Style to automatically update to respond to the layer's new transparency. You may want to adjust the Outer Glow settings to adapt better to the wireframe (**FIGURE 3.15B**). Here's what my Layers palette looks like after completing this exercise (**FIGURE 3.15C**).

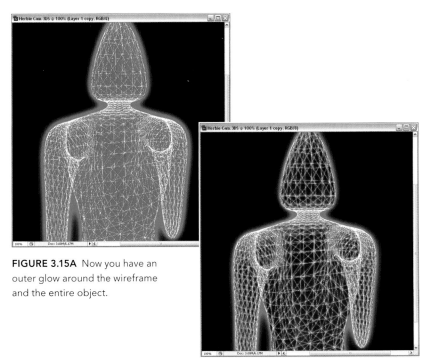

FIGURE 3.15A Now you have an outer glow around the wireframe and the entire object.

FIGURE 3.15B After tweaking the glow to be better suited to the wireframe.

FIGURE 3.15C My Layers palette after completing this exercise.

Making Thicker Wireframes

Because of how Photoshop creates wireframes with transparency, you can also beef up a wireframe, making it thicker. Just add a Stroke effect from the Layer Style dialog (**FIGURE 3.16A**). The Stroke effect draws an outline around the transparency of a layer. Wireframe lines are so thin that the default Stroke setting appears to make the lines thicker.

NOTE   The default color of the Stroke effect is red. You can choose any color you want by simply clicking the color swatch and choosing a different color.

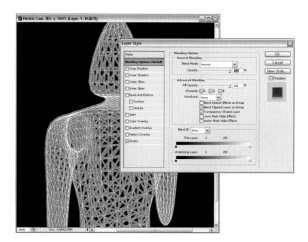

FIGURE 3.16A Adding a Layer Style with a Stroke effect makes a thicker wireframe.

As with Outer Glow, you can access the Stroke options by selecting the Stroke check box on the left side of the dialog. Most of these parameters are self-explanatory, except for Position. You can alter the Position parameter in the Stroke options to adjust how the stroke aligns with the layer. The default is Outside, meaning that the stroke is drawn outside the layer. Center means the stroke is split—half the stroke is on the layer and the other half is drawn outside the layer (**FIGURE 3.16B**). Setting the Position to Inside draws the stroke entirely inside the layer (**FIGURE 3.16C**).

TIP   If you want a wireframe that has a different color but isn't any thicker, add a Stroke effect, change the color of the stroke, and then change the Position to Inside.

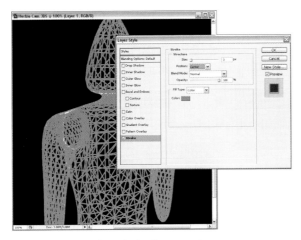

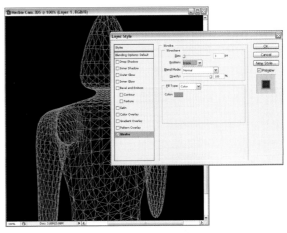

FIGURE 3.16B Stroke with the Center option. Notice how half the stroke is inside the object and half is outside the boundaries of the object.

FIGURE 3.16C With Stroke Position set to Inside, the entire stroke is contained within the bounds of the object.

Creating a Drop Shadow

So far, you've been looking at light that glows against a dark background. But what if the situation was reversed and you had a light object on a light background? That's where drop shadows come in handy.

For this example, open the Plastic_Bottle.obj file in the Plastic Bottle folder in the 3D content folder that ships with Photoshop (**FIGURE 3.17A**).

FIGURE 3.17A The Plastic Bottle model that ships with Photoshop.

1. (Optional) You can transform this bottle a bit to get a more attractive angle, as I did in **FIGURE 3.17B**.

FIGURE 3.17B After repositioning the bottle.

2. Add a white background behind this bottle in the same way that you added black backgrounds behind objects earlier in this chapter (**FIGURE 3.17C**).

FIGURE 3.17C The bottle with a white background.

3. Enter 3D Object mode to change the render mode of the bottle to Line Illustration. Change the Crease Threshold to 13, change the Face Color to white,

and change the Line Color to a blue color. Then use the RGB values of 27, 190, 231 (**FIGURE 3.17D**). Accept the changes and exit 3D Object mode.

FIGURE 3.17D The bottle using the Line Illustration render mode with Crease Threshold set to 13, Face Color set to white, and Line Color set to the RGB values 27, 190, 231.

4. This image looks great; it's super clean and very artistic. The only problem might be that it's just a wee bit too light. So double-click the layer to open the Layer Styles dialog and add the Drop Shadow effect (**FIGURE 3.17E**). The intent of this effect is to add a shadow behind an object to make it appear to be hovering over the page a little.

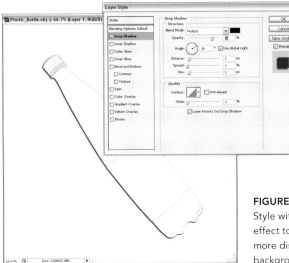

FIGURE 3.17E Add a Layer Style with the Drop Shadow effect to make this bottle more distinct from its background.

Now the problem is that the shadow is too close to the bottle, making it look flat. You'll fix this in the next step.

5. What you need to do is move the shadow away from the object and blur it a little more so that the illusion of depth is not blown by having a drop shadow that is too uniform. Take the Distance slider up to 40 pixels. This will offset the shadow away from the bottle, which will create the illusion that it has more depth (**FIGURE 3.17F**).

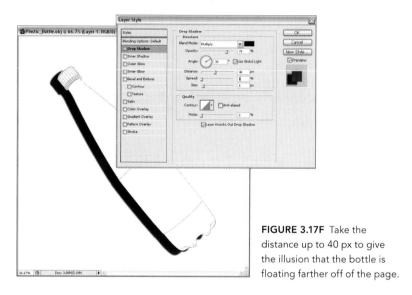

FIGURE 3.17F Take the distance up to 40 px to give the illusion that the bottle is floating farther off of the page.

6. But now the problem is that the shadow is too sharp. Usually, the farther away an object gets from the surface that it is casting its shadow, the softer (i.e., more blurry) the shadow will become. Just like with Outer Glow, the Size value here is like a blur on the drop shadow. Take the Size value to about 20 px or so (**FIGURE 3.17G**).

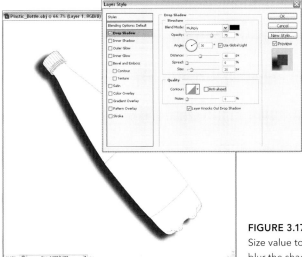

FIGURE 3.17G Increase the Size value to about 20 pixels to blur the shadow's edges.

7. When objects are moved farther from their shadows, the shadows tend to fade away a little. This is because the shadow has more room for ambient light to mix with it. To mimic this effect, take down the Opacity value of the shadow to about 40% (**FIGURE 3.17H**). If the bottle looks like it is made out of a transparent material (like clear glass or plastic), you might want to reduce the opacity further. This will do for now.

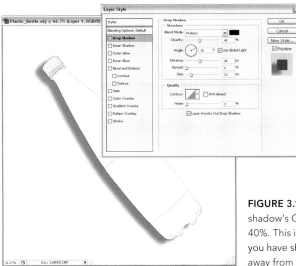

FIGURE 3.17H Reduce the shadow's Opacity value to around 40%. This is a good idea when you have shadows that are far away from their subjects.

More About the Drop Shadow Effect

You need to understand that Drop Shadow works behind the scenes similar to the way that Outer Glow works. Namely, it makes a copy of the layer and allows you to adjust the copy. Because of the similarities, you'll notice many parameters, like Spread, Size, and Contour, that are common between the two effects. But there are two important options that Drop Shadow has that are unique to creating drop shadows. The first is Angle. Drop shadows are created by light coming down at an angle, so this value determines where that light is coming from. By default, the light comes from the upper right, so it makes sense that the default shadow is on the lower left of the object. The other value is Distance. This specifies how far away the shadow is from the object. This creates the illusion that the object is floating farther away from the surface.

NOTE   Because of what Photoshop is doing in the background to create these Layer Styles, these effects can greatly increase the size of your Photoshop documents.

Hacking Layer Styles to Create an Outer Shadow

Drop shadows have a definite angle. But sometimes you might want to create a dark area that surrounds an object uniformly on every side. However, there is no Outer Shadow effect, per se. To create this effect, apply the Outer Glow effect. Next, change the Outer Glow Blend mode to Normal or to one of the darkening Blend modes, like Multiply. Then, simply change the glow color from a light color to a dark color and behold! You've now hacked Outer Glow to become Outer Shadow!

Adding the Bevel and Emboss Effect

At this point, the bottle looks like it exists in a more 3D world, even though you stripped it of its 3D render mode. You can actually use another Layer Style effect, Bevel and Emboss, to add more depth to this bottle.

The purpose of the Bevel and Emboss effect is to add a fake thickness to the edges of a 2D object to give it the illusion of a 3D object. So it would seem that this effect is obsolete when dealing with 3D objects, because they are already 3D. But when dealing with 3D objects like this, it can come in handy. The render mode you added to the bottle gave it a distinct 2D appearance, so a tactful application of Bevel and Emboss will give it a nice touch.

Bevel and Emboss essentially creates its effect by adding a highlight on one side of the object and a shadow on the other side. It gets a little more complicated than that, but essentially, that's what is going on here.

So, if you continue where you left off with the bottle, you can add a little more depth:

1. Add the Bevel and Emboss Layer Style to display the Bevel and Emboss options (**FIGURE 3.18A**).

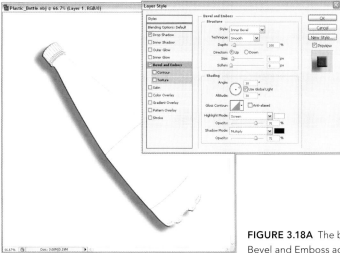

FIGURE 3.18A The bottle with Bevel and Emboss added.

2. From top to bottom, take Depth to 30%, Size to 75 px, and Shadow Opacity (at the very bottom of the dialog) to 30%. The highlight on the right side is very subtle and only discernible where the blue lines on the bottle are. But the shadow area on the left of the bottle adds a nice dimension to this line illustration (**FIGURE 3.18B**).

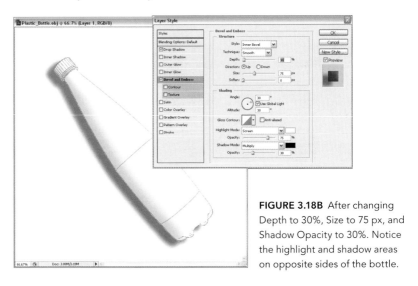

FIGURE 3.18B After changing Depth to 30%, Size to 75 px, and Shadow Opacity to 30%. Notice the highlight and shadow areas on opposite sides of the bottle.

Now you have the best of both worlds: an interesting 2D appearance to your 3D model with added depth thanks to Photoshop's 2D tools.

Making the Drop Shadow an Autonomous Layer

You can take the drop shadow effect a step further and make the Drop Shadow effect its own separate layer, which affords you much more power in the way of compositing 3D elements into a scene.

For this example, let's composite two of my favorite images: a cheesy, circa 1950s UFO and the city of New Orleans.

1. From the Chapter 3 folder, open the Photoshop document UFO over Pontchartrain.psd (**FIGURE 3.19A**).

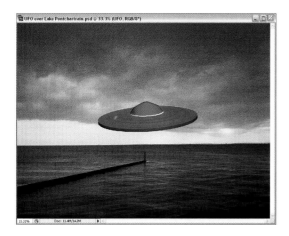

FIGURE 3.19A The UFO over Pontchartrain.psd file.

2. Add a Drop Shadow effect to the UFO layer and increase the Size value to 90 pixels. Now let's take this shadow and bring it down to the surface of the water, separate from the UFO. Because of the distance, you want the shadow to be a little blurry (**FIGURE 3.19B**). Click OK to apply the Layer Style.

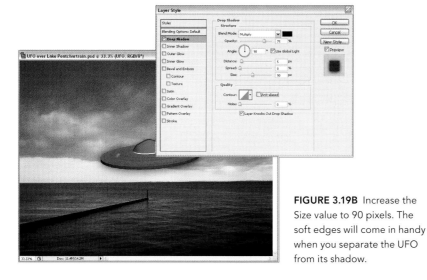

FIGURE 3.19B Increase the Size value to 90 pixels. The soft edges will come in handy when you separate the UFO from its shadow.

FIGURE 3.19C After right-clicking the fx icon, select Create Layer to make the shadow its own distinct layer.

3. In the Layers palette, right-click the fx icon that appears on the UFO layer. From the context menu, select Create Layer toward the bottom of the menu (**FIGURE 3.19C**). A message pops up indicating that the effects may not look exactly the same after you do this. For this particular effect, you won't notice much difference from the original. Any trade-offs in this instance are

worth it. The drop shadow is removed from the UFO and becomes its own autonomous layer, which can then be manipulated independently.

4. Select the new layer, UFO's Drop Shadow. Select the Move tool in the Tools palette and move the shadow around as you please by clicking on it and dragging in the document window. Earlier, I harped for a while about how the Move tool is an enemy of 3D layers. However, once the drop shadow is a separate 2D layer, it is completely legal and acceptable to use the Move tool to move it. You can then move the shadow directly on top of the water to give the illusion that the UFO is actually over Lake Pontchartrain (**FIGURE 3.19D**).

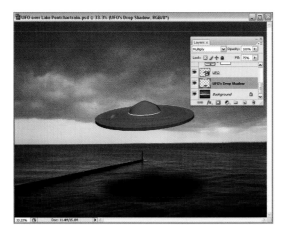

FIGURE 3.19D Once the shadow is separate, select the Move tool and drag and drop the shadow down until it appears to be on the surface of the water.

NOTE   Be aware that once you've used the Create Layer command, you've made a regular old layer (or multiple layers, depending on how many effects you've applied). You will no longer be able to use Layer Style parameters to adjust things like Size or Spread. Giving up that parametric control is worth it for this effect, but it's something you should be conscious of in the future. If you're not ready to part with that kind of control over your Layer Styles, you can always duplicate the layer with the styles, lock it, and turn off its visibility. Then, use the Create Layer command on the duplicate. If things don't work out, you can always go back to the original.

The benefit of making the drop shadow an autonomous layer is that you can have Photoshop's Layer Styles generate a really nice, parametric shadow effect for you automatically. I used a simple UFO here, but imagine the difficulty in creating a shadow on a more complex object.

Really Rad Right-clicking

Right-clicking is pretty much a universal problem solver in Photoshop. You can right-click all over the place. Try it in the document window to access options based on the currently selected tool. You can also right-click tools that are grouped with other tools in the Tools palette (like the Marquee tools, for instance), if you want to access the tools that are not currently visible.

Because right-clicking is so powerful, it can get a little "crowded" when right-clicking in the Layers palette. Right-clicking needs to be very precise here, because you will get different context menus when clicking on the name of the layer, the layer thumbnail, layer masks, or the Layer Styles' fx icon (just to name a few). So be sure you click precisely on the fx icon to get the menu containing Create Layer.

NOTE   For extra credit, try using the wizard lady 3D file instead of the UFO. To make this example look believable, you'll need to transform the shadow layer after going through the preceding steps. You can do this by choosing Edit > Free Transform, or by using the keyboard shortcut, Ctrl/Cmd+T. You can resize the shadow by clicking and dragging on the control points. You can also create a perspective effect by Ctrl/Cmd-clicking on a corner point and dragging it around (**FIGURE 3.20A**). To top this sundae off with the proverbial cherry, add a layer mask to erase the shadow gradually as it goes away from the character (**FIGURE 3.20B**).

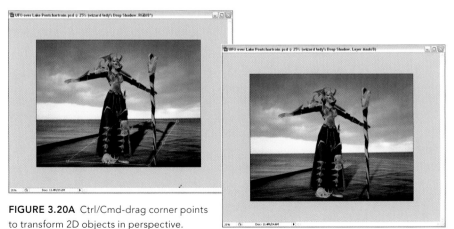

FIGURE 3.20A Ctrl/Cmd-drag corner points to transform 2D objects in perspective.

FIGURE 3.20B
After adding a layer mask to create a gradual fade of the shadow.

This shadow is a great effect. However, notice that the light source in the photo of the lake is coming from a different angle than the shadow suggests. The light is coming from behind the object, but the shadow placement makes it look as if the light is going toward the object. This creates a visual anomaly that you sub-consciously detect without hesitation. In other words, it's a big red flag to how fake this shot is. Particularly if you are new to the world of 3D, this is something to watch out for. In this instance, if you want to add more realism, you could move the shadow closer to the bottom of the screen to give the illusion that the light is coming from behind the UFO. You could also adjust the opacity, shape, and size of the shadow to aid in the illusion.

So here again you can see the benefit of Photoshop Extended—the ability to use standard, familiar 2D tools in conjunction with 3D objects.

Adjusting the Color and Luminance of 3D Objects

Often, you'll want to adjust the appearance of 3D objects for several reasons. Sometimes, after adjusting the lighting in Photoshop, 3D objects still look too dark or too light, or not vibrant enough, or they don't have enough contrast, and so forth. Also, as you composite 3D elements into an existing scene, the matching of the color of the object to the background plays a very significant role in the quality of the final piece.

About Adjustment Layers

In Photoshop, there are generally three ways to make color and luminance (aka brightness) adjustments: with tools from the Tools palette, adjustments from the Adjustments menu (Image > Adjustments), and adjustment layers. The only one of these methods that works on 3D layers is adjustment layers.

Initially, this sounds really terrible. However, even though it is slightly limiting, adjustment layers are the only method mentioned previously that is nondestruc-tive. This means that you can go back at any point and make changes, just like you did with Layer Styles. And as with Layer Styles, adjustment layers can be altered, changed, and removed even after the saved document is closed.

You can apply an adjustment layer from the Layers palette. But you can't do too much in the Layers palette without a layer. So, create a new blank Photoshop document by selecting File > New and choosing the preset Default Photoshop Size, and then clicking OK. At the bottom of the palette is an icon that is a half-black/half-white circle (**FIGURE 3.21**). Click that icon to display all the different types of adjustments that can be applied as adjustment layers. To keep things simple, select Solid Color from the top of the list. This will simply create a layer that is filled with color. Select a color from the Adobe Color Picker that pops up, and click OK. The Solid Color adjustment layer now shows up in the Layers palette immediately above the layer that was selected when you created the adjustment layer.

Notice that all layers beneath the adjustment layer are affected by this solid color. This is very visual and obvious in this example, but remember as you go through this chapter that it is just as applicable to other types of adjustment layers as well. If, for example, you had an adjustment layer that had a lightening effect on it, all layers below it would be affected (and therefore, lightened) by it.

Another feature that is pretty much universal with adjustment layers is the ability to edit them by double-clicking on their icons in the Layers palette. Many types of adjustment layers have unique icons, but their behavior is the same. **FIGURE 3.22** shows the icon for a Solid Color adjustment layer. When you double-click it, the Adobe Color Picker pops right back up and you can change the color if you'd like. How easy is that?

FIGURE 3.21 This half-black/half-white circle icon represents one of the most powerful and important parts of Photoshop: adjustment layers.

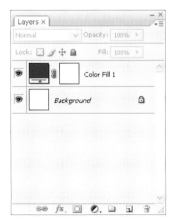

FIGURE 3.22 The square of solid color where the layer's thumbnail should be indicates that this is a Solid Color adjustment layer. Double-click that spot to reopen this adjustment and make changes.

And although the nature and purpose of adjustment layers varies wildly, they all adjust only layers beneath them.

Adjustment layers are extremely powerful. Even when I'm doing 2D work in Photoshop, I use adjustment layers to make color and brightness adjustments about 99 percent of the time. Let's examine a few adjustment layers that I find very useful.

Adjusting Color

When making simple color alterations, there isn't an effect that is easier to use and more powerful than Hue/Saturation.

For this example, reopen a fresh copy of UFO over Pontchartrain.psd from the Chapter 3 folder. Select the 3D UFO layer, click the adjustment layer icon, and add a Hue/Saturation adjustment layer, which is found in the middle of the list (**FIGURE 3.23**).

FIGURE 3.23 Click the adjustment layer icon to see the list of adjustments available as adjustment layers. You'll find Hue/Saturation about halfway down this list.

Before making any changes, make sure that the Preview check box is selected so you can see your results. The first option you see in this dialog (from top to bottom) is Hue. Hue refers to the basic color family (e.g., blue, red, etc.). If you adjust the Hue slider, you will shift all color values proportionally through the color wheel. Use the rainbow colored gradient at the bottom of the dialog for reference.

TIP You can adjust the Hue/Saturation values in three ways. You can manually type in a number, or click and drag on the sliders, or you can click and scrub on the actual name of the value. For example, with the Hue property, just click on the word Hue, and then drag left or right to alter the value. The official name for this functionality is "scrubby slider."

Notice that as you adjust this effect, the UFO *and* the background change. This happens because you selected the UFO layer before applying the adjustment. Remember that adjustment layers affect every layer beneath them and that adjustment layers are created on top of the currently selected layer. So now this adjustment makes sense. I'll talk later about how to control which layers this adjustment applies to.

Return to the dialog and adjust the Saturation value. Saturation is the intensity of a color. A television show for children might have very saturated colors, whereas the art for an emo band would probably be quite desaturated. Notice that adjusting the saturation with this slider universally saturates or desaturates the entire image (**FIGURES 3.24** and **3.25**).

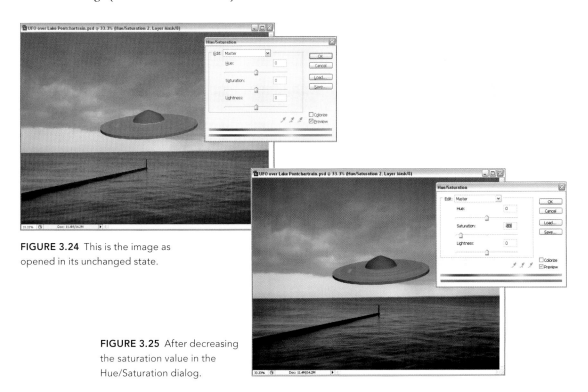

FIGURE 3.24 This is the image as opened in its unchanged state.

FIGURE 3.25 After decreasing the saturation value in the Hue/Saturation dialog.

TIP While you're working with color adjustments (especially with saturation), it's a good idea to frequently select and deselect the Preview check box. Sometimes, you can get a little overzealous when trying to fix your images. Constantly referencing the original will help you keep that in check and will help prevent unrealistic changes.

The Lightness slider is one slider you'll want to be a little careful with. If you have an image that you want to brighten or darken, it may be tempting to try to do that here. I assure you, however, that this is neither the time nor the place for such alterations. The problem with the Lightness slider (as I'll discuss in more detail when we look at adjusting luminance a little later) is that it universally lightens or darkens every pixel. This is generally not a good idea for photos. If you lighten an image, you still want to keep the blackest point of the image black. **FIGURE 3.26** shows what happens when I lighten the UFO image with the Lightness slider. So, this Lightness feature is used for lightening or darkening objects with flat color (like a cartoon) but never on areas of continuous tone (like a photo or a 3D model).

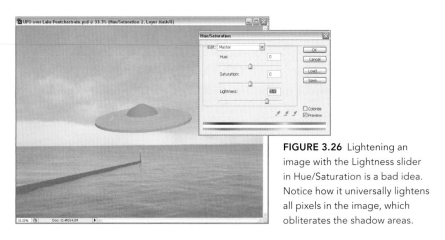

FIGURE 3.26 Lightening an image with the Lightness slider in Hue/Saturation is a bad idea. Notice how it universally lightens all pixels in the image, which obliterates the shadow areas.

One of my favorite features of Hue/Saturation is that it allows you to control which range of color you're adjusting. Let's say you want to adjust the pinkish-orange area of the background image that is free of clouds. With all the soft edges, this would be a challenge using Photoshop's traditional selection tools. With Hue/Saturation, no selections are necessary. You simply click the Edit down arrow in the Hue/Saturation dialog and change the range from Master to the basic color you want to alter (**FIGURE 3.27**).

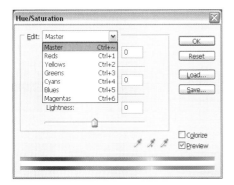

FIGURE 3.27 In Hue/Saturation, you can select a range of colors to process from the Edit drop-down list.

In this instance, the sky is a pinkish-orange, and there is not a pinkish-orange option. In lieu of pink, select Red from the drop-down list. Then as you adjust the Hue or Saturation sliders, you'll notice that only that particular area of the sky is adjusted (**FIGURE 3.28**). If you ever have trouble getting Hue/Saturation to recognize the color you want to alter, simply take your cursor outside the dialog and over to your image. The cursor will turn into an eyedropper. With that tool, click on the area you want to adjust. Hue/Saturation will then adapt to only adjusting that color range.

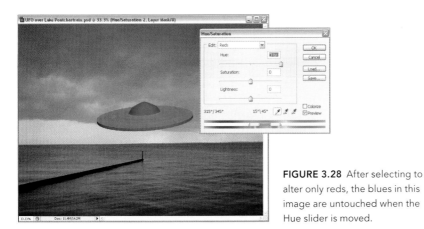

FIGURE 3.28 After selecting to alter only reds, the blues in this image are untouched when the Hue slider is moved.

When you're happy with your results, click OK. And, as expected, the adjustment is applied to both the UFO and the lake.

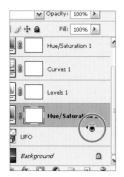

FIGURE 3.29 While holding the Alt/Opt key, you'll see this icon when hovering your cursor over the line in between two layers. This icon indicates that if you were to click here, you would create a clipping mask.

Applying an adjustment layer to only one layer

If you want to apply the Hue/Saturation effect to only the photo of the lake, you could simply drag and drop the adjustment layer beneath the UFO layer after you're done with your adjustments in the Hue/Saturation dialog. But what if you want the same color change to apply only to the UFO? With the adjustment layer immediately above the UFO in the layer stack, hold the Alt/Opt key while clicking the line that divides the layers in the Layers palette. Before clicking, you should see an icon that looks like two overlapping circles with a left-facing arrowhead (**FIGURE 3.29**).

After clicking, the two layers (the UFO and the Hue/Saturation adjustment layer) will form a clipping mask. Basically, that means that the layer on top (the adjustment layer in this case) will only be visible where the layer below it is (**FIGURE 3.30**). The great benefit here is that this relationship is live. So, if you were to move your 3D object around, the clipping mask ensures that the color adjustment still only applies to the area that the UFO takes up. You should even see it update in real time as you transform the UFO.

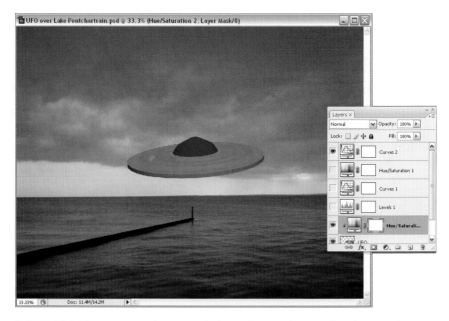

FIGURE 3.30 After creating a clipping mask, the top layer (in this case, the adjustment layer) will only be visible where the layer immediately below it has pixels. The Hue/Saturation adjustment layer was told to only alter red values, but there isn't much red in the UFO, so there isn't much of a difference. But notice the change in the background.

Using clipping masks is extremely important when working with 3D objects. As you are trying to composite a 3D object by matching colors, clipping masks will be very helpful. In those instances, you will not want to change the background color, only the color of the 3D object. This likewise applies to instances where the 3D object is too dark and you want to adjust its luminance independent of other layers. Of all the countless Photoshop documents I've created or worked on in the last few years, I believe every one has at least one adjustment layer with a clipping mask.

Understanding and Adjusting Luminance

Let's take a look at how to adjust luminance problems. Included in this category are objects that are too dark, too light, have too much contrast or not enough, and any combination of these.

Open your old friend the wizard lady.3ds file from the wizard lady folder in the Chapter 3 folder. This file is good to use because she comes in looking a little too dark (**FIGURE 3.31**). Let's look at a few ways to fix her.

FIGURE 3.31 The wizard lady is a shady character. Literally.

But first, you need to understand something very important about highlights and shadows. When you make an object brighter or darker, you do not want to simultaneously adjust the opposite end of the spectrum. In other words, when you make an object brighter, you want to keep the darkest point unchanged. Using the wizard lady, for example, even though she needs some serious lightening, you still want pure black in her shadows. The reverse is also true for darkening an object.

The new and improved Brightness/Contrast adjustment

The easiest way to brighten an object in Photoshop CS3 is to use a Brightness/Contrast adjustment layer (**FIGURE 3.32**). Now, if you're familiar with previous versions of Photoshop, I've probably lost all respect in your eyes by saying that. You see, in previous versions of Photoshop Brightness/Contrast was a terrible effect to use on an image. It universally lightened or darkened every pixel.

But that's all changed in CS3. The good folks at Adobe have gone back and "fixed" the way Brightness/Contrast works so that it now performs intelligently, leaving blacks black and whites white.

I suppose it goes without saying, but when in this dialog (**FIGURE 3.33**), dragging the Brightness slider to the right will brighten your object and dragging it to the left will darken it. To add contrast, take the contrast slider to the right, and to diminish contrast, take the slider to the left. Pretty simple. Just make sure that you don't select the Use Legacy check box. That will revert the behavior of this adjustment to the way it used to behave in previous versions. It would be like buying a movie on VHS tape when you have a DVD player. Nobody wants that.

Using Levels

So, Brightness/Contrast is very easy to use, but it doesn't give you much control. What if you just want to adjust the highlights and not the midtones? You can get more control over luminance adjustments by using a Levels adjustment. Let's add a Levels adjustment layer in the same way you've been adding other adjustment layers—by clicking the drop-down list at the bottom of the Layers palette.

The Levels dialog presents you with something called a histogram (**FIGURE 3.34**). A histogram gives you a readout of how much certain luminance values are used in an image. From left to right, black to white values are represented. So, the far left area of the histogram, where the black triangle is (**FIGURE 3.35**) represents pure black. If the histogram has vertical data above that point, it indicates that there is pure black in your object. The higher the data goes, the more of that shade you have in your image. In this case, the area above pure white (the white triangle on the right) is empty, and all the values are piled up along the left side of the histogram (**FIGURE 3.36**). This tells you that the majority of the brightness values of your image are in the shadow areas. And since there isn't any data over the white triangle, or any on the right side of this chart, you can discern that there isn't any pure white or any highlights.

FIGURE 3.32 A Brightness/Contrast adjustment layer can be created in a way that is similar to the way you created the Hue/Saturation adjustment layer. Simply select it from this drop-down list.

FIGURE 3.33 The simple, new and improved Brightness/Contrast adjustment.

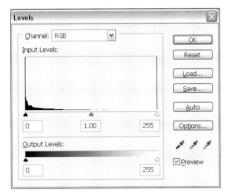

FIGURE 3.34 This chart of sorts is called a histogram.

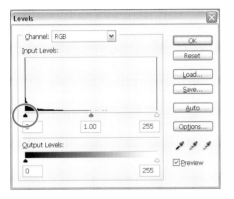

FIGURE 3.35 The leftmost triangle in the Levels dialog represents pure black.

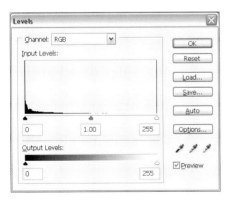

FIGURE 3.36 As you look at the left side of this histogram, you see that there is a disproportionate amount of information in the shadow areas of this image.

NOTE   There is also a Histogram palette in Photoshop, which gives you a constant histogram reading while you work in Photoshop.

So you need to tell Levels to make the point that's currently the brightest (**FIGURE 3.37**) pure white. To do that, simply drag the Highlights slider (the white arrow on the bottom right of the histogram) to the left, and stop right when the slider is under the first area that has data above it (**FIGURE 3.38**). If you were to keep moving the white arrow past that area, it would force all of the values to the right of the Highlights slider to pure white. Doing this would essentially get rid of all the contrast in the highlight areas. That would be bad.

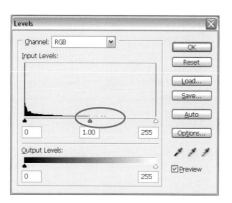

FIGURE 3.37 This shade of light gray is actually the brightest area in the image.

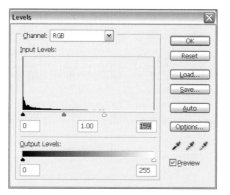

FIGURE 3.38 Drag the Highlights slider over from the right to the brightest point in the image to force it to brighten to white.

After you've adjusted the Highlights slider, you will have successfully adjusted the highlights. If the image didn't have pure black, you could also drag the Shadows slider to the right to get pure black. This is simply the exact opposite of what you did with the Highlights slider.

When you have the white and black values where you want them, it's time to adjust everything in between. Those values are called midtones. To adjust the midtones, click and drag the gray Midtones slider in between the Shadows and Highlights sliders (**FIGURE 3.39**). The rule for adjusting midtones isn't as rigid as it is with pure white and pure black. If you'd like your image darker, drag it to the right. If you want it lighter, drag it to the right. Notice that this doesn't alter the very lightest or very darkest areas of the object. Pretty sweet.

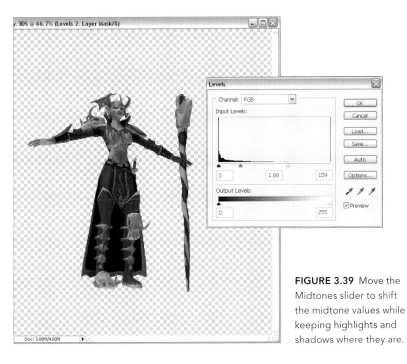

FIGURE 3.39 Move the Midtones slider to shift the midtone values while keeping highlights and shadows where they are.

TIP   As you adjust luminance, you'll notice that often the colors also shift slightly. To fix this, simply change the Blend mode of the adjustment layer from Normal to Luminance, which is done in the Layers palette after the settings are accepted and the dialog is closed. This forces the adjustment layer to only correct brightness and preserves the color values of the underlying layers. You can use this trick on any type of adjustment layer, from Brightness/Contrast to Curves.

Admittedly, Levels is much more challenging to master than Brightness/Contrast, and I haven't even discussed all the options and features here. But all the brain sweat you had to go through to understand this adjustment is worth it because of all the control Levels gives you. The last adjustment you'll use is even more challenging than Levels, but as you might assume, it also gives you more control.

About Curves

The Curves adjustment is the most powerful way to adjust luminance in Photoshop. It can be a tough feature to master. For this reason, many Photoshop users completely avoid it. And to be honest, most luminance issues can be resolved by Levels. But it really pays to go to the extra trouble to get a grasp on how Curves works. Why? Good question.

With Brightness/Contrast you have no control over what values are adjusted. With Levels, you have control over shadows, midtones, and highlights. But what if you want more precise control? What if you just want to adjust a particular area of gray and keep all other values the same? The Curves adjustment gives you that kind of control.

Go ahead and add a Curves adjustment layer. The main interface in this dialog is another chart, this time with a diagonal line. Well, it's actually somewhat similar to the histogram in Levels. As a matter of fact, Photoshop CS3 added a histogram in the background of the Curves interface to help you make adjustments here (**FIGURE 3.40**).

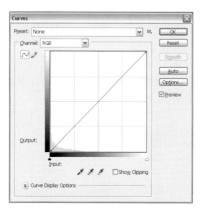

FIGURE 3.40 The all-powerful Curves dialog. That histogram in the background is new to Photoshop CS3.

The key to understanding Curves is knowing what those two gradients along the left edge and bottom of the Curves interface do. The gradient along the bottom of the dialog represents the luminance values in your image, just like with Levels. The gradient along the left edge represents the values that these color are being "remapped," or changed, to. So, by default, you always have that diagonal line because white is mapped to white, black is mapped to black, and so forth. But if you clicked, say, in the middle of the line and dragged the line up, you would be remapping the value shown in **FIGURE 3.41** to the value shown in **FIGURE 3.42**.

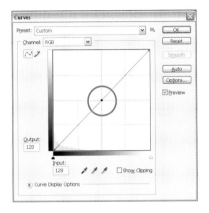

FIGURE 3.41 Using Curves, you can remap this luminance value…

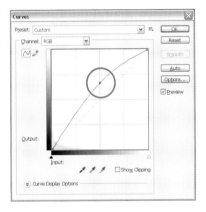

FIGURE 3.42 …to this one.

NOTE Be careful here! A little dab of Curves adjusting will do ya. It's easy to overdo your adjustments in Curves, because the curves you adjust are very sensitive. You might find that you get better results by selecting a point on the curve and moving it by using the arrow keys on your keyboard, which will allow you to create adjustments that are more subtle.

One of the most common Curves adjustments is called an "S curve." This is a really quick and powerful way to increase contrast. To do this, simply click a point about 25 percent of the way into the line from the left edge, and drag down (**FIGURE 3.43**). Notice how subtle the adjustment is. Next, click the line about 75 percent of the way in from the left edge and drag up (**FIGURE 3.44**). The shadows were darkened, and then the highlights were brightened, thereby adding contrast.

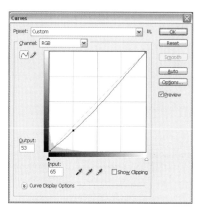

FIGURE 3.43 Click a point about 25% of the way into the curve. Drag it down slightly to darken the shadow areas.

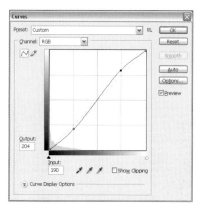

FIGURE 3.44 Click a point about 75% of the way into the curve. Drag it up slightly to lighten the highlight areas.

TIP   If you do get in a pinch and you completely ruin your curve, you can hold the Alt/Opt key to temporarily change the Cancel button to a Reset button. Click the Reset button to reset the dialog box to the way it was when you opened it.

Obviously, the list of color and luminance adjustments you just experimented with is nowhere near exhaustive. But these are the effects that I believe will help you the most when working with 3D objects.

Selecting 3D Outline Pixels

For compositing and masking purposes, it really helps to be able to quickly select the outline of 3D objects. You can do that easily by taking advantage of a great feature of regular layers. That is, you can select the boundary of the layer by holding Ctrl/Cmd while clicking the layer thumbnail in the Layers palette. Photoshop even displays this cool cursor to indicate what you're about to do (**FIGURE 3.45**). After Ctrl/Cmd-clicking, you will have selected the contents of the layer (**FIGURE 3.46**). If the 3D object is displaying a wireframe, the mesh of the wireframe (not the outline of the object) will be selected (**FIGURE 3.47**).

FIGURE 3.45 Hold the Ctrl/Cmd key while hovering your cursor over a layer's thumbnail in the Layers palette to get this Hand-and-Marquee icon. The icon indicates that if you click, you will select the outline of the contents of the layer.

FIGURE 3.46 With the outline of the layer contents selected.

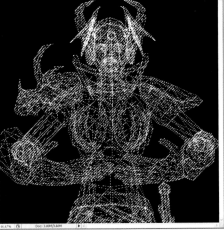

FIGURE 3.47 Using the same technique on a wireframe mesh selects the wires.

This feature can be used for all sorts of cool tricks. Here's just one example of something you can do:

1. Open the file Crazy Wizard Lady.psd (**FIGURE 3.48A**).

FIGURE 3.48A The file Crazy Wizard Lady.psd.

2. Select the outline pixels of this layer by Ctrl/Cmd-clicking its layer thumbnail in the Layers palette (**FIGURE 3.48B**).

FIGURE 3.48B With the outline pixels selected.

3. Make a new blank layer.

4. Select a red color as a foreground color. Fill this layer with the foreground color (**FIGURE 3.48C**). Deselect by pressing Ctrl/Cmd+D or by opening the Select menu at the top of the interface and selecting Deselect.

FIGURE 3.48C A new, blank layer filled with color while the outline of the sorceress layer was selected.

5. Add some Layer Style effects to this layer. Here I added a Gradient Overlay in the Overlay Blend mode, a basic Bevel and Emboss effect, a Drop Shadow effect, and the Satin effect (**FIGURE 3.48D**).

FIGURE 3.48D The new color layer with Layer Style effects applied.

Obviously, this is not one of the intended purposes of the new 3D features in Photoshop Extended. But it can be used to create some really interesting design elements.

You may ask, what is the benefit of using 3D for this? The benefit is the flexibility. Thanks to iPods, silhouettes are a huge design trend right now. If you were going to use a 3D model to create your silhouettes, you could always adjust the angle of the model and change it later. If you trace a photo or use some other 2D means to that end, you do not have the ability to make such changes later.

Saving selections

You can save any selection by choosing Select > Save Selection. In the dialog that pops up, specify a name for your selection so it will be easy to locate at a later time. This creates an alpha channel that is stored in your PSD file. At any time, you can load the selection by choosing Select > Load Selection. In the Load Selection dialog, choose your selection from the Channel drop-down list and click OK. The saved selection is loaded.

TIP   As you can see from the Load Selection dialog, this is another reminder to name files meaningfully in Photoshop. Yes, it takes a little extra time up front, but it easily pays off in the long run. There's nothing more annoying than spending precious near-deadline time trying to decipher what you were thinking weeks ago. Name your files in a way that will be obvious to you in the future!

Using Layer Masks with 3D Layers

Layer masks are another fantastic feature that has been around in Photoshop for years. However, this feature is really reborn when working with 3D files. Layer masks are a nondestructive way to erase a layer's content. They work a little bit differently with 3D layers than they do with 2D layers. Before I get to that difference, let's just have a refresher about layer masks.

Layer mask crash course

Open Tank.psd from the Chapter 3 folder. There is only one layer in this image (**FIGURE 3.49**). By default, Photoshop creates a Background layer out of images that you open. Background layers are locked and will not allow for the movement of the layer, or for layer masks. That might be a little limiting here, so double-click the Background layer. The New Layer dialog appears. You can rename your layer here if you'd like. Either way, this converts the Background layer to a regular old layer.

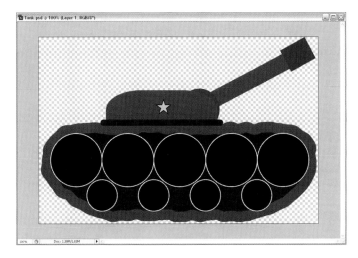

FIGURE 3.49 The Tank.psd file. Notice that there is only one layer in this file.

After the Background layer is converted to a regular layer, click the icon at the bottom of the Layers palette that looks like a square with a circle inside (**FIGURE 3.50**). This adds a layer mask to the layer, which shows up as a white rectangle in between the layer's thumbnail and the layer's name in the Layers palette (**FIGURE 3.51**).

FIGURE 3.50 After converting the Background layer to a regular layer, add a layer mask by clicking the square with a circle inside at the bottom of the Layers palette.

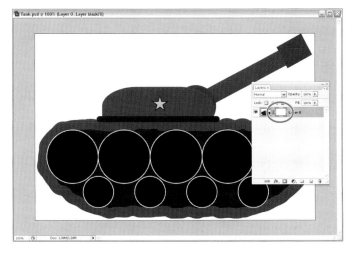

FIGURE 3.51 The layer mask shows up as a white swatch between the layer thumbnail and the name of the layer.

Before going on, you need to make sure that you recognize the difference between activating the layer mask and activating the actual contents of the layer. If you look closely, there are little brackets around the corners indicating which is active. **FIGURE 3.52** shows what it looks like when the layer mask is activated, and **FIGURE 3.53** shows what it looks like after I click the layer thumbnail to activate the contents of the layer.

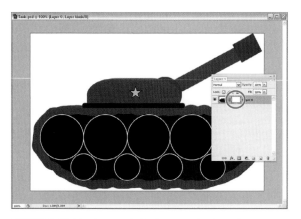

FIGURE 3.52 The layer with the layer mask selected.

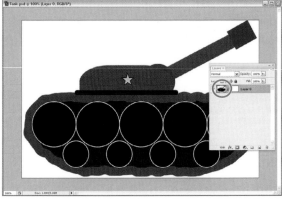

FIGURE 3.53 The layer with the contents of the layer selected.

NOTE You can also look at the top of the document window for an indication as to whether the layer or the mask is active. If your document is maximized, this information appears at the top of the interface in the Photoshop title bar.

Now, onto the magic that is a layer mask. Notice that it is white by default and has no effect on the tank visually. However, if you select the layer mask, select black as your foreground color, select the Paintbrush tool in the Tools palette, and then start painting, you'll notice that you're actually concealing the layer (**FIGURE 3.54**). But don't worry, this is nondestructive erasing. All you have to do is paint with white to recover the areas on the layer that you've erased (**FIGURE 3.55**). For this example, erase the turret and the white background around it so that what you've done with the layer mask will be obvious (**FIGURE 3.56**).

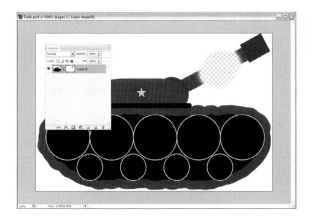

FIGURE 3.54 Painting with black on the layer mask hides parts of the layer.

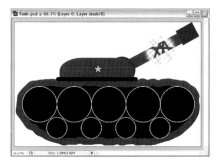

FIGURE 3.55 Painting with white restores the areas that are hidden.

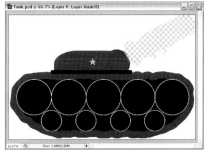

FIGURE 3.56 The tank with the turret "erased" using layer masks.

TIP With layer masks, pure black completely erases a layer, and pure white completely restores it. But shades of gray partially erase and restore. Try experimenting with semitransparency by painting on layer masks with shades of gray. You can also quickly blend two layers together by adding a layer mask to the layer on top and creating a linear gradient on the layer mask that goes from black to white.

If you select the Move tool and move the tank around, you'll notice that the layer mask comes along for the ride. And that's a good thing. If you really did want to get rid of the turret on this tank, you'd want it to stay erased if you moved the tank. This behavior is the default for 2D layers. However, you can change this behavior by clicking the chain icon in between the layer thumbnail and the layer mask thumbnail in the Layers palette (**FIGURE 3.57** on the next page). This unlinks them, so that when you move the tank, the mask you made remains stationary. Most of the time you will probably want to keep them in their default, linked-together relationship.

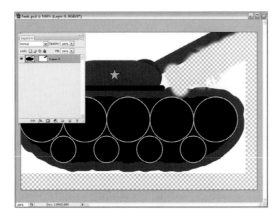

FIGURE 3.57 The chain icon links layers to their layer masks. Click the icon to unlink them, which allows you to move them independently.

Layer masks and 3D objects

Layer masks on 3D objects are unlinked by default, which is the opposite behavior of 2D objects. This may seem really annoying and frustrating at first, but it's actually a great feature. Allow me to demonstrate why this is awesome.

Open UFO over Jackson Square.psd from the Chapter 3 folder (**FIGURE 3.58A**). This is the same UFO you used previously, only now it's terrorizing another great New Orleans landmark. You'll use this little quirk in 3D layer masks to help you composite these two objects together.

FIGURE 3.58A The UFO over Jackson Square.psd file.

1. Select the Background layer and zoom in to the tall, center steeple (**FIGURE 3.58B**).

FIGURE 3.58B Focus on the tallest steeple pictured here.

2. Select the UFO layer and add a layer mask.

3. Select the top area of the steeple. You don't have to take the time to make this perfect, so don't bother selecting the cross at the top. Also, just use the Polygonal Lasso tool to click a few times around the pinnacle to select it (**FIGURE 3.58C**). Or, feel free to use any selection tool you'd like.

FIGURE 3.58C Select the top area of the steeple.

4. Press the letter D and then the letter X on your keyboard. The letter D resets the colors to their defaults, which is white in the foreground and black in the background. Typing the letter X swaps the two colors so that black is your new foreground color and white is your background color. Make sure that the layer mask for the UFO layer is selected and fill the selection area

with the foreground color (black) by pressing Alt+Backspace/Opt+Delete. This will mask out the UFO layer where the steeple is (**FIGURE 3.58D**). Essentially, this creates a steeple-shaped hole on the UFO, giving the illusion that the UFO is coming from behind St. Louis cathedral.

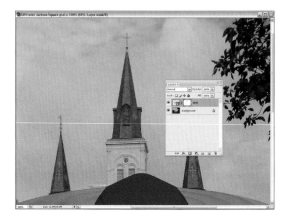

FIGURE 3.58D On the layer mask of the UFO layer, fill the selection with black.

5. Let's say you haven't yet decided where you want the UFO to go. You only know that you want it to appear behind the building. Thanks to the way layer masks work with 3D objects, this is a snap. If you go back into 3D Object mode and move the UFO around, you'll see that the layer mask stays in the same spot (**FIGURE 3.58E**). I love that! Now you can reserve the right to be indecisive because it's so easy to make changes.

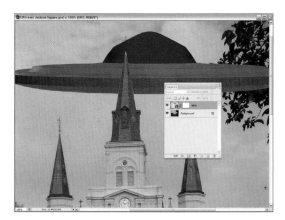

FIGURE 3.58E While in Object mode, moving a 3D layer with a layer mask will not move the mask, only the 3D object. This behavior allows you to easily adjust the placement of your 3D object with minimal fuss.

Playing Back Animations in 3D Files

Depending on the 3D file format you're using, Photoshop allows you to play back animation contained in the file.

As mentioned earlier, I'm a fan of Autodesk's 3DS Max software application. Thankfully for me the .3ds file format output can contain animation that is supported by Photoshop. Some of the other supported file formats (like .u3d) can also store 3D animation.

Open the file Not-so-Merry-go-Round.psd from the Chapter 3 folder (**FIGURE 3.59**). The carousel layer is a 3D file that contains animation. To play it back, you need to be in Object mode. As before, double-click the 3D layer thumbnail in the Layers palette to get there.

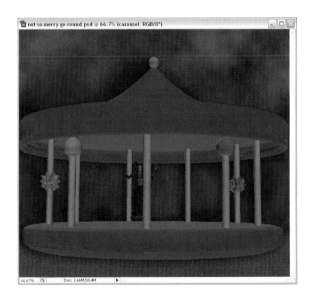

FIGURE 3.59 The Not-so-Merry-go-Round.psd file.

FIGURE 3.60 The 3D animation playback area.

Immediately to the right of the cross section tools, you can see the animation playback controls (**FIGURE 3.60**). From left to right, the first button jumps you back to the beginning of your animation. The next button takes you back one frame. The Play button plays back the animation from the current frame. The button to its right advances one frame at a time. Play the animation back to see that now familiar little sorceress letting off some steam on the not-so-merry-go-round (**FIGURE 3.61** on the next page). Adorable.

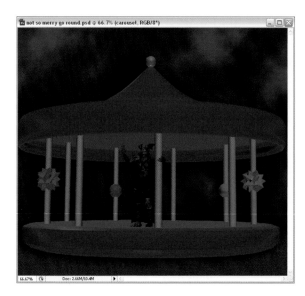

FIGURE 3.61 A different frame in the animation stored in the 3D file.

To the right of these four buttons, you'll see a down arrow. Click the down arrow to reveal a scrubbable mini-timeline that represents the timeline of the animation stored in the 3D layer. Click and drag the arrow to dynamically move in time (depending, of course, on the power of your computer).

Animating 3D Files

I've been training on the new 3D and video features in Photoshop Extended from the day the features were released. The one thing people seem to want to do with Photoshop Extended is to animate the movement of 3D objects in 3D space. I agree that it would be extremely helpful to have that functionality, but unfortunately Photoshop does not allow you to do that in the current version. There are some hacks that you can use to simulate this, and I'll discuss them in Chapter 9 in the video section of the book. But for now, just know that Photoshop is not capable of recording and animating the transformation of 3D layers.

Sorry to be the bearer of bad tidings. I've had several people get upset and send me frustrated emails because Adobe didn't add this feature. For the release of CS4, I'll use my supreme power and influence, and refuse to grant Adobe permission to release Photoshop unless this feature is added.

4

Editing Textures of 3D Objects

In this chapter, you'll look at what is perhaps the most important part of Photoshop Extended for 3D users; that is, the ability to alter textures applied to 3D objects. 3D artists have been using 2D texture maps (usually created in Photoshop) almost since the early days of commercially available 3D software applications. Also since about that time, 3D artists have had to go back and forth from Photoshop to their 3D programs as they made changes to these textures.

However, in the words of the poet, "the times they are a-changin'." As you'll see in this chapter, Photoshop Extended allows you to change textures applied to 3D objects either nondestructively or permanently. You can add scars, buttons, a mustache, freckles, and so on, and see what these objects look like on your 3D model without ever having to go back to your 3D application. This allows you to experiment with textures as much as you'd like without all the hassle and headache.

Don't get me wrong. Textures are amazing. And this is where Photoshop naturally excels, anyway. But from my experience, textures are also the biggest problem area for Photoshop when you're working with 3D objects. So, near the end of this chapter, you'll find a section about the problems you might encounter and how to avoid them. I've done many hours of experiments in this area so you don't have to. My complete lack of a social life is a benefit to all.

Making Changes to Textures

Let's just jump right in. Open the wizard lady.3ds file from the wizard lady folder in the Chapter 4 folder. Make sure it is *not* the wizard lady.3ds file in the Chapter 4 root directory, or you won't see the textures in the following example. We'll use the solo model in the Chapter 4 folder a little later on.

Use the default resolution of 1024 x 1024 when creating your document. If you look at the Layers palette, you'll see that there is a list of the raster texture maps applied to this model (**FIGURE 4.1**). These are what you are going to change.

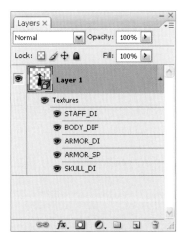

FIGURE 4.1 Looking at the Layers palette with the wizard lady file open, you see a sublist of all the 2D raster textures that have been applied to this object in a 3D program.

Before you change the textures applied to this model, just be aware that you can also just temporarily hide them. If you want to hide a texture applied to this model, all you have to do is click the eye icon to the left of the name of the texture. In this case, click the eye icon to the left of the ARMOR_DI texture. This temporarily hides the texture on her armor, which makes her look like she's wearing Nerf armor (**FIGURE 4.2**). Click the same spot once again to return the visibility to the armor texture.

FIGURE 4.2 Clicking the eye icon next to a texture temporarily hides that texture. Here the character's armor map has been removed.

Next, you'll alter one of the textures applied to this character. This is the good stuff, folks.

NOTE Although these textures can be altered in Photoshop, they must first be applied to the object in your 3D program. You cannot apply textures to 3D objects in Photoshop if those objects do not have textures already applied to them. For more information on why this is, check out the "UVW Mapping" sidebar.

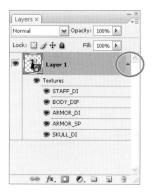

FIGURE 4.3A You can use this arrow in the Layers palette to collapse or expand the list of textures applied to your 3D object.

1. Make sure you can see the textures applied to the object in the Layers palette. If you cannot see them, click the arrow to the right of the layer's name to expand the list of applied textures (**FIGURE 4.3A**).

2. The list of textures refers to all the maps applied to this image. Each item in the list corresponds to a completely different image that has been applied to this object. When you can see the list of the materials applied to this object, double-click the texture map called BODY_DIF. A version of the original image used to create this texture pops up in a new document window. This is the main texture (aka diffuse map) applied to the main body of the character (**FIGURE 4.3B**). In the new window for this texture, you can edit and adjust this texture just as you would any other image in Photoshop. One of the great benefits of this is that the image that was originally applied as the texture is safe. Make all the crazy changes you want here because you won't damage anything. I'll cover how that is and how to change the original images later this chapter.

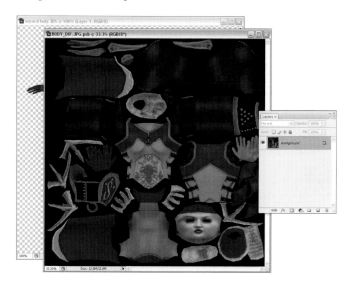

FIGURE 4.3B Double-click a texture in the Layers palette to open it in its own separate window.

3. Now make some changes to the texture. Let's say you want to change the yellow color on her clothing. To do this, add a Hue/Saturation adjustment layer, change Edit to Yellows, and move the Hue slider to the right (to about +145) to turn the yellow color of her clothes to a cyan/blue color (**FIGURE 4.3C**). Of course, you are free to choose any color you want.

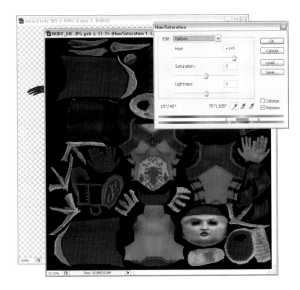

FIGURE 4.3C The BODY_DIF texture with a Hue/Saturation adjustment layer applied. I've changed the Edit drop-down list to Yellows and taken up the Hue to 145 to change the yellow color in the character's suit to blue.

4. Save the image. That's right. Don't be scared. You won't hurt anything. As I mentioned before, you're not affecting the original texture in any way. After saving the image, almost like magic, the color of the texture map applied to the character changes in the other document window (**FIGURE 4.3D**). Go ahead and close the texture map document (not the document window with the 3D character).

FIGURE 4.3D Saving the changes you made in the document window with the texture automatically updates the 3D object's textures to reflect the changes that you made.

5. But wait—there's more! What if you want to undo those changes? Would you have to reopen the texture? No! All you have to do is Undo in the standard way by pressing Ctrl/Cmd+Z. No harm done whatsoever. But let's actually Redo that action by pressing Ctrl+Shift+Z/Cmd+Shift+Z in preparation for the next step.

6. Here's yet another great aspect of being able to make changes to textures. Double-click the BODY_DIF texture in the Layers palette again to open it. It still shows your changes. As a matter of fact, the Hue/Saturation adjustment layer you created is still intact! Just double-click the Hue/Saturation icon in the Layers palette (**FIGURE 4.3E**) to open it back up. You'll see that your settings are exactly the way you left them (**FIGURE 4.3F**). Be careful here. Every time you open this .3ds file, it creates a new instance of this Smart Object (see the next section), and your adjustment layer will no longer be there to edit.

FIGURE 4.3E This icon indicates a Hue/Saturation adjustment layer. Double-click it to reopen your previously accepted settings.

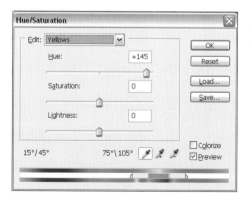

FIGURE 4.3F Notice that the settings are not reset. They are exactly the way you left them.

UVW Mapping

If you are new to the world of 3D, it may seem ridiculous to you that Photoshop can't add textures to 3D objects that don't already have textures applied to them. Equally as frustrating is the fact that you can't move textures around on 3D objects, either.

There is a good reason for this limitation. The way that textures "fit" on a 3D object is actually a very complicated issue. You need to apply what is called UVW mapping to have the materials fit properly on the object. UVW mapping coordinates are essentially just directions for how to cover an object with a texture.

UVW mapping is extremely complex. Certain pixels of an image used as a texture can be mapped to one area (like the face, for example), whereas pixels of the image that are adjacent to the pixels used for the face might be mapped to the feet.

Look closely at the texture map that you altered in the wizard lady.3ds file example. That one image "clothed" the entire wizard lady, but the image didn't look like a person at all. The chest is in one spot, the face is in a different spot, and so on. But in a 3D program, you assign pieces of maps to pieces of 3D mesh.

So this is why Photoshop cannot move textures across an object or apply textures to an object that doesn't have any. Photoshop doesn't have a UVW mapping system that would allow you to give it those kind of instructions. And I'm not sure that you would even *want* to do something that complex in anything other than a completely full-fledged 3D environment.

By the way, in case you are curious as to what UVW stands for, UVW refers to a coordinate system for maps, in the same way that XYZ is a coordinate system for objects and scenes. And actually, UVW functions just like XYZ does, allowing you to move the maps from left to right across a character on the U axis, and so forth. You can imagine the confusion that would ensue if we were to refer to the material's coordinates in the same way that we refer to the object's coordinates.

Understanding the Role of Smart Objects

So now you might be wondering how it is that Photoshop can open a texture and adjust it, even *save* it, and yet leave the original untouched.

Photoshop does this by taking advantage of a relatively new feature: Smart Objects. Introduced in Photoshop CS2, Smart Objects are elements that reference a master element. This is important background information to know, and if you do any other work in Photoshop, you'll want to take advantage of this amazing feature.

What's the big deal about Smart Objects?

In the following example, you'll create a red circle, make it smaller, and then scale it back to its original size. You'll do this once with a regular layer, and then once with the same layer converted to a Smart Object.

1. Create a new document (File > New), and choose Default Photoshop Size from the Presets drop-down list (**FIGURE 4.4A**).

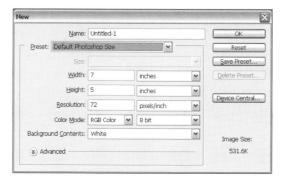

FIGURE 4.4A Make a new document using the Default Photoshop Size preset. This creates a fairly small document size that will be easy to work with.

2. Create a new blank layer by clicking the New Layer button at the bottom of the Layers palette.

3. Select the Elliptical Marquee tool from the Tools palette (**FIGURE 4.4B**).

FIGURE 4.4B Select the Elliptical Marquee tool shown here. It might be hidden underneath the Rectangular Marquee tool. If that's the case, simply right-click the tool to reveal the other tools grouped together here.

4. Click and drag in the document to make an elliptical-shaped marquee selection (**FIGURE 4.4C**).

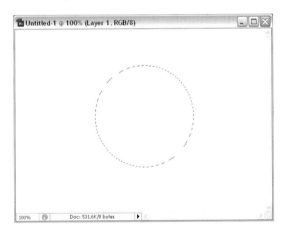

FIGURE 4.4C With the Elliptical Marquee tool selected, click and drag in the document window to create an elliptical selection area.

5. With the new blank layer selected, fill the selection with a colorful foreground color using the keyboard shortcut Alt+Backspace/Opt+Delete (**FIGURE 4.4D** on the next page).

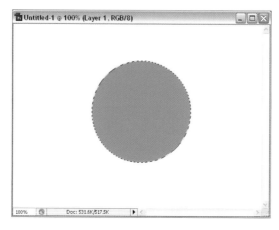

FIGURE 4.4D Fill the selection with the foreground color. You'll probably want to choose a bright color as your foreground color so that this circle pops out from its background. Also, be sure you have the new blank layer selected when you perform this action. It will be critical to following along with upcoming steps.

6. Deselect by pressing Ctrl/Cmd+D.

7. Now let's play with this circle a little. Using the keyboard shortcut Ctrl/Cmd+T, enter Free Transform mode. You can also get to this mode by right-clicking on the object, by using one of the Marquee tools, or by selecting Edit > Free Transform.

8. Grab one of the corner points of the Free Transform box and scale it down while holding the Shift key. The Shift key constrains the proportions as you scale so that the width and the height of the object maintain their relationship to one another. I also like to add the Alt/Opt key while I'm scaling so that the transformation happens from the center rather than the upper-left corner of the bounding box. In this case, scale down the circle quite a bit (**FIGURE 4.4E**). Press Enter/Return to accept the changes made in Free Transform mode.

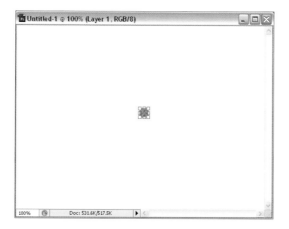

FIGURE 4.4E The circle scaled down.

9. What I want to show you here is that you have actually lost data by scaling. The Free Transform feature in Photoshop is great, but it is destructive (meaning permanent) and destructive (meaning harmful). Using the same method you used in the previous step, enter Free Transform mode again, but this time scale the ellipse back to its original size and press Enter/Return to accept the changes. This looks terrible! Obviously, you've lost some quality (**FIGURE 4.4F**).

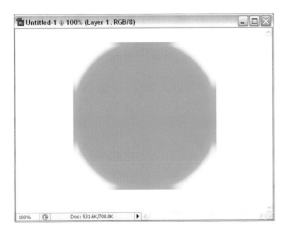

FIGURE 4.4F Yikes! After scaling down your layer and returning it to its original size, it looks awful. Data has been lost in this process.

TIP   To fill a layer with the foreground color, use the keyboard shortcut Alt+Backspace/Opt+Delete. Alternatively, you can right-click inside the selection area and select Fill from the context menu.

I suppose you can't get too angry with these results. After all, this is the way you would expect pixels to behave. If these were vectors (say in Adobe Illustrator or in a 3D program), you wouldn't have any problem scaling these up and down as much as you wanted.

As you might have guessed, Smart Objects changes the situation completely. Using Smart Objects, you can store the data of the original circle so that, as you alter it, Photoshop will constantly reference the original, not the edited version. Let's continue with this circle to see how amazing this feature is.

1. You must first undo the changes you made to your circle and go back to the way it was before you transformed it (**FIGURE 4.5A**).

   TIP To undo one step, press Ctrl/Cmd+Z. To undo more than one step, use Ctrl+Alt+Z/Cmd+Opt+Z. You can also select Edit > Step Backward.

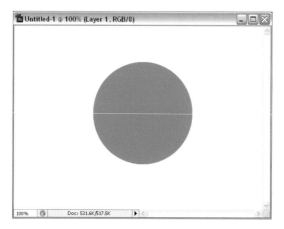

FIGURE 4.5A Using Edit > Step Backward, undo the last several steps to return this circle to its original state.

2. Now, convert the circle into a Smart Object. To do this, right-click on the layer in the Layers palette (not the layer thumbnail), and from the list that pops up, select Convert to Smart Object (**FIGURE 4.5B**). After doing this, an icon appears on your layer thumbnail, indicating that this is now a Smart Object (**FIGURE 4.5C**).

FIGURE 4.5B Right-click on a layer and select Convert to Smart Object to make any layer a Smart Object.

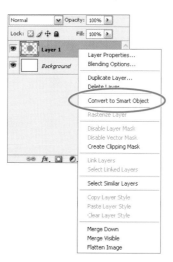

FIGURE 4.5C This icon tells you that this layer is a Smart Object.

3. Free Transform this layer and scale down as before (**FIGURE 4.5D**). Accept the changes by pressing Enter/Return.

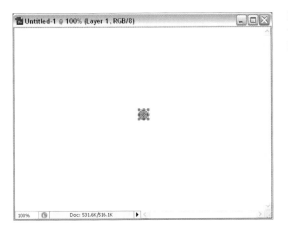

FIGURE 4.5D Scale down the Smart Object as you did before.

4. Here's the moment you've been waiting for. Enter Free Transform one last time to scale the object back up to its original size, and look at that. Absolutely no loss in quality whatsoever (**FIGURE 4.5E**). Again, there is no loss in quality because Photoshop is constantly referencing the original circle. And all this from a raster image, thanks to the power of Smart Objects.

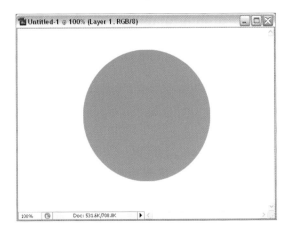

FIGURE 4.5E After scaling it back up to its original size, you'll see that there is no loss in quality, thanks to Smart Objects.

TIP If you import an Adobe Illustrator file by selecting File > Place, Photoshop will automatically convert it to a Smart Object for you.

Just think of the power of this feature! From now on, if you're not sure how small you want to shrink an object, you can just convert it to a Smart Object. This is not just a cool feature, it's the beginning of a revolution in the image editing workflow.

NOTE New to Photoshop CS3 is the long-awaited ability to add filters nondestructively. Simply convert a layer to a Smart Object, or choose Filter > Convert for Smart Filters. Now when you add effects to objects in Photoshop, those effects can be adjusted or removed at any point in time.

NOTE You can actually save Smart Objects as separate files that can be used again and again. Simply right-click on a Smart Object layer and select Export Contents. The layer is saved as a .psb file, a format which I'll refer to again in the next section. In addition, the .psb file format is used to save Photoshop documents that are over 2 GB in size.

NOTE Unfortunately, there are some limits as to what Smart Objects can do. You cannot apply the more robust effects like Vanishing Point and Liquify to Smart Objects. And you can't paint or clone on them, among other things.

Smart Objects and 3D Texture Maps

Now that you understand exactly what a Smart Object is, you'll briefly investigate how they're used when editing the textures applied to 3D objects.

Let's take another look at the wizard lady.3ds file (**FIGURE 4.6**). Double-click the BODY_DIF texture in the Layers palette to open this texture in its own window. Look closely at the name of the file in the document window of the texture (**FIGURE 4.7**). Although this document is based on the file body_dif.jpg, this is actually a completely separate document—a .psb file to be exact, which is the Smart Object file format. Photoshop automatically creates a new Smart Object file based the original texture map so that your original maps are unaltered.

FIGURE 4.6 The wizard lady.3ds file.

FIGURE 4.7 Notice the name of the file (specifically the file extension) at the top of the document window. It is based on the body_dif.jpg file. But if you look closely, you'll see that the file actually has the file extension .psb, the file extension for Smart Objects.

I've provided a lot of information about Smart Objects. The two points that are most critical to understand are that Smart Objects allow you to make image alterations without damaging the original sources, and that Photoshop creates Smart Objects out of textures when you alter them.

Where Are Those Smart Object Files Stored?

So, if Photoshop creates a new, separate Smart Object file with your original texture as its source, then where is it stored? If you can go back to the Smart Object file later and find your adjustment layers still intact, it has to be somewhere, right? Photoshop actually saves the Smart Object in a temporary directory buried on your hard drive.

In some ways, this is a blessing. In the same way that you want to keep your source textures safe to avoid damage, you'll probably also want to keep the updated versions safe as well. Also, most of the time you'll be accessing these Smart Object textures from the Layers palette, and Photoshop knows where they are so you don't have to worry about it.

But in some ways this is a problem. In high-end 3D workflows, you'll want to take textures back to your 3D program for a more high-end rendering solution. You might use Photoshop to get an idea of what your texture will look like or to experiment with textures that are difficult to create from scratch, such as freckles or grass. Then you'll want to take the Smart Objects back into your 3D program. The problem is that your 3D program will not understand that Smart Object file. So I'll show you another way to get these textures into your 3D application coming up next. But in case you want to easily and quickly locate the directory where these are stored, simply select File > Save As to open the directory where they are stored. The directory will differ depending on your OS, but here's where mine is on Windows XP (**FIGURE 4.8**).

FIGURE 4.8 If you ever need to get to the directory where Photoshop creates the Smart Objects when a texture layer is opened, just select File > Save As. Here's where my directory is in Windows XP.

Replacing the Original Textures

What I've covered so far with Photoshop Extended and changing textures is absolutely amazing, without a doubt. But what do you do if you want to actually change and replace the original textures permanently?

For that purpose, there is a convenient feature called Replace Textures. The Replace Textures command actually replaces your original textures with the alterations you have made to the Smart Objects. To use this feature, select the 3D layer that has textures applied to it that you have changed in Photoshop. Select the Layer menu at the top of the interface and choose 3D Layers > Replace Textures.

A word of caution: you must be careful when using this feature. Although this is a very useful feature (some might say it fulfills the real purpose of texture editing in Photoshop Extended), you need to keep in mind that this feature results in a permanent change. So permanent is this command, in fact, that you cannot undo it. You'll even get a dialog warning you of the same when you use this feature (**FIGURE 4.9**).

FIGURE 4.9 This dialog appears when you use the Replace Layers command to warn you of the permanence of the result.

Replace Textures vs. Using the Smart Objects

I've covered two different methods to change the textures of 3D layers. You may be wondering at this point which method to use: Replace Textures or locate and use Smart Objects?

There are pros and cons about each.

With the Replace Layers command, the changes to your source textures are permanent. So, you should probably make a backup copy of them somewhere before executing this command.

On the other hand, I don't believe there are any 3D software applications that can read and understand .psb files, which is the file format for Smart Objects. So you'll need to take those back into Photoshop and resave them in another file format.

In essence, the method you use is really a matter of preference.

Specularity

When creating the textures for a 3D object, almost all 3D programs allow you to also specify the specularity of an object. Specularity is essentially defined as the way highlights look on an object when light shines directly on it.

Look around you right now. As I look around my work space, I see an apple (my reward for finishing this chapter), a plastic water bottle, a wooden desk, and so forth. The highlights of these objects look very different. The pinpoint highlights on the water bottle are very small, indicating that the plastic of the bottle is very shiny. In contrast, the old wooden desk is not nearly as shiny. The highlights are more diffused across the surface of the object. Compared to the glare on the bottle, it's like someone applied a blur to the highlights on the desk. What do the highlights on the objects around you teach you about their surface materials?

Specularity is extremely important when creating 3D objects. It is not very difficult to model a belt in most 3D programs. However, it is far more challenging to create realistic textures for that belt. The specularity of the cloth or leather of the belt should differ greatly from the shine on the buckle of the belt.

Thankfully, Photoshop Extended recognizes the specularity in a 3D file if no texture is applied to it. Let's examine two teapots with different specular values. Other than that one difference, these files are identical.

Open the teapot shiny.3ds file from the Chapter 4 folder. Notice how tiny the specular highlight is (**FIGURE 4.10**). What type of material do you think this might be? It looks like a plastic teapot, perhaps for kids to play with.

Now open teapot flat.3ds from the Chapter 4 folder. This file has no specularity information (**FIGURE 4.11**). With the highlight nonexistent as it is in this image, the teapot doesn't look quite so much like plastic anymore. It actually has more of a matte finish here.

NOTE   Notice that specularity is not a texture. You can't adjust it directly in Photoshop, so be sure to set it up correctly in your 3D program. Consult the Help documentation of your 3D program to learn how your chosen program deals with specularity.

FIGURE 4.10 The specularity settings on this object have created small, pinpoint highlights.

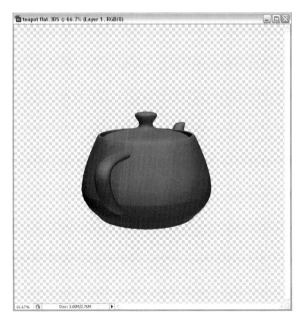

FIGURE 4.11 This is the exact same file except that the specularity has been reduced. This teapot now looks more like clay than plastic.

Troubleshooting Problems with 3D Files

This may seem like a weird spot to put the subject of troubleshooting, but in reality, it is very topical. As you play around more with Photoshop Extended, you'll notice that many times 3D files don't quite come over correctly. Many times they will be hopelessly black, not responding to lighting changes, render mode alterations, or standard Photoshop image adjustments. Sometimes they won't show up at all. Or perhaps you might add a texture element (like a bump map) that causes all other textures to be unreadable for some reason (**FIGURE 4.12**). From my experience, problems with textures are usually to blame.

FIGURE 4.12 If you have some texture elements that Photoshop doesn't accept, Photoshop might not recognize the other textures from the 3D file. Here, the texture doesn't show up because a bump map has also been added.

I've done quite a few experiments in this arena, so let's look at a list of problems you should watch out for.

NOTE I've included a folder in the Chapter 4 folder on the CD called "bad 3D files," which is full of 3D files that don't work. Perhaps you will get different results than those shown in the next few sections.

Location of Texture Maps

You probably noticed that when you needed to access the wizard lady.3ds file in previous exercises, you had to go inside a subfolder to get to the file. In that same folder are tons of additional files that are texture maps for the wizard lady model. Ideally, I would have liked to have stored the textures in the subfolder and stored the .3ds file in the root directory so it would be easier to get to. But Photoshop can't look outside the 3D model's directory for texture maps.

In 3D programs, you can use images for texture maps from anywhere on your hard drive, and the 3D program will keep track of where to find each image. Photoshop does not have that ability. You must keep all images used as textures in the same folder as the models that use them.

If you moved the wizard lady.3ds file to another directory, **FIGURE 4.13** shows you what the model would look like after importing it into Photoshop. Keep in mind that even if the subfolder that contains the needed textures is in the same directory, Photoshop still won't be able to find them. An extra copy of the wizard lady.3ds file is in the root directory of the Chapter 4 folder for you to experiment with.

FIGURE 4.13 This is the wizard lady.3ds file imported into Photoshop when its textures are stored in another directory.

TIP Even though the materials are not recognized if they are not in the same folder as the 3D object when Photoshop opens it, the Layers palette still shows that these textures are applied (**FIGURE 4.14**). If you double-click these texture placeholders, a new document window opens for the texture map. Although it is simply white, if you were to paint on it or add texture and then save the document, you could "repaint" the object's texture (**FIGURE 4.15**).

NOTE In the world of 3D, the terms *textures*, *shaders*, *maps*, and *materials* are often used interchangeably to describe the textures applied to 3D objects.

FIGURE 4.14 Even though Photoshop can't find these textures, they are still listed in the Layers palette.

FIGURE 4.15 When you double-click the textures in the Layers palette, Photoshop opens a placeholder texture if it can't find the original. You can paint on the original to add some texture to the 3D object. Here, I simply scribbled in the document with green and saved it to get this result with the 3D object.

Procedural Maps

In most professional 3D applications, you can apply various types of procedural maps. Procedural maps are maps that use computer-generated patterns to create textures rather than importing an image file. Here's an example of a procedural map called Noise applied to a basic sphere in the software program 3DS Max (**FIGURE 4.16**). In your 3D program, you can adjust various properties of this map (such as the size of the noise, or the amount of noise, for example), because 3DS Max creates this pattern from scratch. Think of them almost like Photoshop filters.

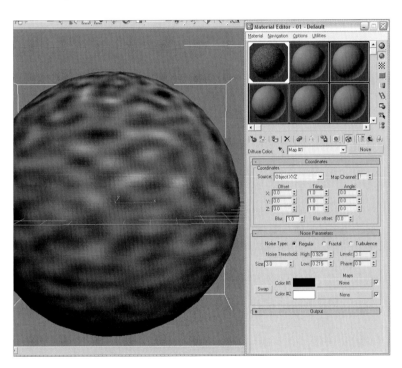

FIGURE 4.16 An example of a procedural map in 3DS Max. Notice all the parameters. This map is being generated by 3DS Max, not by an imported image.

Because of the parametric flexibility of procedural maps, they're very helpful. Unfortunately, they typically don't come over when imported into Photoshop (**FIGURE 4.17**).

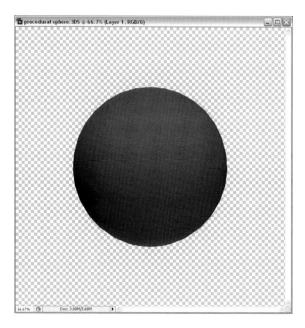

FIGURE 4.17 Procedural texture maps from 3D programs (such as a Noise map from 3DS Max) often don't come across well when applied to objects that are imported into Photoshop. Photoshop doesn't even recognize that this sphere has any textures applied to it.

If you have a procedural texture map that you just can't live without, consult the Help system in your 3D program to find out if your 3D program can convert a procedural map to an image file.

Nonrendering Objects

In most 3D applications, there are a host of objects that you can use as assistants to set up your 3D scene correctly. These might be grids, guides, dummy objects that cameras are parented to, and other such objects, depending on your 3D application. Just like with guides in Photoshop, in the case of most of these "helper" objects, you do not want them to render. 3D programs typically offer options to hide such objects so they don't render. However, even if these objects are hidden in your 3D program, they will usually be visible in Photoshop. And Photoshop does not give you the option to turn them on or off, so you're kind of stuck. You can mask them out (say, with layer masks) in some instances, but if they cover your object, you can't do anything about it.

So keep a close eye on what you have in your scene before exporting your object to a file that Photoshop recognizes. Here are a couple of examples of hidden and nonrendering objects that crept into my .3ds files (**FIGURES 4.18A** and **4.18B**).

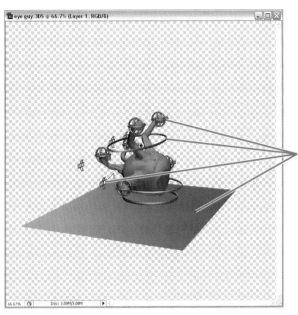

FIGURE 4.18A Here is a sweet eye monster guy, but it's all cluttered by objects in the original 3D file that weren't supposed to render.

None of these spheres and rings, nor this flat ground object, are supposed to be here.

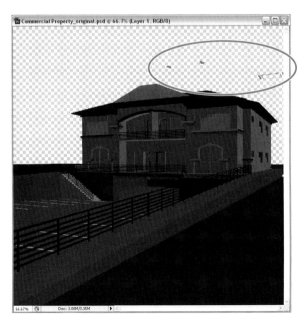

FIGURE 4.18B These little marks at the top of the document are from the AutoCAD file that this property is based on. They are not supposed to render and are hidden in the master 3D file.

NOTE The world of "nonrendering objects" is huge. Depending on your 3D application, items such as bone structures, vector splines, dummy controllers, and paint objects might not be recognized in Photoshop. It's a good idea to break down your 3D objects to a simple mesh before exporting them to Photoshop.

NOTE As you've probably noticed, adding that third dimension does complicate things quite a bit. There's just so much to take in, and it can get confusing. If you find yourself wanting to learn more about the world of 3D, the help documentation that comes with your 3D program is probably the best asset to do this. In Chapter 10, I'll also share some great places to find more information.

Lights

Although Photoshop does recognize lights from 3D programs, it doesn't necessarily recognize every type of light. If, for example, you created lighting with omnidirectional lights in 3DS Max (called "Omni" lights), not only would the light not show up in Photoshop, but it would cause the object to be completely invisible! (See **FIGURE 4.19**.)

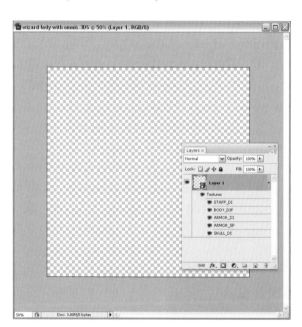

FIGURE 4.19 An omnidirectional light created in 3DS Max doesn't come over too well into Photoshop. Not only are the lights not recognized by Photoshop, but they also prevent my object from coming over. By the way, changing the Lighting and Appearance settings has absolutely no effect on this object. The omnidirectional lights completely prevent the object from being recognized by Photoshop.

Troubleshooting Disclaimer

Keep in mind that the troubleshooting tips provided in the preceding sections are not always consistent. You might be fortunate enough to go through your entire life and never experience Photoshop's unusual reaction to the lights in your scene. However, it's important to be aware of these occurrences in case you experience problems in the future.

5

Creating Textures for 3D Models

So far, we've spent the bulk of time looking at new 3D features in Photoshop CS3 Extended. Before we say good-bye to the 3D portion of this book, I want to cover features of Photoshop's standard version that can also help 3D users, especially when creating textures. Many of the exciting features you'll be using in this chapter are also new to Photoshop CS3 and are not exclusive to Photoshop Extended. This chapter looks at how to refine bump maps and create a realistic eyeball texture, and provides other tips to help you get the most out of using Photoshop in your 3D workflow.

This chapter is mostly for those already working in the 3D realm. You can't use bump maps or displacement maps in the 3D models imported into Photoshop CS3 Extended, nor can you apply textures to imported 3D objects if a texture has not been applied already. So this chapter is mainly for the work you do outside of Photoshop Extended. Therefore, I'll be using many terms and concepts that have no purpose for those of you not using 3D programs.

> **NOTE** Because of the differences in 3D programs, I won't go into specifics about how to set up bump mapping in your 3D program. But rest assured that the concepts covered here are universally applicable to almost all 3D software packages. The Photoshop features discussed in this chapter will be beneficial regardless of your 3D application preference. Remember to look in the Help documentation of your 3D program if you have questions about how to use bump maps, displacement maps, or other such features.

However, I still invite Photoshop and video users to follow along, particularly with the section "Creating Realistic Textures from Scratch" at the end of this chapter. You can always use those concepts to alter the textures on your 3D objects. For example, let's say you are using the planet model that ships with Photoshop. You can create an eye texture to paint over the planet's normal texture (using the methods in Chapter 4, "Editing Textures of 3D Objects") to create an eyeball. Or you could alter the texture map for the planet to make it a basketball, holiday ornament, or whatever spherical object you can think of. The key is knowing how to create the texture in Photoshop. Developing those very skills is at the heart of this chapter.

Bump Mapping

Bump mapping is the process of taking a grayscale map into your 3D application and using it to create "bumpy" surface textures. Imagine having to model every dimple on a basketball's surface—I'd rather go to the dentist. Luckily, you can just use a map to describe how you want an object's surface textured, or "bumped," to your 3D program.

Depending on the 3D program you're using, white areas usually tell the application to raise areas on a surface; black areas on the map are usually unaffected by the map.

Let's look at an example of a bump map in action. **FIGURE 5.1A** shows a 3D model of a sphere. Pretty boring, right? But you can add the texture shown in **FIGURE 5.1B** to make it look like a basketball (**FIGURE 5.1C**). Then you can apply the bump map in **FIGURE 5.1D** to the object's texture to create more realism when it's rendered (**FIGURE 5.1E**). Consult the Help system of your 3D program to learn more about how it handles bump mapping.

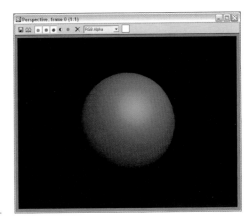

FIGURE 5.1A Just a plain old 3D model of a sphere. In most 3D programs these can be made by simply clicking a button. Nothing special here.

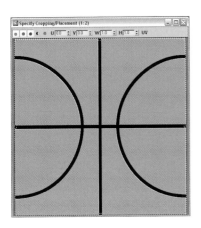

FIGURE 5.1B The basketball texture. Note that the texture doesn't have to be perfect. Photorealism is not a texture's job; that comes later with lights and rendering.

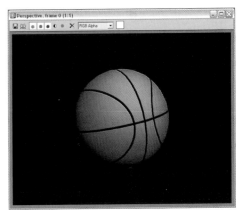

FIGURE 5.1C The sphere with the basketball image applied as a texture.

FIGURE 5.1D The image that you'll be using as a bump map.

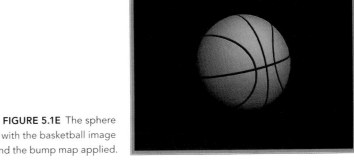

FIGURE 5.1E The sphere with the basketball image and the bump map applied.

Now let's look at how to create better bump maps using the standard Photoshop tools.

Making Better "Bumps" with the New Black and White Adjustment

A new adjustment called Black and White was added to the standard and the Extended versions of Photoshop CS3. The purpose of this filter is to give users more precise control over how color images are converted to grayscale images. Even though Black and White is technically not a 3D feature, you can use it to aid you in creating bump maps to add texture to objects in a 3D program.

Often, when 3D users create a bump map, they use the quick-and-dirty (and inaccurate) way of just duplicating the regular diffuse texture map and desaturating it. For a grungy brick wall texture, this might work well, assuming that the cement in between the bricks is darker than the bricks. **FIGURE 5.2A** shows something similar. The brick wall has had some sprinkler action, so you see variation in the luminance of the cement between the bricks, which might be undesirable. But overall this image will work well for this example. The crags and recesses in the bricks are darker than the bricks, which can help create the indented bumps in the bump map (**FIGURE 5.2B**). But what if the brick wall had yellow

FIGURE 5.2A An image of a brick wall.

FIGURE 5.2B The brick wall with a bump map applied. The bump map was created by simply desaturating the brick wall image.

spray paint on it (**FIGURE 5.2C**)? If that image was converted to grayscale values, the yellow would most likely be much lighter than the bricks (**FIGURE 5.2D**). If you were to use this desaturated version as a bump map, the yellow would pop out and appear raised off the surface, which would be extremely unrealistic (**FIGURE 5.2E**).

FIGURE 5.2C The brick wall with spray paint. Acts of vandalism are digital simulations only.

FIGURE 5.2D When this image with the yellow paint is converted to grayscale, the yellow is much brighter than the rest of the image.

FIGURE 5.2E When applied as a bump map, the yellow appears to raise the surface and look like puffy paint.

The Black and White command allows you to control more precisely how colors convert to grayscale. In the preceding example of the yellow spray paint on a brick wall, you can manually darken the areas that were originally yellow.

To use bump mapping, you'll need a 3D program. However, you don't need anything other than Photoshop to learn about the Black and White adjustment in this exercise.

1. Open the Brick wall.psd file from the Chapter 5 folder (**FIGURE 5.3A**). This is the same brick wall you saw earlier. The extra yellow spray paint is on the yellow paint layer. Make sure that layer's visibility is off for now.

FIGURE 5.3A
The Brick wall.psd file.

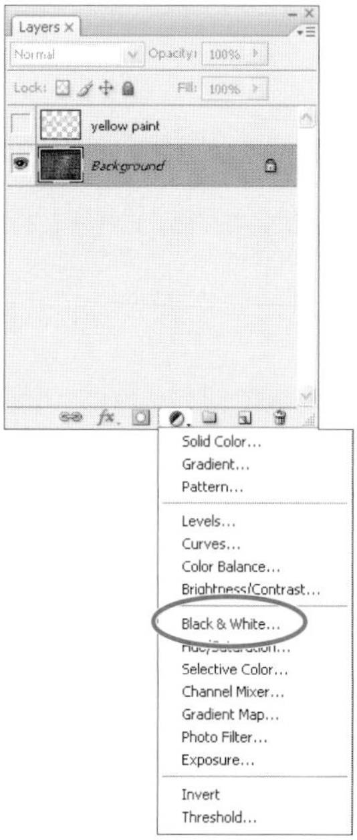

2. With the Background layer selected, add a Black and White adjustment layer by using the adjustment layer drop-down list at the bottom of the Layers palette (**FIGURE 5.3B**).

3. The Black and White dialog is fairly straightforward (**FIGURE 5.3C**). This command converts all colors to grayscale values, but it gives you control over how each color listed converts to gray.

FIGURE 5.3B Add a Black and White adjustment layer by clicking this drop-down menu at the bottom of the Layers palette.

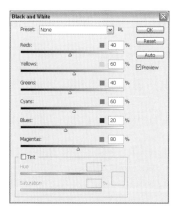

FIGURE 5.3C The Black and White adjustment dialog.

4. Converting these bricks to the default black and white settings without any adjustment results in a lackluster image because of the low contrast between the bricks and the color of the cement holding them together (**FIGURE 5.3D**). This also makes for a weak bump map because all of the "bumps" will essentially be on the same bump plane.

FIGURE 5.3D The brick wall with the default Black and White settings. Nothing revolutionary yet.

5. Increase the contrast of the bricks and cement by adjusting the reds in the document. Move the slider under the red value to 300% (**FIGURE 5.3E**). This doesn't look realistic, but bump maps are never actually seen, so they don't need to look good on their own (**FIGURE 5.3F**).

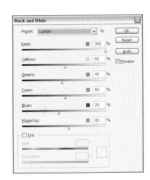

FIGURE 5.3E Brighten only the bricks by taking the red value to 300%.

FIGURE 5.3F The result of increasing the red value.

FIGURE 5.3G With the Black and White dialog open, click on a color in the image window to get a scrubby slider that you can slide to dynamically adjust the brightness of that color range.

6. (Optional) Although this step doesn't help you make a better bump map in this case, there is another great little feature of the Black and White command. In the image, the plants toward the bottom look too dark now that you've lightened the reds. Let's make them more of a light gray rather than the medium-dark gray that they are currently. Trouble is, you might not recall which color they were. That's alright, though, because Black and White gives you another way to choose color. If you click in the actual image window with the Black and White dialog open, you'll get a scrubby slider (**FIGURE 5.3G**). After clicking, drag to the right to brighten that color (**FIGURE 5.3H**), or drag to the left to darken it. Notice how the violet flowers that were clicked on lighten, but the green foliage behind the flowers remain unchanged. The effect with this method is almost as if you click to select a color range, and then as you drag you use an invisible slider to lighten or darken that range. This is really useful for those times when you determine the original color of an area that needs to be adjusted.

FIGURE 5.3H After scrubbing this color range to the right to lighten it.

7. For additional practice, delete the Black and White adjustment layer that you've created in this exercise (or just click Cancel if you are still in the dialog), and start over again after turning on the yellow paint layer. Select the yellow paint layer (so that the adjustment layer you're about to create is created on top of the yellow paint layer). Add another Black and White adjustment layer from the bottom of the Layers palette. As you move the Yellow slider, notice how you can now lighten (**FIGURE 5.3I**) or darken (**FIGURE 5.3J**) the yellow paint. As you do so, you'll notice that there are actually yellow highlights in other parts of the image.

FIGURE 5.3I Dragging the Yellow value to the right brightens this spray paint.

FIGURE 5.3J Dragging the Yellow value to the left darkens the spray paint.

When making bump maps from diffuse texture maps in the future, be sure to take advantage of this Black and White feature to specify how colors are converted to grayscale values. You will get precise results without much effort.

3D Programs and PSD Files

The makers of 3D applications understand how important Photoshop is in practically every 3D user's toolset. For this reason, many 3D programs have the capacity to work with Photoshop documents. For example, in the Autodesk applications Maya and 3DS Max, PSD files can be read natively (without the help of third-party plug-ins) and applied as textures to an object. As a matter of fact, both 3DS Max and Maya allow you to import a PSD file with all of its layers collapsed or select a layer from within a PSD file to use as a texture map.

This is remarkably handy. As mentioned earlier in this chapter, many times you create certain types of maps (specularity maps, bump maps, and so forth) based on the regular diffuse texture map. So it's very easy to create these extra maps by just duplicating the original texture and making changes to the duplicates. You can imagine how helpful it is to be able to create a single multilayer PSD file that stores all of the maps for a particular shader. You can then take that one PSD file into your 3D application (if it supports this feature) and get all the maps for a particular material from the same Photoshop document. That, my friends, is efficiency.

Displacement Mapping

Displacement mapping is extremely similar to bump mapping at first glance. Displacement mapping also uses a grayscale image to create raised surfaces. However, bump mapping is essentially just a lighting trick created when the object is rendered. The actual geometry of the object's mesh is unaffected by the bump map, so bump maps are very limited as to what they can do. Although they can make dimples on a basketball, they cannot create a more drastic alteration, such as the bristles on a tooth brush or the spikes of a punk rocker's hairdo.

Displacement mapping, however, is perfectly capable of such tasks, because it actually changes the geometry of an object. This allows for more radical changes than what bump mapping can accomplish.

Using the New Refine Edge Feature to Enhance Displacement Maps

Like the Black and White adjustment, the Refine Edge feature is new in both the standard and Extended editions of Photoshop CS3. Its purpose is to give you control over the edges of a selection. You can use Refine Edges to feather selection edges, contract them, expand them, smooth them, and so forth.

Black, White, and Gray

So, what does control over selection edges have to do with displacement mapping? As with bump maps, displacement maps are grayscale images where white raises the height of an object, black has no effect, and all grayscale values in between have an effect somewhere in the middle. Those midtone values prove very valuable when making displacement maps. They can provide a gradual transition between white and black. If your displacement map is just pure white (which raises the geometry) and pure black (which does nothing), the edges will look like cliffs. If you have a soft, gray transition between the white and the black, the result will be more like a hill than a cliff. Let's look at an example.

TIP   If you'll be displacing the actual geometry of an object, you need to be sure that there is enough geometry to displace. If your object has a small number of faces (say, 5–10), your displacement results will be very blocky and look terrible (no offense). Add more geometry to your object to get a smoother final result when displaced. This is particularly important when adding gray for a smooth displacement.

FIGURE 5.4A shows the Maze hard.psd file (which is in the Chapter 5 folder), which I'll use as a displacement map. Notice how the maze is only white and black with no intermediary gray values. I created this image by simply creating a black background, and on a separate layer, I filled rectangular marquee selections with white.

After taking the maze into 3DS Max, I applied it to a box with the Displace modifier applied (the method to displace objects varies from program to program). From this example, you can see the power displacement mapping has, and what a boon it can be to your modeling toolset, even though this isn't really modeling (FIGURE 5.4B).

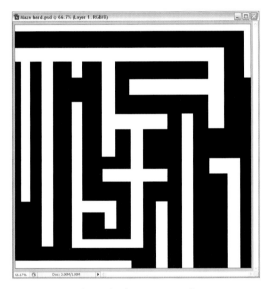

FIGURE 5.4A This is the first image we'll use as a displacement map. This image is only black and white without any gray.

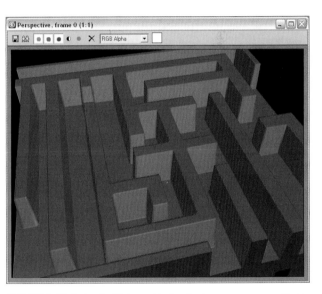

FIGURE 5.4B A simple 3D box with the displacement map applied to it. You gotta love the sweet results with a total lack of effort. Notice that the stark contrast from black to white created a hard edge.

But as cool as this capability is, I'm not super stoked about the harsh edges that have been created by the hard line between black and white in the displacement map. The real power of displacement mapping comes from taking advantage of the soft edges created by gray values.

Let's look at another example. Open Maze soft.psd in the Chapter 5 folder. This is a similar image to the preceding map, only this one has a gradual fade between black and white (**FIGURE 5.4C**). The gradual fades exist because I used the new Refine Edge feature (which you'll learn to use in the next section) to soften and adjust the selection edges before filling them with white. Now, when you go back to the 3D application with this map, you'll see a much smoother result, courtesy of the gray values in the displacement map (**FIGURE 5.4D**).

FIGURE 5.4C We'll use this image as a displacement map. This image has much softer edges than the previous displacement map.

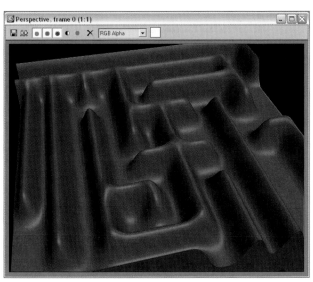

FIGURE 5.4D The soft edges in the displacement map have created smooth transitions from the maze floor to the top of the maze.

The Refine Edge feature

Now that you've seen the difference creating a soft edge can make to your displacement maps, you're ready to use the Refine Edge command. The official purpose of the Refine Edge command is to alter selection edges. That may not sound very impressive, but trust me on this one. The Refine Edge feature holds multitudinous benefits. That's right. I said multitudinous and I meant it. For example, the Refine Edge feature allows you to preview your selection in several different ways. It also allows you to preview the results of your edge refinements before you apply them.

Whenever you create a selection *and* have a Selection tool chosen from the Tools palette, the Refine Edge button appears in the options bar at the top of the Photoshop interface (**FIGURE 5.5**). Click the Refine Edge button. You'll use this command to create a soft-edged displacement map from scratch, but first I'll briefly go over the options in the Refine Edge dialog (**FIGURE 5.6**).

FIGURE 5.5 When you have a selection tool selected and a current selection, you can access the Refine Edge command from the options bar at the top of the Photoshop interface.

FIGURE 5.6 The Refine Edge dialog. Herein lies the power of masterful selection edges.

- **Radius.** This is the most complicated option to understand in this dialog, but it's also the most impressive. Increasing the Radius value refines the area of your selection to pick up greater detail. This is amazingly useful for objects like hair and fur, or for items like fireworks. For a jaw-dropping example of what Radius can do, open the fireworks.jpg file from the Chapter 5 folder (**FIGURE 5.7A**). In times past, selecting just these fireworks would be a little challenging. In Photoshop CS3, this task is quick and easy. Start by selecting a general area around the fireworks. You might want to use the Lasso tool from the Tools palette as I did and pretend you only have ten seconds to select the fireworks. The quality of my selection reflects this (**FIGURE 5.7B**). Click the Refine Edge button in the options bar to open the Refine Edge dialog. Move the Radius value to 250 pixels (px). Although initially

FIGURE 5.7A The fireworks.jpg image.

FIGURE 5.7B I tried to select the fireworks in ten seconds, which resulted in a poor selection.

this parameter seems to just add blur, what it's doing is much more sophisticated. It actually detected the edge of the fireworks automatically for you! (**FIGURE 5.7C**). The Radius value determines how far into the selection area this refinement occurs. Because there is a great deal of variation in the sparks from the fireworks, you moved this value up quite a bit. If you had short, spiky hair as a selection, you would probably use a lower value. Let's keep this image and selection as is to refine it using the next option.

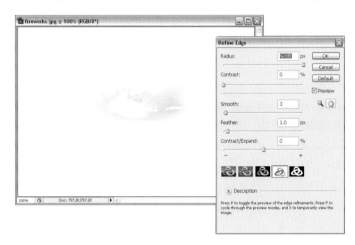

FIGURE 5.7C Increasing the Radius value shrinks the selection to more closely follow the edges of the sparks in the fireworks.

- **Contrast.** Increasing the Radius value left your selection edges a little fuzzy. Contrast reduces the blur in the selection edge. Take the Contrast value to about 30. This is a good balance (**FIGURE 5.7D**). But there is a trade-off. With the current selection, having a low Contrast value keeps all the delicate details of the tiny sparks but keeps a lot of the smoke and background as

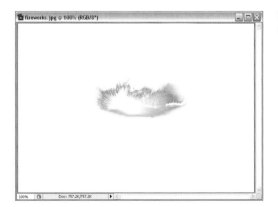

FIGURE 5.7D After taking the Contrast value to 30.

well. Moving Contrast to a high value cleans up the selection nicely but also gets rid of some of the finer sparks on the outer edge of the fireworks (**FIGURE 5.7E**).

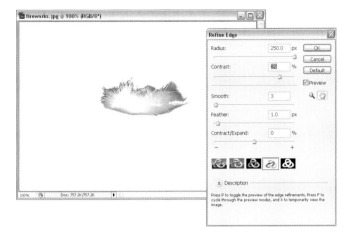

FIGURE 5.7E
If you take up the Contrast value too much, fine details of the sparks will be lost.

■ **Smooth.** This option adds roundness to corners in a selection. **FIGURES 6.7F** and **6.7G** show a pointy selection before and after a liberal dose of the Smooth property.

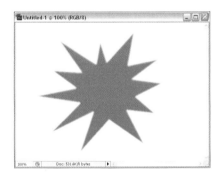

FIGURE 5.7F A selection with several pointy edges.

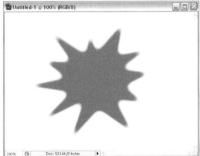

FIGURE 5.7G Increasing the Smooth value rounds out the pointy edges.

- **Feather.** This option blurs selection edges. **FIGURE 5.7H** shows the fireworks after taking the Feather value to stratospheric proportions.

FIGURE 5.7H Raising the Feather value blurs the edges of the selection.

- **Contract/Expand.** By default, Contract/Expand has a value of zero. Moving this slider to a negative value contracts your selection edges (**FIGURE 5.7I**), whereas increasing the value to a positive number expands the edges of the selection (**FIGURE 5.7J**). This is a great feature if your selection has a little fringe around it that you need to get rid of. Be careful with this feature, though. Many times, amateurs use this option to compensate for a poor selection by contracting too much to eliminate the object's edge entirely. Eroding the edges of your object is sometimes just as bad as having extra fringe pixels on the edge of your selection. In most cases, Contract/Expand should be used sparingly.

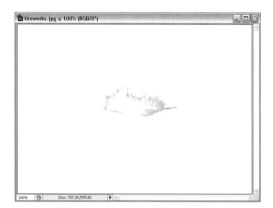

FIGURE 5.7I After Contracting the selection.

FIGURE 5.7J After Expanding the selection.

- **View modes.** It's an amazing feat to be able to see the edges of your selection on a white background. It is much more helpful (in most instances) than just looking at the "marching ants." But Photoshop provides other view modes for you as well. If you're selecting falling snowflakes in a photo, seeing the white flakes on the default white selection background won't be a big help. The five swatches at the bottom of the dialog represent the different methods available to preview selections (**FIGURE 5.7K**). Starting from the left, the first option previews the selection area against the image with no preview background. This is the way selections look when not using Refine Edge. The second button creates a Quick Mask preview, as if in Quick Mask mode. The center button is like the default white background preview, only with black. The fireworks image previews much better against a black background (**FIGURE 5.7L**). The fourth button from the left is the default view mode—against a white background. The rightmost button previews the selection area as a white matte on a black background.

FIGURE 5.7K The five different view modes. Use these buttons to change the view of your selection.

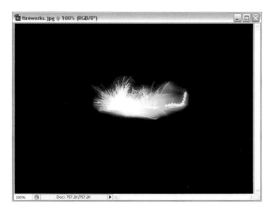

FIGURE 5.7L The fireworks selection with the black background mode selected.

- **The Description area.** At the very bottom of the Refine Edge dialog is the Description area. If it's closed, click the chevron to open it (**FIGURE 5.7M**). The Description area is like a built-in Help area. As you put your cursor over the different Refine Edge options, the Description area provides general information and tips about what the feature does and how to use it. In addition, it shows you images that represent what each parameter does. Radius is a hard property to describe, but the picture provided in the Description area is, as the saying goes, worth a thousand words (**FIGURE 5.7N**). The Description area also provides helpful shortcuts for using the features. For example, pressing F on your keyboard cycles through the various view modes.

FIGURE 5.7M Click this chevron to expand the Description area if it's collapsed.

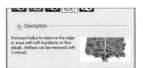

FIGURE 5.7N This little tree picture at the bottom of the Refine Edge dialog appears when your cursor hovers over the Radius property. This image is a great demonstration of what Radius does and is indicative of the great assistance that the Description area provides.

NOTE If you're familiar with earlier versions of Photoshop, you'll know that you've had the ability to Smooth, Feather, Contract, and Expand selections via the Select menu for years. However, Photoshop has never had the capability to preview those selection adjustments, let alone with different backgrounds.

TIP To use a custom color as the selection background, double-click the Quick Mask view mode icon to access the Quick Mask options. Click the color swatch (which is red by default) to open the Adobe Color Picker. Select a color and click OK in the Color Picker and in the Quick Mask options to use your custom color as the background to preview your selection.

Generating Patterns

Patterns are used quite often in 3D textures. If you are modeling a football field, you probably won't use a poster-sized digital image of grass for the field. Instead, you will most likely create a small swatch of grass that can seamlessly repeat. Photoshop is the best tool to help you do this. In this section, you'll learn different ways to generate and manipulate textures using Photoshop.

Making Patterns

Many 3D programs have built-in features for tiling an image. Typically, these tiling features are not intelligent or smooth by any stretch of the imagination, but they do duplicate the texture for you. And if you're just looking for a rote duplication of your texture, it's probably best to use your 3D program (if possible) because it reduces the file size.

However, you can use Photoshop patterns in many facets of the program. You can easily generate and repeat patterns, fill a selection area with them, apply them nondestructively to a stroke (via Layer Styles), apply them as an adjustment layer, and so forth.

Defining a pattern

Let's define a custom pattern.

1. Open the Gravel.jpg file from the Chapter 5 folder (**FIGURE 5.8A**).

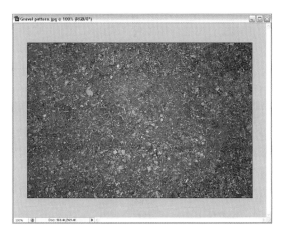

FIGURE 5.8A The Gravel.jpg image.

2. Select the Rectangular Marquee tool from the Tools palette, and make a selection area around that big rock that's in the upper-left area from the center of the image (**FIGURE 5.8B**).

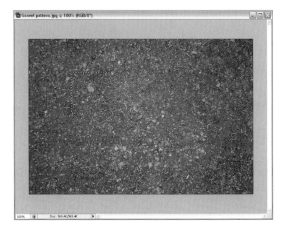

FIGURE 5.8B With the Rectangular Marquee tool selected, click and drag around this rock to select this area.

3. With that area selected, choose Edit > Define Pattern (**FIGURE 5.8C**).

FIGURE 5.8C Select Edit > Define Pattern to make a pattern out of the selection area.

4. A dialog pops up asking you to name your pattern (**FIGURE 5.8D**). Name your pattern, and click OK to define the new pattern.

FIGURE 5.8D Create a name for your pattern and click OK. This will not actually be a file on your computer, so use any characters you'd like.

Filling an area with a defined pattern

Now that you've created a custom pattern, you can put it to work. Fill the Gravel.jpg document with multiple iterations of the pattern you just defined by going to the bottom of the Layers palette and creating a Pattern adjustment layer (**FIGURE 5.9A**). The Pattern Fill dialog appears. Choose the pattern you would like to use to fill the document (**FIGURE 5.9B**). To access the current library of patterns (which contains your custom pattern), click the pattern swatch on the left side of the dialog or click the down arrow immediately to the right of the pattern swatch to open the patterns (**FIGURE 5.9C**). When you create a new, custom swatch, by default it appears as the last pattern swatch in the current pattern library. You'll need to scroll down to get to it (**FIGURE 5.9D**). Click it to select it, and then click OK to close the dialog. The entire image fills with repetitions of the pattern you created (**FIGURE 5.9E**).

FIGURE 5.9A Create a Pattern adjustment layer from the bottom of the Layers palette.

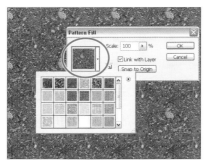

FIGURE 5.9C Click the pattern swatch or the arrow next to it to access the current pattern library.

FIGURE 5.9B The Pattern Fill dialog. From here you can select a pattern to use as a fill and make a few adjustments as well.

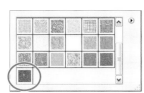

FIGURE 5.9D The created pattern hides out at the bottom of the current pattern library.

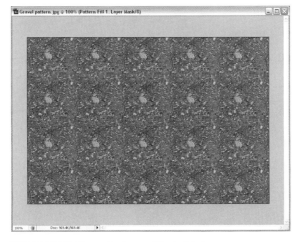

FIGURE 5.9E The entire image filled with the custom pattern.

FIGURE 5.10A The icon for the Pattern adjustment layer. Double-click it to open the Pattern Fill dialog again.

If you want to fill the image with more repetitions (thereby making the pattern smaller), you can adjust the Scale value of the Pattern adjustment layer. To do this, double-click the icon for the Pattern adjustment layer in the Layers palette (**FIGURE 5.10A**). The Pattern Fill dialog appears again. Click in the Scale field to type in a new Scale value, or click the arrow next to the word Scale to access a slider to adjust Scale more dynamically. Look at the difference in the pattern when it is scaled down to 50% (**FIGURE 5.10B**).

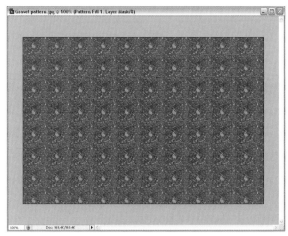

FIGURE 5.10B The Pattern adjustment layer with the custom pattern scaled to 50%. Notice how scaling down the pattern adds more repetitions of the pattern.

NOTE Patterns are accessible everywhere! For example, you can apply them from the Layer Style dialog in several ways. You can apply a Pattern Overlay effect, or you can apply a Stroke effect, and then change the Fill Type from Color to Pattern.

TIP You can also fill a layer or a selection area by first selecting either a layer in the Layers palette or a selection area in the image window, and then choosing Edit > Fill. Note, however, that this is destructive. You can't adjust this later. For this reason, I prefer to use adjustment layers.

The Pattern Flyout Menu

In virtually any area in Photoshop where you can select patterns, you'll find a little circle containing an arrowhead. This is the Pattern flyout menu, which includes several options when dealing with patterns.

Patterns are stored in pattern libraries, and many pattern libraries ship with Photoshop. You can access them from the bottom of the Pattern flyout menu.

When loading another library, Photoshop asks whether you would like to replace the current library with the one you're opening or whether you would like to "append" it. If you select Append, Photoshop just adds the new library at the bottom of the currently opened one.

You can also load other pattern libraries by selecting the Load Patterns option. The file extension for a pattern library is .pat.

You can save a pattern library by selecting Save Patterns. Photoshop saves the current pattern library, which now includes our custom preset. You'll find out how to access free additional pattern libraries In Chapter 10, "Plug-ins and Resources."

Textures for Video Games

When creating textures for video games, be sure to keep the size of the document that contains the texture to a minimum. Video game engines are very picky about sizes, and they are usually in multiples of two. So, common textures might be 256 pixels x 256 pixels, or 512 x 512. Some video game engines even allow textures up to 1024 x 1024.

If you're new to the world of video game design, these sizes might seem small. But remember that the pixel dimensions of a standard TV are 720 x 480, which means that textures that are 1024 x 1024 will never be seen at full size on a standard TV set, so you never want to create textures larger than they will be rendered onscreen. Keep in mind that video game engines render video games on the fly, so it's very important that all 3D meshes and textures be as small and streamlined as possible.

Seamless Patterns

When creating patterns, you typically want those patterns to repeat seamlessly. In the previous example, you made a pattern based on the biggest rock in the image so that the pattern would be obvious as you filled an area with it. But usually those types of obvious pattern indicators make poor patterns. If you're making a dungeon for a video game for instance, you don't want the same cracks and stains on every wall. Patterns work best when no one knows they're patterns.

What makes a good seamless pattern?

The best images to use to create seamless patterns are those that have areas with no distinguishing features. In the gravel image, that one rock is so much bigger than the others that it draws attention to the fact that you're using a pattern. It seems like a small detail, but once repeated, it will be obvious (**FIGURE 5.11**). So, details are the first thing to look out for.

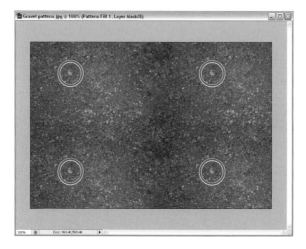

FIGURE 5.11 Watch out for details like this rock. When repeated, the pattern becomes obvious.

Another detail to consider when trying to make seamless patterns is variations in light. Sometimes these lighting variations are so subtle that you don't notice them until you see problems in the repetitions of your patterns. Using the same Gravel.jpg image as a pattern, look at the seams in **FIGURE 5.12** when the pattern is scaled down to 20%.

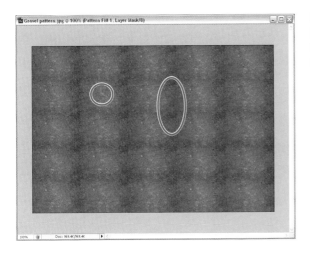

FIGURE 5.12 Even though lighting detail may be subtle, it can be a big issue when making a pattern.

TIP If you use the Eyedropper tool to hover over different areas of your image, the Info palette will give you information about the colors you are hovering over. You can use this palette to compare lighting information in different parts of an image.

One other issue that often ruins an otherwise seamless pattern is perspective. Open the Field.jpg file from the Chapter 5 folder (**FIGURE 5.13**). At first glance, it seems like this image might perfect to use to create a seamless texture. No obvious features appear in the grass, and the lighting across the grass is pretty consistent. The problem is that there is a great variation in perspective. The grass at the bottom of the image is very close to the camera. But it looks like the grass

FIGURE 5.13 The Field.jpg image.

in the center of the image is in another zip code. If that grass goes back that far that quick, you can bet that any decent size swatch of this image will not make a good seamless pattern.

Cleaning up images to use as seamless patterns

Sometimes, there's only a small blemish that keeps an image from being used to create a great seamless pattern. Photoshop has a huge toolset to fix such issues with an image. You can paint over a flaw, copy other image data over it, clone it out, and so forth. But the fastest way to get rid of a little blemish in an image is to use the Spot Healing Brush tool in the Tools palette. Don't confuse this tool with the Healing Brush, which looks almost identical (**FIGURE 5.14**).

FIGURE 5.14 Select the Spot Healing Brush tool for this exercise, not the regular old Healing Brush.

When used correctly, this tool is perhaps the fastest image editing tool in Photoshop. The purpose of the Spot Healing Brush is to paint over areas that are out of place (e.g., pimples, out of place rocks as in the previous example, and other blemishes). The Spot Healing Brush blends the texture of areas around the blemish into the areas where the blemish is. Often, this process removes the blemish and any trace that it ever existed—like a Witness Relocation Program for visual anomalies.

But beware that black and white are like the kryptonite to this super tool. Avoid spot healing areas that have big glints or shadows. They tend to create streaks in the results that are often worse than the initial blemish.

Let's fix that big rock in the Gravel.jpg image.

1. Open the Gravel.jpg image from the Chapter 5 folder (**FIGURE 5.15A**). Zoom in to the rock by holding Ctrl/Cmd and the spacebar and clicking on the rock.

FIGURE 5.15A The Gravel.jpg image.

2. Select the Spot Healing Brush tool and click and drag to paint an area that encompasses the entire rock but not too much more than that (**FIGURE 5.15B**).

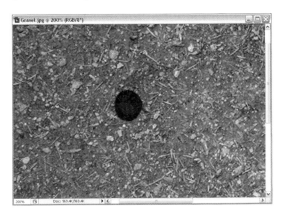

FIGURE 5.15B Paint an area that encompasses the blemish. In this case, cover the rock entirely and a little bit outside of the rock.

3. When you release the mouse, your blemish is gone (**FIGURE 5.15C**). If some artifacts remain, repeat the process as necessary. And that's it. That's all there is to removing blemishes in Photoshop. The Spot Healing Brush is just that powerful.

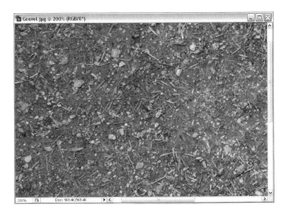

FIGURE 5.15C After using the Spot Healing Brush tool to get rid of the rock.

Brushes and the Spot Healing Brush Tool

The Spot Healing Brush, as the name implies, is a brush. It uses a limited version of Photoshop's awesome brush tools to do its work. Therefore, you can use the keyboard shortcuts [and] to reduce and increase the size of your brush, respectively. You can also right-click in the image to access a pop-up dialog that allows you to adjust the diameter (size) of your brush. You might prefer to use the keyboard shortcuts, because that method allows you to see the size of your brush as you're adjusting it. Right-clicking and using the slider is a little more of a guessing game.

Sometimes when spot healing with this tool, you might want a softer edge or a less blurry edge. The Hardness parameter in the context menu controls this effect. A higher Hardness parameter creates a harder-edged brush. A lower value blurs the brush. A soft-edged brush can sometimes blend in healed areas better. I prefer to use the keyboard shortcut Shift+[to decrease brush hardness or Shift+] to increase it.

Using the Pattern Maker to create seamless patterns

The Pattern Maker is a filter in Photoshop that generates seamless textures for you. It's just as quick and automatic as it sounds. However, for it to be so efficient, it takes some liberties with your pattern. But if you want to create seamless patterns for objects like water in a distant body or stars in space, look no further than the Pattern Maker.

1. Open the Gravel.jpg file from the Chapter 5 folder (**FIGURE 5.16A**)

FIGURE 5.16A The Gravel.jpg image (opened anew, without changes).

2. Open this texture in the Pattern Maker filter by selecting Filter > Pattern Maker. The Pattern Maker dialog opens (**FIGURE 5.16B**).

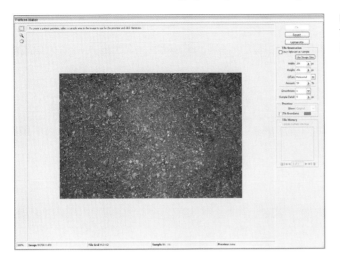

FIGURE 5.16B
The Pattern Maker.

3. Select an area with the Rectangular Marquee tool inside the Pattern Maker filter. You'll find it in the upper-left corner of the Pattern Maker window (**FIGURE 5.16C**). Click and drag to select a region to use as the repeating tile in your pattern. I opted to confine my selection to the brighter area in the center of the image so I didn't get any of the shadows around the edges (**FIGURE 5.16D**).

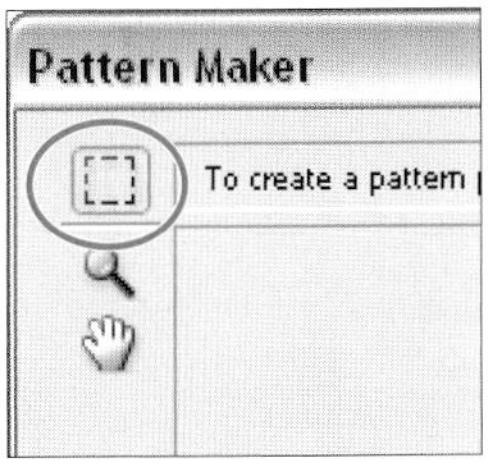

FIGURE 5.16C The Rectangular Marquee tool in the Pattern Maker filter.

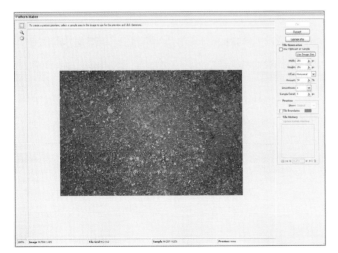

FIGURE 5.16D
Before the Pattern Maker can generate patterns, you first need to select an area to use as a repeating pattern.

4. When you've defined an area to create a pattern from, generate a pattern by clicking the Generate button in the upper-right area of the interface. The initial results are usually decent (**FIGURE 5.16E**). But this filter is fairly flexible, and there's a lot you can change quickly and easily to get results that are more along the lines of what you're looking for. From here on, we'll just fine-tune this pattern.

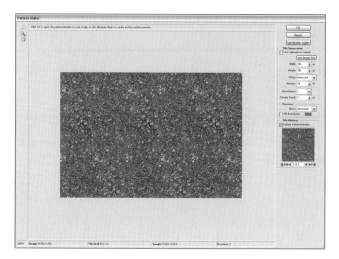

FIGURE 5.16E
The initial results from the Pattern Maker.

5. The initial results show a lot of detail. If you'd like to reduce the nooks and crannies of the pattern to make this pattern even more seamless, increase the Smoothness value on the right side of the Pattern Maker filter. You can use a setting of 1, 2, or 3. Since 1 is the default, take this value to 3. You'll notice that simply changing this value has no effect on the pattern. You need to click the Generate Again button (formerly the Generate button, when this filter was first applied) each time you make changes to generate a pattern using the settings you've altered. So go ahead and click the Generate Again button to see your pattern with maximum smoothness (**FIGURE 5.16F**). Notice that the edges are now much softer and blend together better. Although this result looks great, sometimes increasing the Smoothness value reduces fine details in the pattern. On the other hand, when creating a repeating tile that will be viewed from a distance, that's exactly what you want. For now, take the Smoothness level back to 1, and click Generate Again.

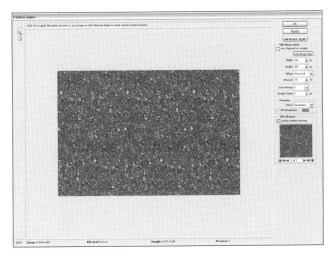

FIGURE 5.16F
The pattern with
a Smoothness
value of 3.

6. You can also use the Pattern Maker to specify the size your pattern should be. So far, you've been using the video game pattern size of 256 x 256. But you might want a seamless pattern that is the size of the entire image. Simply click the Use Image Size button, and click Generate Again (**FIGURE 5.16G**). Your entire image becomes a single, repeatable tile. To benefit from this new size, you would then have to take this document into another, larger document and repeat it. For the purposes of this exercise, take the size back down to 256 x 256, and click Generate Again.

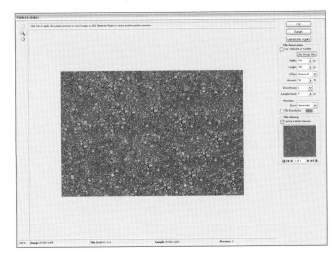

FIGURE 5.16G
The pattern
with the tile size
adjusted to be
the size of the
entire image.

7. If you find that your settings are about right, but you'd like to get another version of your pattern, just click the Generate Again button until it gives you a pattern you're happy with.

8. If you find that you liked a previous iteration of your pattern better than the current version, go to the Tile History area in the Pattern Maker filter (**FIGURE 5.16H**). Each time you click Generate/Generate Again, the pattern that is generated is stored in the Tile History area. Previously generated patterns can be accessed at any time by using the navigational arrows below the tiles. Be aware that when you close Tile History, the history is wiped away and starts over again the next time you open the Pattern Maker.

FIGURE 5.16H The Tile History area in the Pattern Maker filter. This is the equivalent of a History palette in this filter.

TIP   If you want to save a pattern you've created with the Pattern Maker, use a marquee selection to define a pattern as you did earlier in this chapter.

9. When you're done adjusting and fiddling with your pattern, click OK to fill the current layer with that pattern. If you specified a smaller pattern size, your pattern will still fill the entire document, but each tile of the pattern will be the size you specified, just as in the Pattern Maker filter window.

TIP   You can also have an area selected when you launch the Pattern Maker, and the Pattern Maker can use that selection to create its patterns. However, patterns must be rectangular. If your selection area is nonrectangular when you launch the Pattern Maker, the Pattern Maker converts that selection to an equivalent rectangular selection.

Creating Realistic Textures from Scratch

Now, I'll talk about creating something from nothing in Photoshop, which is one of my favorite topics to discuss. Many times, the textures you create will be based on photos you've taken (or swiped from a Google image search—don't act like you haven't done it!). But many times you won't have that luxury. When creating the basketball texture used earlier, for example, I couldn't use a photo. Even the best photo of a basketball couldn't be used as a texture, because a rectangular version of it was needed. So I had to create it from scratch in Photoshop. In this section, we'll explore a few innovative ideas for creating organic, synthetic textures from nothing.

Smart Filters

Most of the time when creating synthetic textures out of whole cloth, you use Photoshop's great wealth of filters to work your mojo. In previous versions of Photoshop, this has been a double-edged sword. Filters are powerful and important, but they have always been destructive. After you applied them to a layer, there was no way to make adjustments or remove them without deleting the layer. This has been especially frustrating for 3D users, because they typically use multiple effects applied to the same layer to achieve the results they're looking for.

But Photoshop CS3 puts an end to all that frustration. It does this by providing the ability to apply filters nondestructively to Smart Objects. Or, you can select Filter > Convert for Smart Filters, which converts a layer to a Smart Object. There really aren't any filters that are "smart." The "smartness" comes in the way the filters are applied.

To see how this works, press the letters D and then X on your keyboard. The letter D resets your colors to the defaults (black as the foreground and white as the background), and X swaps them so that black is your background color. Next, create a new Photoshop document by selecting File > New. Change the preset to Default Photoshop Size. Change the Background Contents drop-down list to Background Color. Click OK to create a new document with a black background. Next, select the Filter menu at the top of the interface and choose Convert for Smart Filters to convert your layer to a Smart Object. Now you're ready to add some nondestructive filters to this baby, so take a deep breath and prepare for the goodness.

Make sure your layer is selected, and then choose Filter > Render > Clouds (**FIGURE 5.17A**). Even though there isn't anything different about the Clouds filter, something magical has happened in the Layers palette (**FIGURE 5.17B**). You now have all sorts of gizmos and doo-hickeys all over the place!

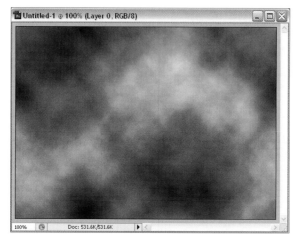

FIGURE 5.17A The Clouds filter applied to this layer.

FIGURE 5.17B The Layers palette after applying the Clouds filter to a Smart Object.

Let's first look at the actual effect. You can now see it as its own object in the Layers palette. Double-click the name of applied filters to adjust their parameters. Clouds doesn't have any parameters, so double-clicking just reapplies a new version of Clouds. If you want to delete Clouds, you can just drag it to the trash can icon in the Layers palette. You can also just temporarily make it invisible by clicking the eye icon next to its name in the Layers palette. You can also click the eye next to the words Smart Filters in the Layers palette to toggle the visibility of all filters applied to this layer. Notice that to the right of the name Smart Filters in the Layers palette is a white rectangle. This is like a layer mask that only affects effects, not the layer itself as you've seen previously.

NOTE   The Clouds filter is generated randomly. If you find an application that you like, save it. You may never be able to duplicate that exact pattern again.

One of the most interesting aspects of Smart Filters is the icon shown in **FIGURE 5.18**. Double-click this icon to open the Blending Options dialog. Here you can reduce the opacity of the effect or change its Blend mode. Previously, the only way you could perform such functions was to select Edit > Fade *immediately* after applying an effect. And you could never go back and adjust those blending changes once applied. But in Photoshop CS3, not only are the effects nondestructive, but so are their blending options.

As you go forward now and create synthetic effects, remember the power and flexibility of Smart Filters. The ability to go back and adjust the third of 20 effects applied should not be taken for granted.

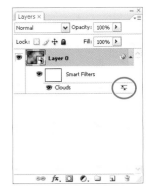

FIGURE 5.18 The Blending Options icon for filters. Double-click it to nondestructively change the Blending and Opacity options for this effect.

Using Reference Images

Using reference images is a topic of Herculean importance and always bears repeating. Reference images are images of real-world objects that you use as reference when trying to re-create them digitally. In Example 1 in this chapter, you create realistic wood from scratch. If you were doing this in a real-world

scenario, you would want to have an image like this displayed at the same time for constant reference.

Years ago, when I first started getting into 3D, I assumed that using reference images was a form of cheating, as if it was a crutch that the pros didn't lean on. How young and foolish I was. The truth

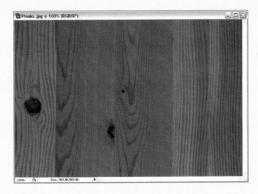

is that all the great digital artists, from Pixar to others in the film industry, use reference images to make a more believable final result.

This doesn't mean that you should try to necessarily copy the reference image. The reference image is just that—a reference. So you might use the wooden planks image just to get ideas about the way rings of wood grain are spaced out, or ideas for color variations, and so forth.

Example 1: Creating a Wooden Plank

In this mini-tutorial, you'll start out by making a texture that could be used for a wooden object.

1. Create a new Photoshop document by selecting File > New. From the Preset drop-down list, select Default Photoshop Size. In this case, don't worry about the Background Contents because you'll be fixing that in the next step.

2. As you create this wooden texture, feel free to use the Planks.jpg file in the Chapter 5 folder as a reference. Your goal is to create a wooden plank that realistically resembles one of the planks in the photo. Try to mimic this photo by selecting foreground and background elements that resemble the wood and grain colors in the photograph. Click the foreground color swatch to open the Adobe Color Picker. Select a color that matches the base color of the wood (not the lines of wood grain). I chose the RGB values of 174, 142, 79. Click OK to accept this color. With the background layer selected, fill it with this color by pressing Alt+Backspace/Opt+Delete.

3. Create a new layer by clicking the Create a New Layer icon at the bottom of the Layers palette. **FIGURE 5.19A** shows what you should have thus far.

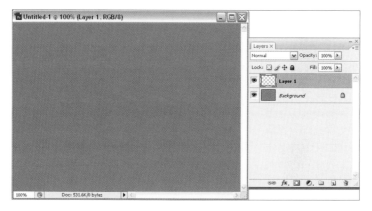

FIGURE 5.19A For your wood texture, you should now have a wood colored background and a separate blank layer.

4. On this new blank layer, add the lines for the wood grain. Select a new foreground color that will be better for the lines of wood grain. I chose a slightly darker brown with the RGB values of 138, 91, 41.

5. Now select an artistic brush to create the grain. Select the Brush tool in the Tools palette. Then go to the Brushes palette. Select the Spatter 39 pixel brush (**FIGURE 5.19B**).

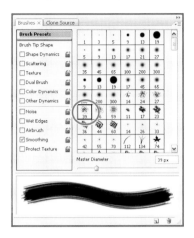

FIGURE 5.19B Select the Spatter 39 pixel brush to paint the lines of grain.

6. With the new layer selected, draw three straight, horizontal lines from the left edge to the right edge (**FIGURE 5.19C**). As you can see, they don't need to be (and probably shouldn't be) perfectly straight and uniform.

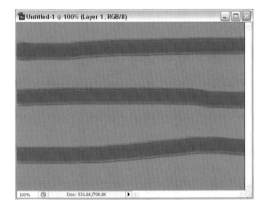

FIGURE 5.19C These horizontal lines will become the wood grain.

7. Use the Photoshop filters to warp these lines. That will look better (and will be much faster) than if you were to draw the grain lines manually. With the paint strokes layer selected, choose Filter > Distort > Wave. Several settings are available to use, and you'll probably get different results every time. So keep adjusting parameters until you find the effect you like. I recommend using Sine as the wave type, because Triangle and Square don't return results that look much like a wood grain texture. The settings I used are shown in **FIGURE 5.19D**.

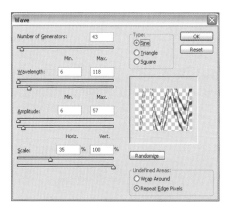

FIGURE 5.19D The settings for the Wave filter that I used to turn my paint strokes into wood grain.

8. From this point on, you need to treat both layers as one object. And since flattening layers is the most destructive thing you can do to a Photoshop document (it goes against my moral value system), I have a better way to use these two layers as one. Select one of the layers, and then while holding the Shift key, click the other layer so both are selected. You'll convert the two layers into a single Smart Object layer. Select Filter > Convert for Smart Filters. Technically, this is still a destructive change, but like Thelma and Louise, if these layers are going to be forced into a destructive edit, at least they'll both go together. And as you add filters to this Smart Object, the filters will be nondestructive.

9. With this new Smart Object layer selected, choose Filter > Noise > Add Noise. Take the Amount to 20% with Gaussian selected and Monochromatic selected as well. **FIGURE 5.19E** shows what the image should look like.

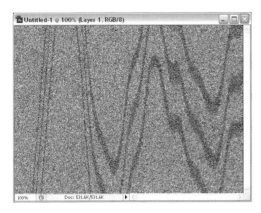

FIGURE 5.19E The image thus far with Add Noise applied.

10. With the layer selected, choose Filter > Blur > Motion Blur to apply some motion blur to this texture. This effect helps simulate the texture of the wood. Use an Angle value of 90 (to make the blur happen vertically) and a Distance (blur amount) value of 25 (**FIGURE 5.19F**). Now the image is starting to look halfway decent.

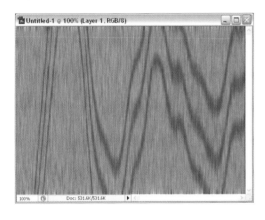

FIGURE 5.19F The wood texture after applying the Motion Blur filter.

11. Let's put some finishing touches on the wood grain by horizontally scaling the image so it resembles a plank. Select the layer and press Ctrl/Cmd+T to enter Free Transform mode. A pop-up dialog informs you that you can't view Smart Filters while you're transforming this object. Go ahead and click OK. Now drag the center points on the side until you have something that resembles a plank (**FIGURE 5.19G** on the next page).

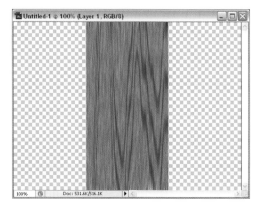

FIGURE 5.19G Free Transform the wooden texture to make it more of a plank shape.

FIGURE 5.19H
The Liquify toolset.

12. The image looks pretty good as is, but there is a little more you can do. You'll first have to convert it to a regular layer. Right-click on the name of the Smart Object layer and select Rasterize Layer. Then select Filter > Liquify. You can use Liquify to make manual, organic deformations of your image. Use the tools in the upper-left area of the Liquify filter to make those changes (**FIGURE 5.19H**). The Forward Warp tool is selected by default. Use the Forward Warp tool to click and drag on areas to smear the pixels around like paint. You can also use the Twirl Clockwise tool, which is the third tool down from the top in the tools area of the Liquify filter. Click and hold to twirl an area until it creates a knot in the wood, as you saw in the reference image. Click OK to accept the Liquify alterations (**FIGURE 5.19I**).

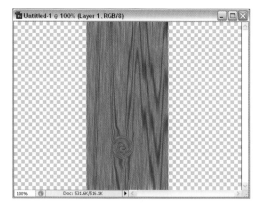

FIGURE 5.19I After adding a knot in the wood by using Liquify.

TIP To make this Liquify adjustment nondestructive, duplicate the layer and apply Liquify to the duplicate.

13. You can then burn the wood a little bit to make it look more realistic. Be aware that you are not trying to create highlights and shadows. You'll get much better results by saving that for your 3D program. See the sidebar "Textures and Lighting Effects." Select the Burn tool from the Tools palette in Photoshop. Click and drag over the knot to "burn" it a little bit, and maybe burn in a few other places to add some more character to the plank (**FIGURE 5.19J**). You can also use the Dodge tool to add more character by lightening areas. And that's it! You now have realistic, organic wood from scratch that will look phenomenal when used as a texture for a 3D program. **FIGURE 5.19K** shows what this texture looks like when applied as a texture to a simple box in 3DS Max. As you can see, 3D programs are very forgiving of many imperfections in texture maps.

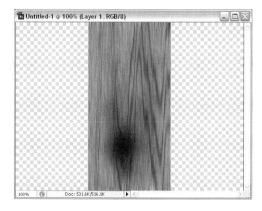

FIGURE 5.19J Use the Burn tool to add darkness to the knot in the wood and in a few other places, and you're done!

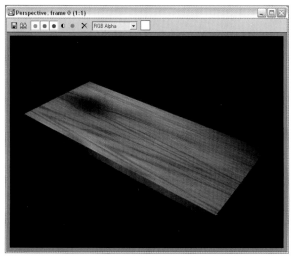

FIGURE 5.19K The wooden plank used as a texture in a 3D program.

If you are creating textures for a 3D program, leave all lighting effects off! Textures look much more realistic on their own when you add the Lighting Effects filter, or gradients, or other methods to simulate natural lighting. But although that will make the texture look better on its own, it will actually make the results look worse if the texture is being used as a 3D texture. The lighting in 3D programs is much more powerful and realistic than what you can create in Photoshop. In addition, if you add artificial lighting in Photoshop, it will most likely conflict with the 3D lighting in your 3D program. So leave off the lighting information in your textures. If your textures come out looking a little cartoonish and fake because of it, that's okay. It's amazing what good lighting can compensate for.

Example 2: Making an Eyeball Texture

Now, let's create something a little more interesting—a human eye. Actually, you'll just create the texture for the eye. You can then apply this texture to a model in a 3D program or replace the texture of a sphere model you've imported into Photoshop.

1. Open the Eye start.psd file from the Chapter 5 folder (**FIGURE 5.20A**). This is a basic Photoshop document with a white background. Guides have been set up to make it easier to create an eyeball in the center. If you don't have

FIGURE 5.20A The Eye start.psd file. Make sure that you can see the cyan colored guides.

cyan crosshairs in your document (as shown in the figure), select View > Show > Guides to ensure that Guides has a check mark next to it. This check mark indicates whether guides are on or off.

2. Create a new layer by clicking the Create a New Layer button at the bottom of the Layers palette, and make sure the layer is selected. Select the Elliptical Marquee tool in the Tools palette. Using the keyboard shortcuts Alt/Opt (to make the selection area scale from its center) and Shift (to constrain the selection area to be a perfect circle), click in the center of the image and scale out to create a round selection area. Press D to reset the default colors, and then press Alt+Backspace/Opt+Delete to fill this selection with black. Press Ctrl/Cmd+D to deselect your circle (**FIGURE 5.20B**). This black circle will be the background of the eye.

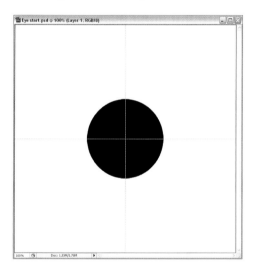

FIGURE 5.20B Create an elliptical selection in the center of the document and fill it with black.

3. Create another new layer and make sure it's selected. The next step is to create another circle that is the same size as the black circle, and fill it with green. The easiest way to do that is to select the boundary of the black circle layer by holding the Ctrl/Cmd key and clicking the layer thumbnail of the black circle layer. With that selection active, select a foreground color that will be the base color of your eye. For this example, select a green color.

Make sure the new blank layer is still selected (not the black circle layer), and fill it with the foreground color by pressing Alt+Backspace/Opt+Delete (**FIGURE 5.20C** on the next page).

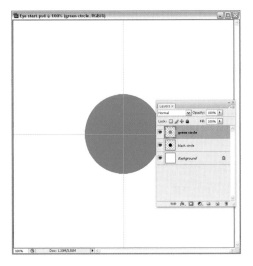

FIGURE 5.20C The document and Layers palette after step 3.

NOTE I named my layers so that you would know what's going on, but this step is optional. Rename a layer by double-clicking its name in the Layers palette and typing a new name.

4. Now you can add some filters to the green circle layer. But you might want to make adjustments to those filters later, so first convert this layer for Smart Filters. Select the green circle layer and choose Filter > Convert for Smart Filters.

5. With the green circle layer selected, add some noise by choosing Filter > Noise > Add Noise. Use 60% for the Amount setting with both Gaussian and Monochromatic selected (**FIGURE 5.20D**).

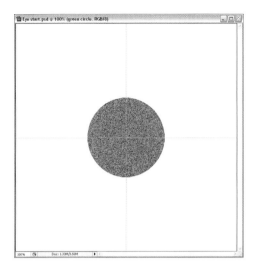

FIGURE 5.20D After adding some noise to the green circle layer.

6. With the green circle layer still selected, make the magic happen by choosing Filter > Blur > Radial Blur. Change the Blur Method to Zoom. That will give the noise the old sci-fi "warp to light speed" effect. Change the quality to Best and the Amount to 70 (**FIGURE 5.20E**). After applying the blur, you should start to see the beginnings of a cornea (**FIGURE 5.20F**).

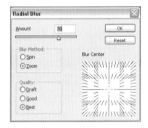

FIGURE 5.20E Radial Blur settings.

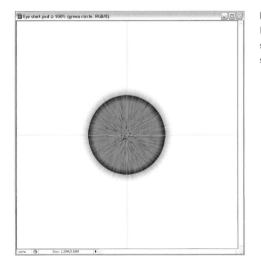

FIGURE 5.20F After adding Radial Blur, you can start to see how this can become a sweet-looking eye.

7. The green circle layer looks great, but it's too big. Scale it down by pressing Ctrl/Cmd+T to enter Free Transform mode. Click OK when the pop-up dialog appears. Click on the corner points to scale it down. As with selecting, you can use the keyboard shortcuts Alt/Opt (to scale from the center) and Shift (to constrain proportions, keeping this a perfect circle). I'll scale it to about there (**FIGURE 5.20G**). Press Enter on the numeric keypad or click the check mark in the options bar to accept your changes. Your Smart Object will again show the effects applied to it (**FIGURE 5.20H**).

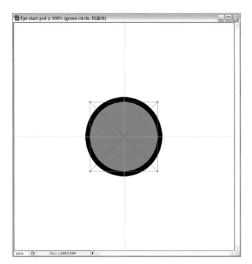

FIGURE 5.20G Free Transform the green circle layer to scale it down to about here.

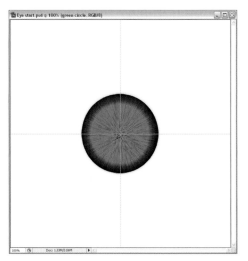

FIGURE 5.20H After Free Transforming.

8. You can now add more variation to the green color. Ctrl/Cmd-click the layer thumbnail of the black circle layer to select its boundaries. Choose Select > Modify > Contract. Enter 16 and click OK.

9. Make a new layer, and with that new layer selected, fill the selection area with a cyan color (click the foreground color swatch in the Tools palette to get the color picker to change colors).

10. Repeat steps 4–6 for the cyan circle layer, except this time when you apply Add Noise, deselect Monochromatic so that you get a little bit of color variation in the eye. Then select the cyan circle layer and take the Opacity value in the Layers palette down to 60% to blend these radical color values into your previous green eye color (**FIGURE 5.20I**).

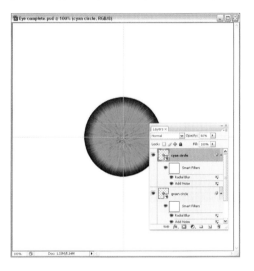

FIGURE 5.20I The project up to this point.

11. Create one more new layer, and make sure it is selected. This layer will hold the pupil. Press D on your keyboard to turn your foreground color black. Make a small, pupil-sized selection in the center of the document and fill it with black (**FIGURE 5.20J**). Press Ctrl/Cmd+D to deselect.

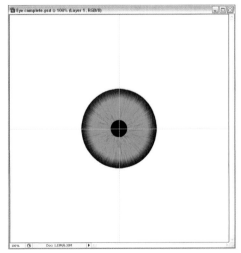

FIGURE 5.20J The formation of the pupil.

12. With the new pupil layer selected, choose Filter > Blur > Gaussian Blur, and change the Radius value to 6 pixels. Your eye is now complete (**FIGURE 5.20K**). **FIGURE 5.20L** shows what this texture looks like when applied to a sphere in a 3D program.

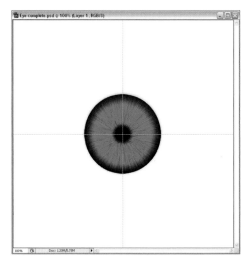

FIGURE 5.20K Soften the pupil to blend it in to the background, and the eye is done!

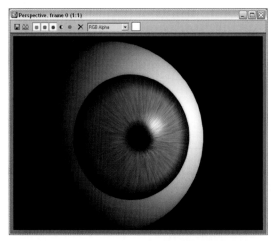

FIGURE 5.20L The finished eyeball texture applied to a simple sphere in a 3D program.

NOTE   I've placed a PSD file called Eye complete.psd in the Chapter 5 folder. It contains a completed version of the eye project.

Video Basics

6

And now we begin the journey into the world of video. The good news is that working with video is much easier than working with 3D in Photoshop. After all, video is essentially just a series of still images (called frames) played back in rapid succession. And Adobe is already a big player in the video world with industry-leading tools like After Effects, Flash, Premiere Pro, and Encore. So it's no surprise that the video aspects of Photoshop are a little easier to understand and to work with. In this chapter, you'll learn all the basics: how to import video, play it back, create new video documents, and export video. You'll also learn the great secret about audio in Photoshop Extended.

Video in Photoshop Extended

Photoshop has actually offered you the ability to animate for a while, using the Animation palette. Video editing and animation still happen in the Animation palette, but now there are two different sides to the palette. Understanding the way these two palettes work is the foundation of working with video in Photoshop Extended.

NOTE QuickTime plays a huge role when working with video in any Adobe product, and Photoshop Extended is no exception. Don't even think about working with video in Photoshop Extended without having the latest version of QuickTime on your computer! You can download a new version free of charge from www.quicktime.com.

Animation (Old vs. New)

Let's take a walk down memory lane and look at the way you had to animate in times past, and compare it to the new way. I won't go into detail about the old way of doing things because that method of animation is now archaic. For more information on how to animate frames, consult the Photoshop Help documentation.

The two sides of the new Animation palette are Animation (Frames) (**FIGURE 6.1A**) and Animation (Timeline) (**FIGURE 6.1B**). When animating in previous versions of Photoshop—now in the Animation (Frames) palette—you would have to specify states of a layer and create "tweens." The old way to animate was not flexible or intuitive. The Timeline side of the Animation palette is where you rotoscope, play video, and create high-end, keyframe-driven animation. The Timeline side is only available in Photoshop Extended.

FIGURE 6.1A The Frames side of the Animation palette.

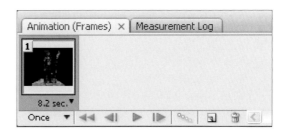

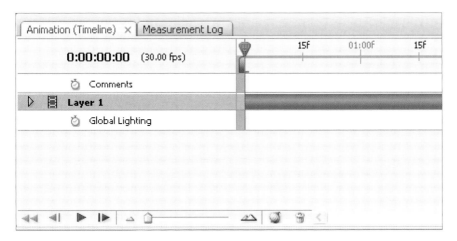

FIGURE 6.1B The Timeline side of the Animation palette. This is where the good stuff is.

Even though the Frames side of the Animation palette is outdated, this way of animating is still available to you in Photoshop (in both Photoshop standard and Photoshop Extended), but this method is not compatible with animating video! You can switch back and forth between the Frames side and the Timeline side of the Animation palette by clicking the button at the bottom-right corner of the Animation palette (**FIGURES 6.2A** and **6.2B**). You never need to be concerned about upgrading from the Frames side to the Timeline side. But as you switch from the Timeline side to the Frames side, you will lose a great deal of functionality. As you'll see as you go through the following material in this book, converting your video or animation from the Timeline side to the Frames side is akin to flattening the layers in a standard Photoshop file.

FIGURE 6.2A Click this button to switch from the Frames side of the Animation palette to the Timeline side.

FIGURE 6.2B Click this button to switch from the Timeline side of the Animation palette to the Frames side.

Importing and Playing Back Video

Importing video is just as easy as importing any other file. Select File > Open to find a video file to import. On Windows, you can open the Files of Type drop-down list to see all the types of files that you can now import into Photoshop Extended (**FIGURE 6.3**). Notice that most of the video formats fall under the QuickTime heading. This is another reminder of the importance of having the most recent version of QuickTime installed on your computer.

FIGURE 6.3 All the file types that Photoshop Extended can import. That's pretty big list!

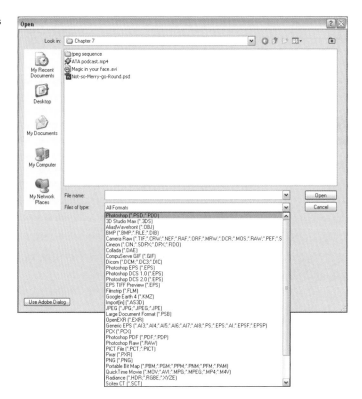

Navigate to the Chapter 6 folder and open the Magic in your face.avi video file. It opens just like a regular image file (**FIGURE 6.4**). This movie file depicts the wizard lady getting revenge for all the times we teased her during the 3D portions of this book.

FIGURE 6.4 The Magic in your face.avi file.

Video Formats Recognized by Photoshop

Here's a list of the video file formats that Photoshop Extended can import:

- MOV

- AVI

- MPEG-1

- MPEG-4

- FLV (This is the Flash Video format. Import is only possible if you have Adobe Flash 8 or later installed.)

- MPEG-2 (This is the file format recognized by DVDs. This format is only able to be imported into Photoshop if you have an MPEG-2 encoder installed on your system. Several free MPEG-2 encoders are available on the Internet.)

Later in this chapter I discuss the various formats that Photoshop can export to, and there are a lot more options there.

To play this movie in Photoshop, simply press the spacebar on your keyboard (**FIGURE 6.5** on the next page). Press the spacebar again to stop playback.

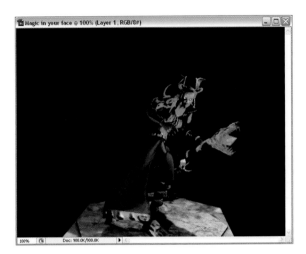

FIGURE 6.5 A later frame from the video layer. The wizard lady doesn't look very happy.

In the same way that 3D layers are denoted by a 3D cube on their layer thumbnail, video layers are so designated by a film icon on their layer thumbnails (**FIGURE 6.6**). All of the video frames for the layer shown in the figure are stored on this video layer. Unlike with 3D layers, there is no "mode" to enter with video.

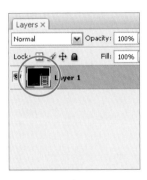

FIGURE 6.6 This icon on a layer's thumbnail indicates a video layer.

Are Imported Videos Embedded into PSD Files?

When you looked at 3D files, you saw that the 3D files were embedded in the Photoshop document once the PSD file was saved.

Video works differently in Photoshop and in most major video applications. Only a link to the original file is stored in the Photoshop document because of the size of video files. It's not uncommon for video files to be over 2 GB in size. If Photoshop embedded a 2 GB video file into the PSD when saving the file, it would increase the size of the PSD by 2 GB. That would fill your hard drive before you knew what hit you.

Because the video file is not embedded in the PSD file, it's very important that you respect the link that the PSD file has to your video files. Do not move, rename, or delete the source video files or your Photoshop document will not be able to locate them. In Chapter 8, "Intermediate Video Editing in Photoshop," you'll learn how to fix broken video links in case you run into problems in this area.

Playback might seem a little slow at first depending on your system and the imported video file. When you initially play a video file, Photoshop attempts to cache the frames of the video so that they can play back more quickly. Frames that are cached can play back in real time and will have a green line above them.

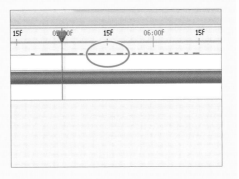

See Chapter 8 for other ways to get better playback performance.

Video Navigation

You know that the spacebar can start and stop video playback, but just being able to start and stop video playback isn't that helpful. Photoshop offers a whole host of ways to zip around a timeline.

The Current Time Indicator

The most important navigation tool is the Current Time Indicator (CTI). The CTI is the red vertical line with the blue handle on top that indicates where you currently are in the timeline (**FIGURE 6.7**). Dragging the CTI to the right moves further in time, whereas dragging to the left moves you earlier in the video. You can jump large amounts of time or go to the very next frame.

You can click on the blue part of the CTI and drag it anywhere in the timeline, or you can click at the top of the timeline to quickly jump to a particular place in time

It's important to know where you are in the video for trimming, painting, animating, and other editing tasks. Where your CTI is will make a significant difference when using the video features of Photoshop.

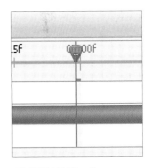

FIGURE 6.7 The Current Time Indicator.

What Is a Timeline?

A timeline is a graph that displays time. On the left side of the graph, or timeline, is the beginning of a video, whereas the far right side displays the end of the video. Practically every program that can contain animation, video, or audio, or that has anything that shows objects with a duration, will have a timeline of some sort. Using the Current Time Indicator, you can navigate to specific points in the timeline to make events occur at various points in time.

The Current Time area

In the upper-left corner of the Animation (Timeline) palette is the Current Time area (not to be confused with the Current Time Indicator), which displays the timecode of the current frame (**FIGURE 6.8**). Timecode is a way to display time in video. If I were to tell you that the current time of day is 3:12 p.m., you would know exactly when in the day that is. Timecode does the same for video.

Timecode is displayed as four sets of numbers separated by colons. From left to right the timecode is read as hours:minutes:seconds:frames. So the number 0:03:14:22 would indicate 3 minutes, 14 seconds, and 22 frames.

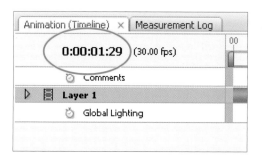

FIGURE 6.8 The Current Time area.

When you put your cursor over the Current Time display in the upper-left corner of the Animation (Timeline) palette, an alternate version of a scrubby slider appears (**FIGURE 6.9**). Click and drag left and right to scrub backward and forward in time, respectively. As in other areas in Photoshop, holding the Shift key while scrubbing will scrub through time much faster (ten frames at a time), and holding the Ctrl/Cmd key while scrubbing will scrub you through the timeline at a slower rate.

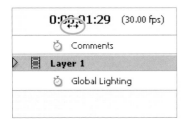

FIGURE 6.9 This icon is actually a scrubby slider, even though it's missing a hand. Click and scrub left and right to adjust the Current Time Indicator.

If you want to jump to a particular frame, you can double-click the numbers in the Current Time area to access the Set Current Time dialog. You can manually enter the timecode of the frame you'd like to jump to. Once you enter the timecode and click OK, the CTI automatically jumps to that point in the timeline.

To the immediate right of the Current Time area, Photoshop displays the frame rate of the current project. The frame rate indicates how many images (frames) play back per second and is therefore often abbreviated as fps, or frames per second. The higher the frame rate, the faster the video will play back. If the video has to display 30 images in 1 second, it will have to display those images much faster than if it only had to display 5 images per second. I'll discuss how to adjust the frame rate of a project, and a little more about frame rates in Chapter 8, "Intermediate Video Editing in Photoshop."

TIP   If you clear out the current time in the Set Current Time dialog and type a single number (like 5, for example), the Set Current Time dialog will interpret that as frame 5 and will take you there. If you type in 50 and click OK, your CTI jumps to 0:00:01:20, assuming your project is 30 frames per second. This is because 30 (fps) can be divided into 50 frames 1 time, with 20 frames left over.

FIGURE 6.10 The playback buttons in the Timeline side of the Animation palette.

The playback buttons

In the bottom-left corner of the Animation (Timeline) palette are a few useful playback buttons (**FIGURE 6.10**). The one on the far left is my personal favorite. This little helper zaps your CTI to the beginning of your animation, which you'll want to do constantly. Moving to the right, the next playback button (the Selects previous frame button) takes you back one frame at a time each time you click it. The button to its right is simply a Play/Pause button (the spacebar does the same thing, and it's easier to get to). The rightmost button (the Selects next frame button) advances the video one frame at a time each time you click it.

TIP When clicking the Selects previous frame or Selects next frame buttons, you can hold the Shift key to go to the previous/next second instead of the previous/next frame.

Zooming into and out of the timeline

Depending on the task at hand, you may want to see each frame of your timeline, or you may want to see huge 20 minute chunks at a glance. You can zoom into your timeline to see smaller increments of time or zoom out to see more of your video footage. The little mountains with a slider in the middle to the right of the playback area can be used to do just that (**FIGURE 6.11**). Either click the small mountains on the left or drag the slider to the left to see more of your timeline. Alternatively, click the large mountains or scrub the slider to the right to zoom in to do more precise editing.

FIGURE 6.11 Click the mountains (or use the slider) to zoom into and out of the timeline.

Zooming in or out is more helpful than it might seem on the surface. Let's say you're timing the animation of a lens flare in Photoshop to sync up to the tail of a rocket in a video. You'll probably want to zoom in really close to ensure that each frame matches precisely, so you would click the large mountains or drag the zoom slider to the right. On the other hand, if you're editing a video of a whale-watching trip, unless you find some magical spot where whales incessantly congregate, I'm guessing you'll have a lot of boring video to get rid of. If you want to remove large chunks of unwanted video in one fell swoop, you'll want to zoom out quite far so you can see huge video chunks at a glance. To do this, click the small mountains or drag the slider to the left.

Integrating Animated 3D and Video

In Chapter 3, "Even Cooler 3D Tricks," you looked at playing back animations stored in 3D files. But now that you have more information about video, there's actually an easier way to do this that doesn't involve getting into 3D Object mode.

Open the Not-so-Merry-go-Round.psd file from the Chapter 6 folder (**FIGURE 6.12**). This is the same file that you saw in Chapter 3 and is also copied to the Chapter 6 folder for your convenience. With the Animation (Timeline) palette

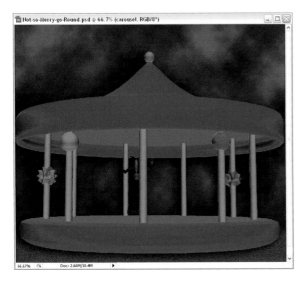

FIGURE 6.12 The Not-so-Merry-go-Round. psd file.

open, press the spacebar to play this animation. No need to enter 3D Object mode at all! Of course, here you have the best of both worlds because you can still edit this object in 3D, and you can also edit it like video.

TIP   There is a lot going on in the Not-so-Merry-go-Round.psd file, so it may take a while to load and play at regular speed.

About Image Sequences

Often when dealing with video, you don't actually import, edit, or export video files. Instead, you might use an image sequence, which is exactly what it sounds like—a series of still images. In an image sequence, each frame of a movie is rendered out to a separate image file. In contrast to the single file that a video file will create, image sequences export to many images—one for each frame in the timeline. If you exported a 10 second project with a frame rate of 30 frames per second, that would be a total of 300 frames (10 seconds x 30 fps). If exported to an image sequence, this would make 300 separate files!

When that series of frames is imported back into Photoshop (or another video program), the series of images is treated just like it was a movie clip. You'd never know the difference.

So, you're probably wondering why anyone would want to use an image sequence instead of a regular video. Well, there are actually several reasons, and personally, I prefer to deal with image sequences in many instances.

For one, file corruption isn't as big of a problem with image sequences. If you send a client a 10 GB video (which actually happened to me a couple weeks ago), and the video file gets corrupt, you'll have to start the transfer process from the beginning again. That can cost precious time and money that your job most likely won't allow. If you were to use a 10 GB image sequence however, and one of the many images in the sequence became corrupt, it wouldn't be that big of a deal. One or two images in the sequence could easily be emailed to remedy the situation without any loss of time or money.

The idea of file corruption is also important when exporting from your video or 3D program. When exporting really flashy projects to video, computers can take a long time to render those projects and will frequently crash in the process. If the program crashes when rendering a video file, you'll have to start the render all over again. If you render to a still image sequence, you can just pick up from where the program crashed.

NOTE   The term "render" is common in video and 3D circles, but not in the standard 2D Photoshop workflow. In a nutshell, render just indicates the process of converting your project to a video or still image format that other programs can understand.

NOTE   Rendering, discussed later in this chapter, is the process by which video is exported.

Also, when transporting video to a remote location, image sequences come in handy. Because they are just a bunch of separate images, you can break them up as necessary, which you can't do with a solitary video file. Let's say you had a video file that was 5 GB in size. How would you save, transport, and store that file? You would have to use either a small hard drive or a next generation DVD format, which is ridiculously expensive at the time of this writing. However, if you used an image sequence, you could just split the images onto two DVDs, or maybe even a DVD and a CD. The total cost would be less than $1.

If you're coming from a solid Photoshop background, it might be easier for you to render to image sequences because you're more familiar with different types of image compression than video compression. For example, if you've ever sent a project to a professional printing press, you've probably (I hope) used TIFF files because they have a lossless compression algorithm. Basically, that means that they look really good. And you also are probably aware of JPEG files that are lossy (meaning that data is lost when saved) but are great for those times when you need an image to look decent and file size is an issue. You can leverage this knowledge when creating image sequences. If you need an image sequence for a Web video project, try using a JPEG sequence. If you're creating a project for broadcast, a TIFF sequence might be a good choice.

Using image sequences

Using image sequences in Photoshop is a piece of cake. After all, handling images is what Photoshop does best. To import a sample video sequence, select File > Open and navigate to the Chapter 6 folder. In that folder is another folder called JPEG sequence, which contains billions of images. Well, actually there are only 68, but it looks like a lot more. Click only once on the first image in the sequence, which is 05-weight_00024.jpg, to select it. Notice the Image Sequence check box in the Open dialog (**FIGURE 6.13**). When you select this check box, Photoshop searches for a numbering or alphabetized system in the naming convention of your image files. It's best to use a series of sequentially numbered images as I have in the JPEG sequence folder. Click OK to open the image sequence.

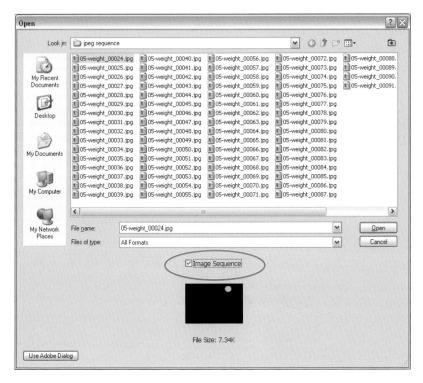

FIGURE 6.13 In the Open dialog, select the Image Sequence check box to import a sequence of still images and have them function as a video file would.

A dialog pops-up asking you what you would like the frame rate for the image sequence to be. Keep this at the standard 30 fps, and click OK. If another pop-up dialog about pixel aspect appears, click OK in that as well.

With the Animation (Timeline) palette open, press the spacebar to preview the animation. No one would ever know that it wasn't originally a video clip. And thus you see that image sequences are perfectly compatible with video programs (like Photoshop is now) and can be used interchangeably with video files.

I'll talk momentarily about how to export to image sequences from Photoshop in the upcoming section on exporting.

Image sequences and Bridge

I have to be honest. When Adobe Bridge first shipped with Photoshop CS2, I was not a big fan. But I've since seen the light, repented, and come into the full circle of fellowship with Bridge.

Adobe Bridge is the ultimate Adobe file browsing application, and it ships with most Adobe products. It also previews the file formats for most Adobe applications, including PSD files, Adobe Illustrator files, video files, audio files, and many others.

Bridge CS3 introduces the amazing ability to preview image sequences. I don't know of any other way to preview image sequences without opening them.

To preview an image sequence in Bridge, you first have to launch Bridge. Click the Go to Bridge button in the options bar in Photoshop (**FIGURE 6.14**). Bridge takes a while to open, especially the first time. And there's no welcome screen, so just click this button with authority and wait patiently for Bridge to open. Like me, the button does unexpected things when you keep poking it repeatedly.

FIGURE 6.14 The Go to Bridge button in the options bar. Click this button to launch Adobe Bridge CS3.

Using the buttons on the left side of the Bridge interface (**FIGURE 6.15**) and the folders in the main window, navigate to this book's disc or to your hard drive (if you've copied the files there) until you get to the JPEG sequence folder in the Chapter 6 folder. You should see something like the screen shown in **FIGURE 6.16**.

FIGURE 6.15 You can use the buttons on the left side of the Bridge interface to jump to important areas on your hard drive. You can also use the drop-down list here as well.

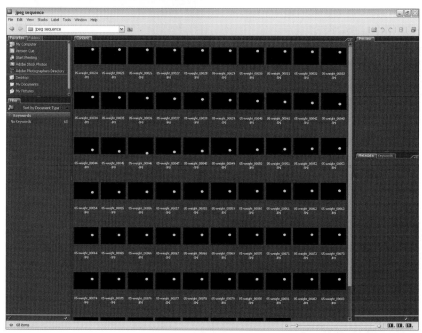

FIGURE 6.16 The JPEG sequence image sequence as seen in Bridge.

Click once on one of the images, and press Ctrl/Cmd+A to select all of the images in the JPEG sequence folder (**FIGURE 6.17**). With the images selected, go to the Stacks menu at the top of the Bridge interface and choose Group as Stack. Bridge then displays all of the images as one object, and it displays the number of images in that stack at the top of it (**FIGURE 6.18**).

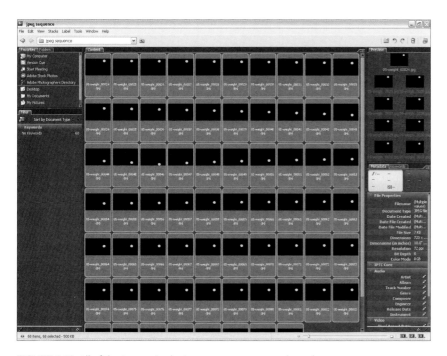

FIGURE 6.17 All of the images in the image sequence are selected.

FIGURE 6.18 The image sequence after being grouped as a Stack in Bridge. The number 68 represents the number of images grouped in this Stack.

The Group as Stack feature is great for photographers to use to clean up multiple images of the same camera shoot. But Bridge also allows you to see this stack as a movie. The key here is that you need to first increase the size of the thumbnail. You do that by clicking on the slider at the bottom of the screen and dragging to the right (**FIGURE 6.19A**). Increase the size of the thumbnail until you have a mini-timeline at the top of the stack thumbnail, as shown in **FIGURE 6.19B**. Note that you won't see this timeline until you let go of the slider and place your mouse back over the stack.

FIGURE 6.19A Use the slider at the bottom of the Bridge interface to increase the size of the Stack thumbnail.

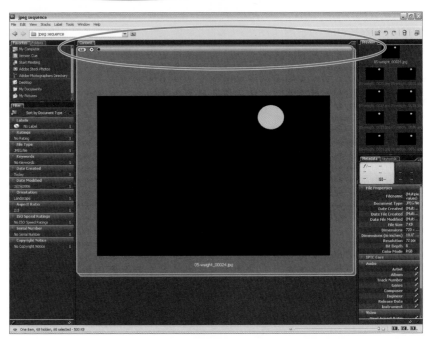

FIGURE 6.19B Increase the size of the thumbnail until you get a bar at the top of the thumbnail that represents a tiny timeline.

Now you can click the Play button next to the tiny timeline at the top of the stack thumbnail to play back the stack. You can even manually scrub the little timeline at the top of the stack thumbnail to look at whatever section of your image sequence that you want to. Amazing! But it gets even better. You can also select Stacks > Frame Rate to select a new frame rate to use to play back your stack.

Stacking is completely nondestructive. If you want to ungroup your stack, select it and choose Stacks > Ungroup from Stack. If you want to just temporarily see all the files in your stack (maybe to delete one that shouldn't be there), you can choose Stacks > Open Stack. To close the stack so it becomes a previewable stack again, select Stacks > Close Stack. Bridge, please forgive me for my earlier misjudgment.

Creating Files for Export to Video

When creating Photoshop documents that you know you will use in other video programs such as After Effects, you must carefully set up your document with the end in mind. Photoshop provides several templates for common video output media. And Photoshop CS3 is even better organized than earlier versions, so creating documents for video is even easier.

Create a new video document by selecting File > New; the New dialog pops up (**FIGURE 6.20**). In previous versions of Photoshop, Adobe crammed presets for every type of media in one long list. In CS3, these presets are more orderly and

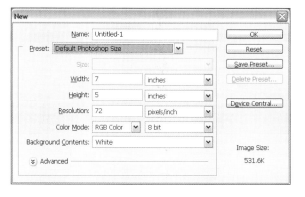

FIGURE 6.20 The New dialog.

easier to access. From the Preset drop-down list, choose Film & Video (**FIGURE 6.21**). You can then choose from a list of document presets from the Size drop-down list (**FIGURE 6.22**). Select a preset that matches your output medium. If you don't see a preset for your particular project (like iPod video, which is missing from this list), you can manually type in the dimensions of your output medium.

FIGURE 6.21 Choose Film & Video from the Preset drop-down list to access all of the film and video document presets.

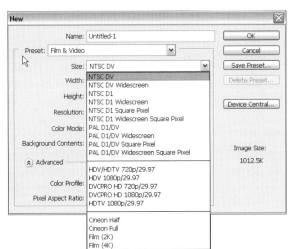

FIGURE 6.22 From the Size drop-down list, you can select preset video document templates.

Notice how the Size drop-down list is divided into three sections (**FIGURE 6.23**). The top area with NTSC and PAL presets is for standard-definition video projects. The middle area is for high-definition video projects. And the bottom area is for projects intended for film.

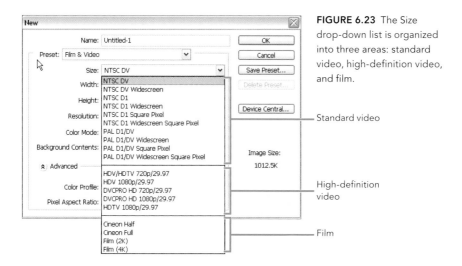

Standard video

High-definition video

Film

Click the chevron next to the word Advanced at the bottom of the New dialog to see the Pixel Aspect Ratio for the new document. Thankfully, these Size presets come with the correct pixel aspect ratio built in. See the "Pixel Aspect Ratios" sidebar for more information about this important video concept.

Video Standards

When dealing with video standards, you will often see NTSC and PAL, which represent the video standards in different regions.

NTSC (National Television Standards Committee) is the standard for North America and Japan. The pixel dimensions for NTSC video are 720 wide x 480 high. The frame rate is 29.97 fps. The pixel aspect ratio is 0.9 for full screen and 1.2 for wide screen.

PAL is the standard in most of Europe (except France) and in many other countries throughout the world. The pixel dimensions are 720 pixels wide x 576 pixels high. The frame rate is 25 fps. The pixel aspect ratio is 1.07.

Although not technically a video standard per se, film has a frame rate of 24 fps.

Make sure you create your video project with your intended audience (and its hardware) in mind.

Pixels, short for "picture elements," are the building blocks of images and what you see onscreen—the little squares that you see when you zoom in too closely. These little guys can cause all sorts of problems when working with video.

The problem is that pixels on a computer monitor are square; they're exactly as wide as they are tall. However, the pixels on most TV screens are rectangular. Not only that but the size of the pixel depends on the video standard you're using.

The pixel aspect ratio also has a bearing on the frame aspect ratio. For example, for regular full-screen TV, the pixel aspect ratio is 0.9. This means that the pixels are slightly taller than they are wide. This creates a frame aspect ratio of 4:3. Using the exact same number of pixels, and only widening the pixel aspect ratio to 1.2 (slightly wider than tall), will create a wide-screen video with a frame aspect of 16:9.

It is *very* important that you create your Photoshop document with the correct pixel aspect ratio. If you change your mind later, it will profoundly distort your image!

Exporting to Video

Talking about exporting video is getting a little ahead of myself at this stage in the game. You haven't even made anything to export yet. However, from my training experience, people are usually most interested in this utilitarian issue, so let's cover this up front.

More good news: Photoshop can actually create more types of video than it can import. Also, the dialog used to export video is well organized and easy to use. That's a small thing, but it does help to make an intimidating topic feel more conquerable.

To export video, choose File > Export > Render Video. The all-important Render Video dialog appears (**FIGURE 6.24**). This dialog contains four sections: Location, File Options, Range, and Render Options.

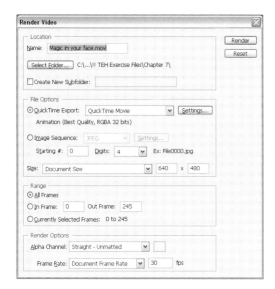

FIGURE 6.24 The Render Video dialog.

Location

The Location area is an easy one. Click the Select Folder button to tell Photoshop where to save your video or image sequence. If you'll be saving an image sequence, Photoshop even allows you to create a new folder in which to save the images, just in case you forgot. To create a new folder, select the Create New Subfolder check box and type in the name of the new folder in the area to the right. Photoshop creates a new subfolder within the folder that you selected after clicking the Select Folder button.

File Options

The File Options area is arguably the most important. This is where you select what type of file you'll export and the quality of that file. You first select whether you want to render to a video file (using QuickTime Export) or to an Image Sequence. For now leave it set to QuickTime Export.

Don't let the QuickTime portion of the name fool you. Photoshop exports to many other file formats besides QuickTime. This is just another reminder of how important it is to have QuickTime on your computer, because Photoshop uses QuickTime components to import and export to many video formats, not just QuickTime.

To see the list of formats that Photoshop can export to, click the drop-down list next to QuickTime Export (**FIGURE 6.25**). Here you see all the standards like MOV, FLV, and AVI. But you also see some impressive extras, such as 3G (used for exporting video to cell phones and other mobile devices), iPod, and Apple TV.

FIGURE 6.25 The long list of video formats that Photoshop can export to.

The bottom of the File Options area allows you to change the document template and the pixel dimensions. This allows for great flexibility, but I don't recommend changing these settings here. Most likely, it will yield results that are stretched and undesirable.

File compression and codecs

Even more important to the quality and size of the final video than the format is the way the video is compressed. From the drop-down list with the various file formats, choose QuickTime movie as the file format. Next, click the Settings button (**FIGURE 6.26**) to look at all the ways to compress this file format. From the Movie Settings dialog that pops up, click Settings again to get to the real compression options (**FIGURE 6.27**). In the Standard Video Compression Options, click the Compression Type drop-down list at the top of the interface (**FIGURE 6.28**). Yikes! And you thought there were a lot of options for file formats!

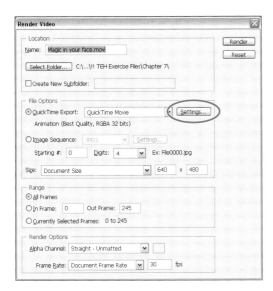

FIGURE 6.26 Click the Settings button to access to the available compression options.

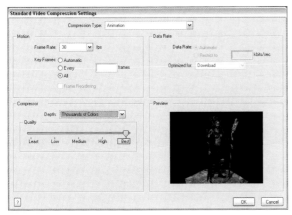

FIGURE 6.27 The Standard Video Compression Options dialog.

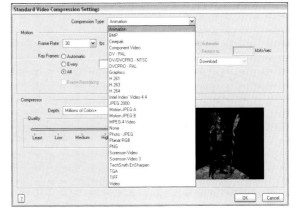

FIGURE 6.28 The long list of compression options available for QuickTime movies.

These compression settings are also called "codecs," short for COmpression/ DECompression. Whatever method you use to compress this file when it is saved must also be used to decompress it when it is viewed. If you use a codec to compress it, but others using your video don't have that particular codec installed on their machines, the video will not play correctly, if at all.

So which codec should you use? Unfortunately, that answer is a little beyond the scope of this book. The huge list of codecs you saw in Figure 6.29 are for

QuickTime movies only. If you were to export to an AVI file, you would have another long list of codecs, completely different than the codecs available for QuickTime. In Chapter 10, "Plug-ins and Resources," I'll share a few resources that you can use to get up to speed with codecs.

TIP   In the Help documentation for Photoshop, there is an entry called Export Video. There you can get more information on many of the video formats that Photoshop can export to, as well as definitions of each format's options.

For now, with QuickTime selected as the format, change the codec to Animation (**FIGURE 6.29**). The Animation codec is a lossless compression algorithm used for high-end video work. With this codec selected, click the Depth drop-down list on the left side of the dialog to see all of the options for color depth (**FIGURE 6.30**). Color depth is basically the number of colors in your video. The more colors your video has, the smoother it looks. Millions of Colors is the most colors you can choose from this list, but there's also an option called Millions of Colors+. What is that about? The "+" sign represents an alpha channel, which is transparency data. I'll talk more about alpha channels in Chapter 8.

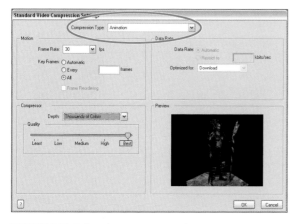

FIGURE 6.29 Select the Animation codec.

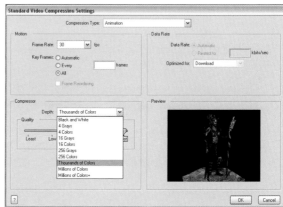

FIGURE 6.30 The Depth drop-down list. From here you can select the number of colors used in your video.

Choosing the Image Sequence option

Now select Image Sequence instead of QuickTime Export. Click the drop-down list to the right to see all the formats that Photoshop can render an image sequence to (**FIGURE 6.31**). You can also click the Settings button to the right of the drop-down list to adjust the compression settings for each format.

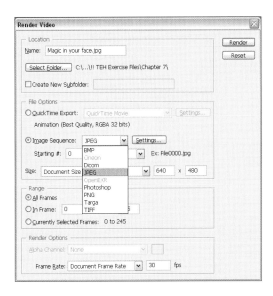

FIGURE 6.31 The various image files you can render to an image sequence.

The Starting # field allows you to select a starting number to use in the names of your image sequence. This number does not have a bearing on which frames of your video get rendered, only the number they start with. This feature can be helpful if you are creating a special effects shot that will then be edited into a larger video project. You can start numbering from the frame number of where the image sequence will be inserted, so you can keep track of where that particular image sequence will be placed.

To the right of the Starting # field is the Digits field. Here you can specify how many digits will be used when numbering the image sequence. If you'll only be rendering 45 frames, it will make for a cleaner Explorer or Finder window to change this value to 2 so only two digits are assigned to each file. For example, if you choose five digits to render a 45 frame project, your file names would be 00001.jpg, 00002.jpg, and so forth. If you select only two digits, you will have much cleaner names: 01.jpg, 02.jpg, and so on.

Range

In the Range area you can choose All Frames, which renders all of the frames in your video. Or you can choose In Frame, which allows you to specify a range of frames to use. The In Frame value is the first frame that will be rendered, and the Out Frame value is the last frame of your video that will be rendered. The Currently Selected Frames option refers to the work area, which is discussed in Chapter 8.

Render Options

The Render Options area at the bottom of the Render Video dialog provides two choices: Alpha Channel and Frame Rate. Choosing Alpha Channel allows you to embed transparency information into your video file in the form of an alpha channel. But this option is only available when you have selected a file format that supports alpha channels, such as a QuickTime movie with the Animation codec, or a TIFF or Targa image sequence. Several options are available to you when creating an alpha channel; we'll look at those in Chapter 8.

Frame Rate is pretty self-explanatory. If you want to enter a new frame rate for your video, you can do so here. The default option is to use your document's frame rate, but you can also click the drop-down list to choose from common frame rates, or manually enter a custom frame rate in the field to the right.

NOTE The rendering process often takes a while; it's not just your computer. Generally, the more you compress video (making a lower-quality file), the faster the rendering process. The higher the quality of the final output file, and the more effects and animation you have applied in your project, the longer the project will take to render, generally.

TIP It's extremely important to create a new folder when rendering to an image sequence. If you're using the standard video frame rate of 30 fps, you would create 600 separate images for only 20 seconds of animation. That's a lot of images, which could mean a lot of computer clutter if you don't plan ahead and organize them well.

Using Audio

Ladies and gentlemen, for this section, I invite you to lean in a little closer as I share with you a great secret about using audio in Photoshop Extended. In the actual Help documentation that ships with Photoshop, you'll read that "although the Audio option is available in the pop-up menu below the File Format menu, Photoshop Extended CS3 does not support audio tracks." Throughout the Help documentation, you'll find several such discouraging statements that all point to the same idea: There is no audio in Photoshop Extended.

Well, thanks to some behind-the-scenes information from one of Photoshop's programmers, Michael Clifton, I've learned that this is not the case. The audio features of Photoshop Extended were added right before it shipped, so there wasn't time to really flesh out the features or even include information about working with audio in the Help documentation.

The good news is that not only can you preview audio in Photoshop, but you can also export video with audio as well. Here's the trick. Open the file ATA podcast.mp4 from the Chapter 6 folder (**FIGURE 6.32**). This video with audio file is an episode of the All Things Adobe podcast that I created. More about this podcast is explained in Chapter 10.

FIGURE 6.32 A frame from the ATA podcast.mp4 file.

NOTE   The podcast episode is about how to get to the 3D models that ship with Photoshop. The entire episode is provided for your benefit.

To play back audio while your video previews, hold the Alt/Opt key while pressing the Play button in the playback area (**FIGURE 6.33**). Although you have no control over volume, panning, or audio characteristics, the ability to play back audio makes the video features of Photoshop Extended a complete feature set. Thank you, Michael Clifton.

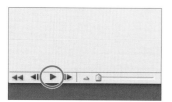

FIGURE 6.33 Hold the Alt/Opt key while pressing this button to play back audio along with video.

To export video with audio is a little more tricky. No matter which file format you output to, the audio options are grayed out. This might lead you to believe that audio is never rendered and included with the video. But this is not true, because Photoshop Extended does in fact have the capability to render audio. But it is a little hit or miss as to when it will do that. When I experimented with FLV and AVI files, audio was never rendered with the video. When I switched the file format to QuickTime, audio was not rendered when I used the H.264 or the MPEG-4 codecs. However, when I used the Animation codec, audio was rendered to the MOV file. So it's inconsistent, but Photoshop does have the ability to render video files that have their audio tracks intact.

Now you know the secrets behind what I call Audiogate. If anyone asks, you didn't hear it from me.

Animating

7

If the video capabilities in Photoshop Extended were limited only to the import and editing of video files, it would still be impressive. But such is not the case. Photoshop also gives you the ability to animate with many tools and features to help you accomplish this task. You can animate six properties: Position, Opacity, Style (i.e., Layer Styles), Layer Mask Position, Layer Mask Enable, and Global Lighting. This chapter discusses each of these properties.

NOTE You cannot animate other standard properties, such as Scale and Rotation.

Before I get into the details of animating, I want to stress that you can animate just about any layer in Photoshop. Let's say you've made a great outer space scene in Photoshop, complete with stars, planets, rockets, and so on. No matter what method you used to create these layers, you can bring them to life with the new features of Photoshop Extended. Whether creating video for the Web, mobile devices, broadcast, DVD, or any other medium, don't underestimate the power that you now have to play Dr. Frankenstein and bring static images to life.

About Animation

To thoroughly understand how animation works in Photoshop, it's a good idea to first take a look at how animation works in general.

In traditional hand-drawn animation, skilled animators (those who were paid the most) would simply draw the most important frames, called the "key" frames. These keyframes were then sent on to junior animators or interns (those who were paid much less) who would then create the frames between the keyframes. Because they created the frames in between the keyframes, this process was called "tweening." So, an expert animator might create keyframes of a bomb and an explosion, and the junior animators would then create the frames of the bomb exploding.

In digital animation, software users are the equivalent of the highly paid animators. You determine the keyframes, and the software programs figure out the rest. In this case, Photoshop is the tweener. In Adobe programs, however, the process of tweening is called interpolation.

With this background, you're ready to learn how to create animation in Photoshop. You'll be amazed at how simple this is.

Animating Properties

The most important part of animating is the Time-Vary Stopwatch icon next to an animatable property in the Animation (Timeline) palette (**FIGURE 7.1**). If you do not see these stopwatches, click the right arrow next to the name of the layer in the Animation palette while in Timeline mode.

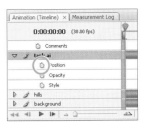

FIGURE 7.1 This stopwatch indicates that this property is animatable and plays a significant role in animation.

You use the stopwatch to tell Photoshop whether or not you want this property to change over time (animate). When the stopwatch is not clicked, the property will not change over the course of the video. Its current value will be constant. Clicking the stopwatch tells Photoshop that this property will change over time. For example, if you have clouds in a background and you want them to move across the screen, you need to click the Time-Vary Stopwatch. If you move the clouds without clicking the stopwatch, you would just change their new, permanent position.

After clicking the stopwatch and then creating an animation, clicking the stopwatch again to deselect it would delete all of your keyframes. So, be careful not to click this icon a second time unless you are sure that you want to delete all of the animation that you've created. Again, a deselected stopwatch tells Photoshop that you don't want that property to animate, so all keyframes applied to that property are deleted.

The process of creating an animation is really just three simple steps:

1. Click the Time-Vary Stopwatch icon next to a property's name in the Animation (Timeline) palette.
2. Move the CTI (Current Time Indicator).
3. Change the value.

And that's all there is to it. Steps 1 and 3 add keyframes. Keyframes are denoted by the diamond shapes in the timeline. These diamonds show up automatically. Repeat steps 2 and 3 to add more keyframes. Let's look at how to animate several different properties. Keep in mind that the methods used to animate them are exactly the same.

TIP If your Animation palette keeps reverting back to the Frame side instead of the Timeline side, remember to click the button in the lower-right corner of the Animation palette to switch between them.

Animating Position

Open the Tank.psd file from the Chapter 7 folder, and open the Animation (Timeline) palette (**FIGURE 7.2**). You'll animate this tank by moving it across the screen from left to right. You first need to put the tank in the right spot, so you need to select the tank layer before you can do that.

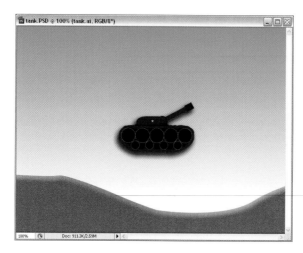

FIGURE 7.2 Open the Tank.psd file and the Timeline side of the Animation palette.

FIGURE 7.3 The highlight indicates that the tank layer is selected in the timeline.

1. Click the tank layer in the Layers palette or select its layer (or "track") in the timeline. When layers are selected, a highlight appears around the layer's name in the timeline (**FIGURE 7.3**).

2. Select the Move tool from the Tools palette and move the tank to the left side of the screen on top of the hill (**FIGURE 7.4**). With the tank in place, you're ready to animate.

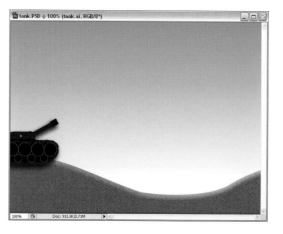

FIGURE 7.4 Move the tank layer into place.

3. Click the arrow next to the word tank in the timeline to expand this layer (**FIGURES 7.5A** and **7.5B**). You should see all of the animatable properties for this layer.

FIGURE 7.5A Click this arrow to reveal the properties you can animate on this layer.

FIGURE 7.5B The animatable properties display after expanding this layer.

4. Click the stopwatch next to Position to tell Photoshop to animate this property. A diamond appears in the actual timeline area (**FIGURE 7.6**). This diamond is a keyframe, and it is Photoshop's way of telling you that it will remember the current value at the current time.

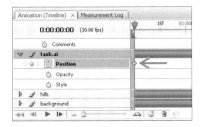

FIGURE 7.6 Create another keyframe by moving out in time and changing the Position value.

5. Move the CTI out to about two seconds in time.

6. Change the value of the property by moving the tank to the edge of the ridge (**FIGURE 7.7** on the next page). Notice that a new keyframe is created for you in the timeline as soon as you change the value because the stopwatch was clicked.

When you move in time and change the value of a property, a new keyframe is generated automatically. Even better is that you've already created animation.

FIGURE 7.7 The animation at the two second mark.

7. Drag the CTI to the beginning of the timeline and press the spacebar to preview your animation thus far. Look at that tank go! Let's keep this party going by finishing this animation.

8. Repeat steps 1 and 2, moving the CTI and changing the value.

9. Drag the CTI to four seconds into the timeline and take the tank to the bottom of the ditch (**FIGURE 7.8**).

10. Take the CTI to the six second mark and take the tank back up to the top of the ledge (**FIGURE 7.9**).

Congratulations. You have just completed your first animation. Feel free to add or adjust keyframes as desired to achieve a smoother and more realistic animation.

Creative possibilities

Animating the position of objects is probably the most common animation task. You might use the Position property to animate vehicles moving on a course, advertising slogans sliding in from offscreen, or all the pieces of a Web site layout gathering together.

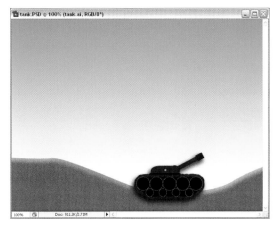

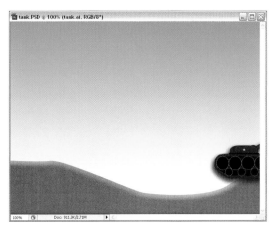

FIGURE 7.8 The animation at the four second mark.

FIGURE 7.9 The animation at the six second mark.

Animating Opacity

Animating the transparency of a layer is just as easy as (if not easier than) animating position.

Open the lightbulb.psd file from the Chapter 7 folder (**FIGURE 7.10**). If you get a pop-up dialog related to pixel aspect ratio, just click OK. You'll be making this lightbulb gradually fade from off to on.

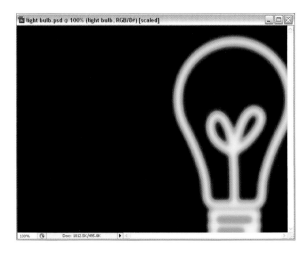

FIGURE 7.10 The lightblub.psd file.

1. Select the lightbulb layer, and using the top of the Layers palette, set the Opacity value to 0% (**FIGURE 7.11**).

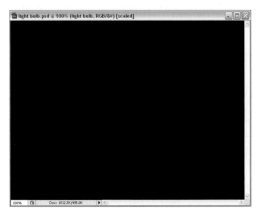

FIGURE 7.11 In the Layers palette, set the Opacity value for the lightbulb to 0%.

2. With the lightbulb layer selected and the CTI at the beginning of the time-line, take the Opacity of the layer to 0%.

3. Click the stopwatch for Opacity in the Animation (Timeline) palette (**FIGURE 7.12**).

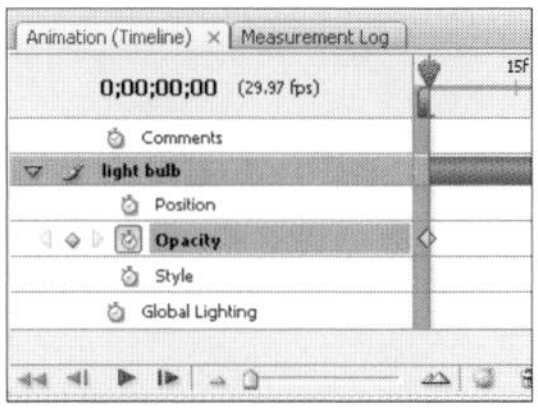

4. Drag the CTI to three seconds in, and then change the Opacity value to 100% (**FIGURE 7.13**). You've just created a lightbulb that fades onscreen.

FIGURE 7.12 Click the stopwatch for the Opacity value at the first frame to create a keyframe.

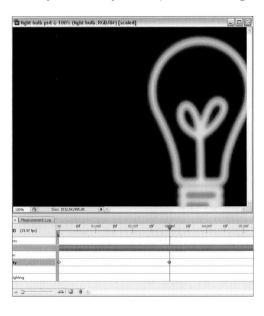

FIGURE 7.13 After creating a keyframe with a value of 100% at approximately the three second mark.

Creative possibilities

Animating opacity is another animation tool that is used frequently. You can use the Opacity property to make logos or titles fade in or out, or you can crossfade two video layers to create a cross dissolve transition between them. Adjustment layers can also be animated. Just for fun you could create a Hue/Saturation adjustment layer on top of a person's face that made his or her skin appear green in color. You could animate the opacity of the adjustment layer to fade in, making it look like the person is getting sick. Not super attractive, but a cool trick nonetheless.

Animating Layer Styles

The ability to animate Layer Styles opens a huge treasure box of fun and creativity. You can animate any type of Layer Style from Outer Glow to Drop Shadow, and so on. There's also a component of Layer Styles called Global Lighting that you can animate separately from other Layer Styles. Global Lighting is discussed in detail a little later in this chapter.

To animate Layer Styles, you simply click the Time-Vary Stopwatch icon, move in time, and then change anything about the Layer Style.

NOTE   Layer Styles were discussed in Chapter 3, "Even Cooler 3D Tricks," in case you need a refresher to follow along with this exercise.

To see this in action, follow these steps.

1. Open the werewolf for glow.psd file from the Chapter 7 folder (**FIGURE 7.14**).

FIGURE 7.14 The werewolf for glow.psd file.

2. Select the werewolf layer and open its animation properties in the Animation (Timeline) palette.

3. With the CTI at the first frame in the video, click the Time-Vary Stopwatch icon for the Style property. This tells Photoshop that you want to animate Layer Styles applied to this layer.

   The only thing is, you haven't even added any Layer Styles yet! No matter. Photoshop will still be able to animate any Layer Styles applied later, which is why I set up this exercise like this. Photoshop is extremely flexible when animating Layer Styles.

4. Move the CTI out to two seconds in the timeline.

5. Double-click the werewolf layer in the Layers palette to the right of the name of the layer. The Layer Style dialog pops up.

6. Turn on Outer Glow, and click the yellow glow swatch to change the glow to a red color. Change the glow Size value to 35 pixels to create a creepier and more pronounced glow. Click OK to accept your new red glow.

   Photoshop recognizes your alteration to the Layer Styles applied to the layer and automatically creates a keyframe to retain that value (**FIGURE 7.15**). Isn't that awesome? But it doesn't end there.

FIGURE 7.15 Because you made a change to the Layer Style with the Time-Vary Stopwatch icon clicked, Photoshop automatically creates a new keyframe for you when you add this red glow.

7. Move your CTI out to four seconds.

8. Double-click the fx icon on the werewolf layer in the Layers palette to reopen the Layer Styles dialog.

9. Make another change. You can make any change you want (even add additional effects), and Photoshop will animate between the red glow you had previously and your current style. Let's just change the Outer Glow color to green.

10. Click OK. Another keyframe is automatically generated. Play back your animation to see Photoshop interpolate between the red glow and the green glow (**FIGURE 7.16**).

FIGURE 7.16 This frame of the animation is between the keyframe with the red glow and the keyframe with the green glow. Notice how Photoshop interpolates between colors.

Creative possibilities

The possibilities for interesting animations with Layer Styles are practically endless. You could animate the Distance value of a Drop Shadow effect to simulate an object moving closer to or farther away from the viewer. You could animate the Depth value to simulate light sweeping across a 3D object. You could add the Texture property to Bevel and Emboss and animate the Scale value to create the effect of a texture moving across an object. Perhaps you could use this technique to simulate reflections moving across an object's surface. Unleash the creative monster inside you and explore the potential of animating Layer Styles.

NOTE   In the preceding exercises, you moved your CTI to whole seconds, like two or four, which was only for ease of following the exercise. There's nothing special about these numbers.

Animating Layer Mask Position

The ability to animate Layer Mask properties is not immediately obvious. You can only animate Layer Mask properties if your layer has a layer mask applied to it. Unfortunately, the Photoshop Help documentation does not explain much on this topic. So, that's why you have this nifty book to fill you in on this stuff.

NOTE   As with Layer Styles, layer masks were introduced and explained in Chapter 3. To keep up with these examples, you may need to quickly jump back to Chapter 3 to get up to speed.

You can animate two properties of layer masks: Position and Enable. In this section, you'll animate the Layer Mask Position. But before you can animate the Layer Mask Position, you have to know what it is.

Open the layer mask position.psd file from the Chapter 7 folder (**FIGURE 7.17**). In this PSD file, a gun turret is about to shoot out some serious fire. For now, it's just a static image, but you'll add some action by animating Layer Mask Position. Notice that the FIRE! layer group already has a layer mask applied for you (**FIGURE 7.18**). This layer group contains the layer of fire, and the layer mask is currently concealing that fire. You'll animate the layer mask so that it reveals the fire in a way that makes it look as if the fire is being shot out of the gun.

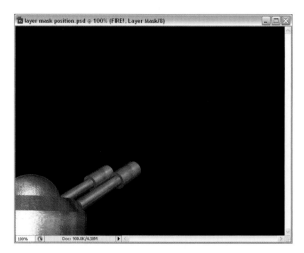

FIGURE 7.17 The layer mask position.psd file.

FIGURE 7.18 The layer group FIRE! already has a layer mask applied for you.

In Chapter 3, I talked briefly about how an object can be unlinked from its mask by clicking the chain icon in between the layer's thumbnail and the layer mask thumbnail (**FIGURE 7.19**). Once the chain is gone, you can move the mask independently from the contents of the layer, and vice versa. The animation property Layer Mask Position allows you to animate the movement of an unlinked layer mask. As you'll see in the following example, this is much different than just being able to animate the position of a layer.

FIGURE 7.19 Click the chain icon to unlink the layer contents from the layer mask applied to the layer. That way you can move the layer mask independently of the layer contents.

Before you animate, you need to see the animatable properties for a layer. However, in this example, the layer mask is not applied to a layer but a layer group. Layer groups are folders that contain other layers. Yes, you can even animate properties of layer groups. In the Animation (Timeline) palette, click the arrow next to the FIRE! layer group to reveal its animation properties (**FIGURE 7.20**). Since you can't move entire layer groups as a whole or apply Layer Styles to them, you can't animate Layer Styles for layer groups. The properties you can animate for layer groups are Opacity, Layer Mask Position, and Layer Mask Enable.

1. With the CTI at the beginning of the timeline, click the Time-Vary Stopwatch icon for the Layer Mask Position property.

2. Move out in time to one and a half seconds.

3. Make sure that the layer group and the layer mask are unlinked. Click on the layer mask for the FIRE! layer group to select it.

4. Select the Move tool in the Tools palette, and then click and drag the layer mask up to the top right of the document window until all of the fire is exposed (**FIGURE 7.21**).

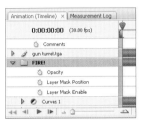

FIGURE 7.20 Click the arrow next to the FIRE! group in the Timeline side of the Animation palette to reveal its animatable properties.

FIGURE 7.21 After animating the position of the FIRE! layer group's layer mask to reveal the angry blast of fiery fury.

5. Click the Selects first frame button in the bottom-left corner of the Timeline side of the Animation palette to jump the CTI back to the beginning of your animation.

6. Press the spacebar to preview your animation.

The turret appears to shoot out the fire. Pretty cool, especially considering that this animation started out as a still image.

Creative possibilities

The ability to animate the position of a layer mask opens many doors. You can animate the Layer Mask Position for a regular layer, for a 3D layer, for a layer group (as you just saw), and also for an adjustment layer. Just animating the Layer Mask Position of an adjustment layer alone can yield amazing results. You could animate a layer mask on a Levels or Curves adjustment layer to make parts of an object lighter or darker. Or you could play on the possibilities that are available because of the shape of a layer mask. You might make a layer mask that made holes in a layer until it looked like fog was on top of it. Then, as you animated the position of the layer mask, it would look like moving fog, but it would still keep the layer's contents in the same spot.

Animating Layer Mask Enable

When using layer masks, you can disable and enable them by holding the Shift key and clicking on the layer mask in the Layers palette. This allows you to quickly see the differences in a layer before and after a mask.

Photoshop CS3 Extended gives you the ability to animate the enabling/disabling of layer masks. At first, this doesn't sound very useful, or at least it didn't to me. But this feature is actually quite helpful because it uses Hold keyframes, which I discuss a little later in this chapter. Basically, Hold keyframes don't interpolate, they just jump to the next value. So if you want to create an object appearing out of nowhere or just flashing onscreen, you could use Hold keyframes.

For this example, open the layer mask enable.psd file from the Chapter 7 folder (**FIGURE 7.22**). When you open this file, you'll see a bullet hole in the document. If you look in the Layers palette, you'll see this layer duplicated many times and repositioned throughout the document (**FIGURE 7.23**). You'll animate the Layer Mask Enable property to simulate an old gangster movie shoot-out in this document. Each bullet hole duplicate layer has a layer mask that hides the bullet hole. As you animate the layer mask by turning it off, it will look as if the document was shot. I know it's sad. But that's what this document gets for squealing.

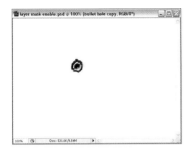

FIGURE 7.22 The layer mask enable.psd file.

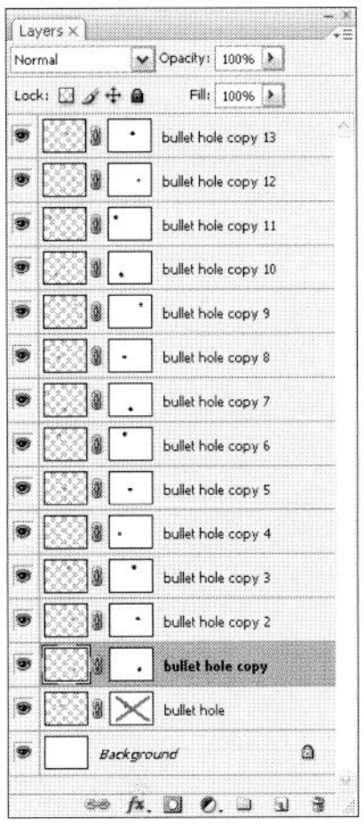

FIGURE 7.23 The Layers palette with the layer mask enable.psd file open. Notice all the duplicates of this bullet hole.

TIP You can disable/enable layer masks by right-clicking on them in the Layers palette.

In previous examples in this chapter, you set up keyframes at the first frame, but there are so many layers here that I've gone ahead and done that for you. All you have to do to is drag out to a different time in the timeline, select a bullet layer (either in the Animation palette or in the Layers palette), and Shift-click its layer mask to disable it. To get the real shoot-out effect, stagger the frames that reveal bullet holes. So, you might uncover the first bullet hole at five frames in, the next hole at 13 frames in, and so forth. **FIGURE 7.24** shows an example of the project a little later in time after animating some bullet holes. Notice how the keyframes are staggered in time.

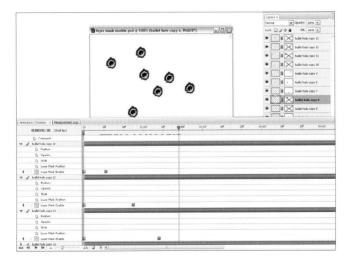

FIGURE 7.24 Note how the keyframes are not lined up so that they appear at different times to add to the shoot'em up factor.

NOTE The keyframes are square because they are a different type of keyframe. These are Hold keyframes, which are discussed later in this chapter.

Creative possibilities

You can use Layer Mask Enable to animate objects appearing or disappearing instantly, as you did in the bullet hole example. But you can also use this feature to animate pieces of an object appearing or disappearing, like a character's head or fingers. For a nonhuman character, this feature could be used to extend or retract spikes. Try animating Layer Mask Enable to create a typewriter effect using type characters. You can also use it to animate invisible object footprints (or paw prints) walking across the screen.

Vector Mask Animations

Photoshop is an equal-opportunity animator. You can animate Vector Mask Position and Vector Mask Enable for vector-based masks just like you can with raster layer masks. Vector masks can be created by using the vector drawing tools and can be seen in shape layer and regular vector masks.

Global Lighting

Global Lighting, a more obscure property, is technically part of Layer Styles, but it can span multiple layers. So Photoshop generously offers it as its own separate animatable property that is not tied to a layer. Instead, you animate Global Lighting for an entire document. But even if you never animate Global Lighting, it's helpful to know about it.

What Is Global Lighting?

In certain Layer Style effects, the angle of the lighting is important. Let's take Drop Shadow as an example. The drop shadow Angle value indicates where the light source is coming from. **FIGURE 7.25** shows a Drop Shadow effect applied to some text. The fact that the drop shadow appears at the bottom right of the text suggests that the light source is shining down onto the text from the upper left. If the drop shadow was on the upper-right side of the text, you would assume that the light source was coming from the lower-left area and pointing up toward the text (**FIGURE 7.26**).

FIGURE 7.25 Text with the Drop Shadow effect applied. Notice how the angle of the drop shadow suggests the direction that the lighting is coming from.

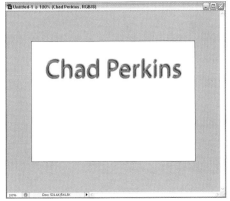

FIGURE 7.26 This shadow indicates that the light source is on the bottom-left area of the text and is shining up.

If you added a Bevel and Emboss effect, which also uses a lighting system, you'd see that Bevel and Emboss has its own Angle value (**FIGURE 7.27**). Bevel and Emboss uses the Angle value to determine where it should place the highlights and shadows that it creates to simulate a 3D bevel effect. If you applied a Bevel and Emboss effect and a Drop Shadow effect on the text at the same time, you'd want ensure that they were using the same lighting angle. It would be unprofessional to have Bevel and Emboss telling the eye that the light is coming from one direction while the Drop Shadow is indicating that the lighting is coming from a different source, as is the case in **FIGURE 7.28**.

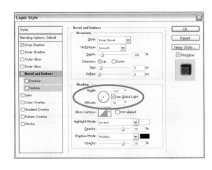

FIGURE 7.27 The Bevel and Emboss options in the Layer Style dialog. In the Shading area, you'll find an Angle value similar in purpose to the Angle value for the Drop Shadow effect.

FIGURE 7.28 In this image, the Bevel and Emboss effect is created from light coming from the upper-right area of the image, but the Drop Shadow effect indicates that the light is actually coming from the upper-left area. Notice the shadow on the left edges of the text. This image looks terrible.

Global Lighting makes all Layer Styles use the same lighting direction, so you don't even have to think about it. And not only does Global Lighting unify the lighting source across effects, but it also uses the same angle for every effect on every layer!

Let's say you're trying to composite several elements into a scene. You want all of them to have a consistent light source. So, in any effect that uses a light source, make sure that Use Global Light is selected while you're adjusting the Angle value (**FIGURE 7.29**). Then all effects throughout your document that use Global Lighting will automatically use that same value.

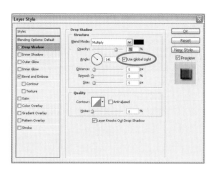

FIGURE 7.29 Select the Use Global Light check box to activate Global Lighting for a particular effect.

To change the Global Lighting value, simply change the Angle value with the Use Global Light check box selected, and it will update all effects in your document that use Global Lighting. If you want an effect to have its own independent lighting angle, simply deselect the Use Global Light check box for that particular value.

Because Global Lighting affects an entire document, you only have to animate it once to affect all effects on all layers that use it.

Faking Time Lapse by Animating Global Lighting

In the following example, you'll simulate a time lapse effect by animating Global Lighting.

Open the time lapse.psd file from the Chapter 7 folder (**FIGURE 7.30**). There's a lot going on in this file, and some of what you see is animated already. The clock hands go around in a circle, the simulated "sun" in the upper-left corner goes from left to right, the color changes according to the time of day, and so forth. The problem is that the Layer Styles in this entire document correspond to the position of the sun at the first frame but stay the same throughout the animation. To make all of the Layer Styles sync up to the sun, you only have to animate one property: Global Lighting.

FIGURE 7.30 The time lapse.psd file.

1. Click the Time-Vary Stopwatch icon next to Global Lighting in the Animation (Timeline) palette (FIGURE 7.31).

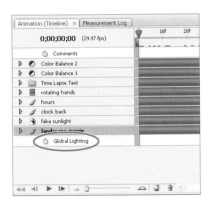

FIGURE 7.31 Click the stopwatch next to Global Lighting to animate Global Lighting for the entire document.

2. Drag the CTI to the very end of the timeline.

From this point, all you need to do is change the angle of any effect on any layer that uses Global Lighting.

3. Double-click the fx icon for the hours layer in the Layers palette (FIGURE 7.32). The Layer Style dialog opens.

4. Click Drop Shadow on the left side of this dialog, so that you can see the various parameters of the Drop Shadow effect.

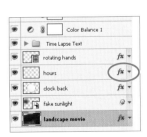

FIGURE 7.32 Double-click the fx icon on the hours layer in the Layers palette to open the Layer Style dialog so you can adjust the Global Lighting value.

5. Make sure that Global Lighting (next to the Angle value) is selected. Currently, the Angle value is at 127 degrees. Change this value to 40 degrees (**FIGURE 7.33**) to make the light source appear to come from the upper-right area of the image and match the lighting that is already in the scene.

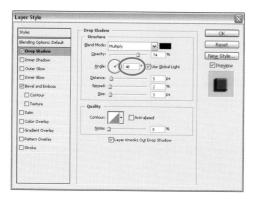

FIGURE 7.33 Change the Angle value of the Drop Shadow effect to 40 degrees to create a new Global Lighting keyframe.

6. Click OK to close the dialog.

   A new keyframe is added for you to the Global Lighting property, and your animation is complete.

7. Take the CTI to the first frame of the timeline, and press the spacebar to preview your animation.

Notice how all Layer Style effects—Bevel and Emboss on the clock, Drop Shadow on the text, Drop Shadow on the hands of the clock, and so forth—move together as Global Lighting changes (**FIGURE 7.34**).

FIGURE 7.34 After only changing the Global Lighting value of one effect on one layer, all Layer Styles that use Global Lighting are now changed as well.

Adjusting Keyframes

After all the practice you've had using keyframes in the previous examples, you're now ready to learn some intermediate tricks for working with and adjusting keyframes.

Moving Keyframes

Many times you'll want to move a keyframe. You can move keyframes closer to each other to create faster animation (see the sidebar "Changing the Speed of Your Animation"). Or you might want to simply change the timing of an animation, perhaps to match an audio event.

To move a keyframe, just click on it and drag it left or right in the timeline. Remember that keyframes retain their values. So if you move a keyframe to the left, Photoshop will have to reach that value earlier in time. Moving it to the right gives Photoshop more time to interpolate to that value.

NOTE When keyframes are selected, they will be gold in color instead of gray.

You can also Shift-click multiple keyframes to select more than one keyframe at a time. You can then move all selected keyframes in time, keeping their respective relationships to each other.

Changing the Speed of Your Animation

If you find that your animation is moving too quickly or too slowly, you can fix this by changing the distance between keyframes. Keyframes represent the values of a property at a particular time. Click and drag keyframes closer together to speed up animation, or drag them farther apart to slow it down.

This may seem awkward and difficult to remember, but try to think of this in real-world terms. Assume that you need to drive ten miles from your house to get to work. If you had eight hours to get there (assuming you weren't in Southern California), you could take your sweet time—maybe even go out to eat or go for a walk first. But if your boss called and said that he needed you there immediately, you would have to go much faster to cover the same ten miles in ten minutes.

The point is that if you want to go the same distance in a shorter period of time, you need to increase your speed. As you begin your study of animation, remember that there is an important relationship between time, distance, and speed.

Adjusting Existing Keyframe Values

You can adjust the value of a keyframe that already exists by going to the frame that has the keyframe and changing the value. Photoshop automatically recalculates the interpolation for you.

It's very important that you have your CTI on the exact frame that has the existing keyframe. If you are even one frame off, Photoshop will create a new keyframe instead of adjusting the old one. This will create undesirable "jumps" in your animation.

Next, I'll talk about the Keyframe Navigator, which helps you know for certain whether or not you are on a frame with a keyframe.

Using the Keyframe Navigator

The keyframe navigator is a little helper in the timeline that serves several purposes.

FIGURE 7.35 The music notes.psd file.

Its official purpose (as the name implies) is to help you navigate keyframes. To help you grasp this tool's purpose, open the music notes.psd file from the Chapter 7 folder (**FIGURE 7.35**). In the Animation (Timeline) palette, open the green notes layer (the top layer) to see the keyframes of the Vector Mask Position on this layer (**FIGURE 7.36**). To the left of the words Vector Mask Position is the keyframe navigator (**FIGURE 7.37**).

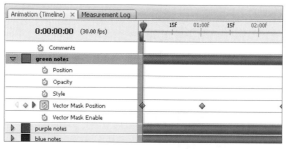

FIGURE 7.37 The keyframe navigator.

FIGURE 7.36 The Vector Mask Position keyframes of the green notes layer.

If you click on the right arrow of the keyframe navigator, you'll jump to the next keyframe of this property. If you click on the left arrow, your CTI jumps to the frame where the previous keyframe is. This truly is a great way to navigate keyframes.

Another purpose of the keyframe navigator is to let you know when you're actually on a frame that has a keyframe applied. When your CTI is currently on a frame with a keyframe for a particular property, the center of the keyframe navigator displays an embossed gold diamond (**FIGURE 7.38**). When this area is hollow, you will create a new keyframe by adjusting this value.

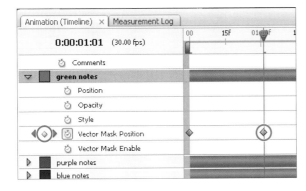

FIGURE 7.38 When the center diamond is illuminated, you know that your CTI is currently on a frame that this property has a keyframe on.

The keyframe navigator has one other great purpose: to create keyframes without having to change values. To demonstrate this, close the music notes.psd file and open the opacity pump.psd file from the Chapter 7 folder (**FIGURE 7.39**). This file contains a pump movie and a static balloon image layer. Since you can't animate the scale of the balloon, you'll animate the pump pumping opacity into the balloon.

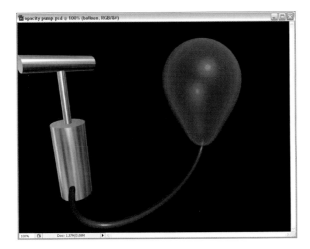

FIGURE 7.39 The opacity pump.psd file.

I've already set up a few keyframes for you on the balloon layer. Open the balloon layer in the Animation (Timeline) palette to see them (**FIGURE 7.40**).

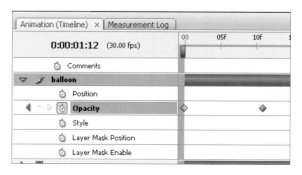

FIGURE 7.40 The keyframes already applied to the Opacity property of the balloon layer.

The problem is that the pump does its pumping thing and then holds a moment before pumping again. If you were to move in time to the end of the next pumping motion (at 0:00:01:21) and set a keyframe for a higher opacity value, Photoshop would start to animate from your last keyframe. That's way too early. You don't want Photoshop to start increasing the opacity until the pump starts pumping again (at 0:00:01:12).

You can use the keyframe navigator to help you fix this dilemma. Go to frame 0:00:01:12 where the pump starts pumping again. Go to the keyframe navigator and click the hollow diamond in between the two arrows to create a new keyframe at the current value. With that keyframe in place, you can go out to the 0:00:01:21 mark and change the opacity value to 75% (**FIGURE 7.41**). Now the balloon won't start animating until the pump starts pumping again. (There is one more round of the pumping action if you'd like to practice and get that balloon up to 100% on your own.)

FIGURE 7.41 A look at the timeline after the project is done.

You can select multiple keyframes in several ways:

- You can click and drag to marquee select several keyframes. This works well when you want to select a range of adjacent keyframes.

- You can hold the Shift key while clicking multiple keyframes. This is good for those times when you want to select noncontiguous keyframes.

- You can use one of my favorite methods to select all the keyframes of a given property by clicking the name of that property in the timeline. For instance, if you had many Position keyframes on a layer, you could select them all by going to the Animation (Timeline) palette and clicking on the word Position on the left side of the palette.

Copying, Pasting, and Deleting Keyframes

You can copy and paste keyframes between layers to make tedious tasks, like animating snowflakes falling, a little easier. You may not choose to use the exact same animation, but sometimes tweaking an existing animation is easier than creating keyframes from scratch, especially since Photoshop has made this process so easy.

1. Reopen the music notes.psd file from the Chapter 7 folder.

2. Open the green notes layer in the timeline. This layer has some sweet animation data that needs to be shared with its little purple sister to the right.

3. Click on the words Vector Mask Position on the green notes layer to select all of its keyframes. You should see a row of golden keyframes, indicating they are all selected (**FIGURE 7.42**).

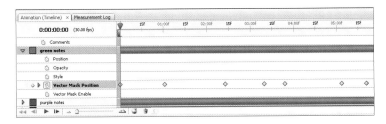

FIGURE 7.42 After selecting all of the keyframes for the Vector Mask Position property on the green notes layer.

4. Right-click on one of the selected keyframes and select Copy Keyframes.

5. Open the properties for the purple notes layer. Click the stopwatch next to the purple notes layer's Vector Mask Position property.

6. On the newly created keyframe, right-click and select Paste Keyframes. All the copied keyframes from the green notes layer are pasted here (**FIGURE 7.43**).

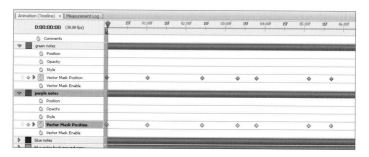

FIGURE 7.43 After pasting the keyframes from the green notes layer.

7. To create greater randomization, select all of the keyframes for the purple notes layer's Vector Mask Position property and scoot them on down the timeline a little bit (**FIGURE 7.44**). You can also move the layer with the Move tool.

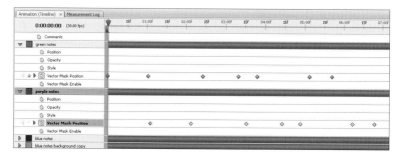

FIGURE 7.44 You can move the pasted keyframes down the timeline to create more randomization in the animation.

If you want to delete keyframes, simply right-click on them, and select Delete Keyframes. Note that pressing the Backspace/Delete key on your keyboard (which usually does a good job of deleting stuff in Adobe programs) will not work for this purpose.

Keyframe Interpolation

As mentioned earlier, interpolation is nothing more than a nerdy term meaning how something gets from point A to point B. In Adobe programs (except Adobe Flash), interpolation replaces the traditional animation term of tweening.

Different Types of Interpolation

Photoshop provides two types of keyframe interpolation: Linear and Hold. So far, you've primarily dealt with Linear keyframes, which are denoted by their diamond shape. Linear keyframes go from one keyframe to another at a constant velocity.

But for those times when you don't want keyframes to interpolate, you also have the option of using Hold keyframes. Hold keyframes don't interpolate at all, and they look like squares instead of diamonds. The Layer Mask Enable keyframes you saw earlier were Hold keyframes. You can manually change keyframe interpolation from Linear to Hold.

1. With the music notes.psd file still open, open the animation properties for the blue notes layer in the Animation (Timeline) palette.

2. Click on the Vector Mask Position property to select all of its keyframes.

3. Right-click on a keyframe and change the interpolation from Linear to Hold (**FIGURE 7.45**). This changes all the diamonds (Linear keyframes) to squares (Hold keyframes) (**FIGURE 7.46**).

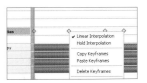

FIGURE 7.45 Select Hold Interpolation from this menu to change the selected keyframes from their default Linear Interpolation.

FIGURE 7.46 When you've changed the interpolation from Linear to Hold, the diamonds turn into squares.

Now when this animation plays back, the blue notes will jump from position to position instead of smoothly animating.

Creative possibilities

Obviously, you will probably use Linear interpolation most of the time. But Hold interpolation definitely has its place. For example, you could have used

Hold interpolation instead of the keyframe navigator to fix the problems with the opacity pump animation earlier. You can also use Hold interpolation to create edgy graphics that jump across the screen. Or try using Hold keyframes to create flashing lights. You might not use Hold keyframes in every project, but it's great to know that they're there waiting for you when you need them.

"Roving" Keyframes

Adobe After Effects has a great animation feature called Roving Keyframes that allow you to scale an animation. Well, there is a similar feature in Photoshop, but it's kind of hidden, so it doesn't have its own name.

Open a fresh copy of music notes.psd from the Chapter 7 folder. If you've already been working on this file, just select File > Revert to return to the last saved version. The animation of the green notes is a little too short; it ends at about four seconds. You could click and drag the last keyframe to the end of the timeline, but that would just make the last movement really long. You can scale an entire animation while keeping all keyframes in their relative positions and times. To do this, select all of the keyframes for the Vector Mask Position property on the green notes layer. Then click and drag on the last keyframe while holding the Alt/Opt key. You can also drag the last keyframe to the end and all the keyframes will likewise scale, keeping their relative relationships.

Creative possibilities

"Roving keyframes" is a great feature to use anytime you've spent lots of time creating many keyframes and realize that you want to shorten or lengthen the entire animation. Let's say you've spent hours upon hours creating many different random Opacity keyframes to create a jittery, scary animation. But after previewing the entire animation you realize that you've spaced the keyframes too far apart, and the animation looks more suited for a lullaby than a scare. Scale all animations in one fell swoop to speed up the entire animation.

NOTE One of the reasons I'm such a fan of Adobe products is that the integration between programs is unparalleled. If you are familiar with After Effects or Premiere, most of this chapter has probably been review. Also, in the case of Roving Keyframes, you use the same Alt/Opt keyboard shortcut to perform the same action in After Effects.

8

Editing Video

When using raw video, often there are pieces of that video that you don't want. Sometimes they are at the beginning of the video and sometimes at the end. Most of the time, those unwanted bits of video are scattered throughout the piece. In this chapter, you'll learn about all the various options that Photoshop offers to get rid of the undesirables in your video. I'll also discuss how to tailor your timelines to better suit your needs and explain a few ways to work more efficiently with video in Photoshop CS3 Extended.

Cutting Video

The concept of cutting video is almost as old as video itself. When footage is shot, it is hardly ever perfect and ready to distribute as is. Editing is the process of telling a story with your video. Let's look at two basic video edits in Photoshop: trim edits and splitting layers. Later in this chapter you'll learn a few more advanced techniques for editing video.

How to Cut (Trim) Video

The most basic edit, and perhaps the most common edit, is the trim edit. This is where you cut off a little from the beginning or a little from the end of a video clip. Think of this edit like a banana. A banana is great for making smoothies, it's high in potassium, yada yada. But whenever you peel a banana, there's always that weird black plug thing at the end that you don't want to eat; so, you slice it off. Also, sometimes the top tip gets a little squished during the all the trauma of opening it, so you might chop that off as well.

My point is that trimming a banana is a lot like trimming video. You crop the edges to get rid of the parts you don't want. In video, you might have a director yelling out the take number at the beginning. Like the nasty banana plug, you lop off that chunk to make a better video.

In Photoshop, select File > Open to open the army of zombies.mov file from the Chapter 8 folder (**FIGURE 8.1**). This movie clip is from George Romero's classic

FIGURE 8.1 The army of zombies.mov clip imported into Photoshop.

zombie film, *Night of the Living Dead*, which is now in the public domain. When I extracted this clip from the original movie, I cut it a little weird. It starts out with the zombies from the Figure 8.1, but they are only onscreen for five frames. That's not long enough for viewers to acclimate to this scene, so let's cut out this section. To trim video, all you need to do is to put your mouse over the beginning or the end of a video layer in the Animation (Timeline) palette. When you do, a double-headed arrow icon appears (**FIGURE 8.2**). While this icon is visible, if you click and drag to the right, you will trim (or in other words, hide) the frames that you drag past. Don't worry: This is all nondestructive. At any time, you can just drag the edge of the video back to where it was to restore the trimmed frames.

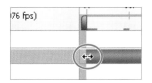

FIGURE 8.2 When you place your cursor over the beginning or the end of a video layer in the timeline, this icon indicates that you are ready to trim!

TIP   To move a clip in time, simply click on the inside of a video layer in the timeline (not on the edges) and drag to the desired location. You could use this technique with the zombie video to drag the new In point of the layer to the beginning of the timeline, so that it starts playing at the beginning of the video.

NOTE   When video is cut, the area that is cut appears faded. That faded color lets you know that there is still video information available that you can get back at any time, but it is currently hidden. This is like a mask, but for time.

Trimming tricks

I've explained how to trim, but there are a few tricks that might help you edit better. You might try clicking the Zoom In button at the bottom of the Animation (Timeline) palette to zoom in to the timeline. This allows you to cut with more precision. Sometimes when you edit, if you're zoomed out too far, it's as if you are a surgeon performing surgery from across the room. As with surgery, getting a little closer can help you make more exact cuts.

Another trick is to move the CTI exactly to where you want to make the cut. Then trim the edge to the CTI. It's like when a barber uses a comb as a guide when cutting hair. Think of the CTI as a comb for cutting footage. In this instance, you could move the CTI to 0:00:00:05 because this is where the next batch of zombies appears, and you want this to be your new In point for this video layer. Then drag the In point of the layer to the CTI to make a more precise cut (**FIGURE 8.3**).

FIGURE 8.3 After trimming the first five awkward frames using the CTI as a guide.

NOTE The left edge of a video layer is referred to as the In point because it is the place where the video begins to play. The right edge is called the Out point.

NOTE Video editing in Photoshop CS3 Extended is totally nondestructive. As with imported 3D files, your original video remains unchanged by Photoshop. Photoshop only stores your edits to the video.

Splitting Layers

So now you know how to cut the ends of a piece of video, but what happens when you have a rotten spot in the center of your banana (so to speak)? If there is a bad section inside your video clip, you can split the layer to remove the unwanted portion.

Open the barring the door.mov file from the Chapter 8 folder (**FIGURE 8.4**). This clip is also from *Night of the Living Dead*. It shows the main character barring the door to prevent zombie intrusion. In this small fragment of video is a quick cut to a woman's face. In the context of the entire scene, the cut to her face works fine. But in this small piece, it seems out of place. So, let's get rid of it.

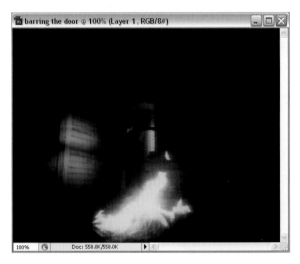

FIGURE 8.4 The barring the door.mov file.

The video cuts (or changes) to her face are at 0:00:02:22—two seconds and 22 frames in, so put the CTI at that point (**FIGURE 8.5**). Now click the all-important

Animation (Timeline) palette menu (**FIGURE 8.6**), and choose Split Layer (**FIG-URE 8.7**). Photoshop splits that one layer into two layers at the current CTI point.

FIGURE 8.5 Put the CTI at two seconds and 22 frames (0:00:02:22).

FIGURE 8.6 The Animation (Timeline) palette menu button. Click to get a wealth of video options.

FIGURE 8.7 Choose Split Layer from the Animation (Timeline) palette menu.

Let's finish the job by selecting the top layer and moving out to five seconds and four frames (0:00:05:04). This is the frame after the last frame of the clip with the woman. Make sure the top layer (and only the top layer) is selected, click the

Animation (Timeline) palette menu and select Split Layer. Now the entire shot of the woman is a separate, distinct clip in the timeline (**FIGURE 8.8**). Select the middle layer in your Photoshop document (which is the clip with the woman) and drag this layer to the trash can in the Layers palette, as you would a standard Photoshop layer.

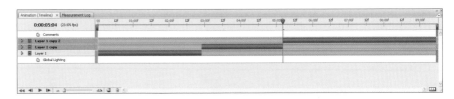

FIGURE 8.8 After splitting the video on either side of the cut with the woman's face. This clip is now a separate layer that you can delete independently from the other parts of the video.

Filling Gaps in Video

You deleted the scene with the woman's face, but now you have a huge gap in the video project (**FIGURE 8.9**). To fill the gap, just click and drag the top clip to the left until its In point comes immediately after the Out point of the bottom layer (**FIGURE 8.10**).

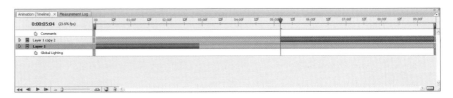

FIGURE 8.9 After deleting the scene with the woman, you're left with a gap between clips.

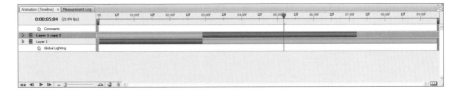

FIGURE 8.10 After moving the top clip to fill the gap between the two clips.

In this case, these two clips back to back create what is called a "jump cut," because there is a sudden awkward jump that doesn't look right. From this stage you could continue cutting both clips to find a better cut point between them that would make the video flow more smoothly.

NOTE You might have noticed that the layers in the timeline correspond to the layers in the Layers palette. Changes such as moving, renaming, or deleting will appear in both palettes. To accomplish such tasks, you can use whichever palette you feel most comfortable with.

NOTE The Animation (Timeline) palette menu holds the bulk of options and features for working with video in Photoshop Extended. You'll be spending the majority of time in the rest of this book learning about and using the options in this menu.

Working More Efficiently

Videos can be hours long. Many videos can be hours and hours long. Sifting through numerous clips and editing them can consume your entire life. Here are some tricks and features to help you become more efficient when working with video.

Keyboard Shortcuts for Video

When working in a full-fledged video program, keyboard shortcuts are probably the most important tool in speeding up your production. However, you might be frustrated to learn that the standard keyboard shortcuts in video editing programs don't work in Photoshop. Typically, the Home key jumps you to the first frame, and the End key jumps you to the end of your timeline. In After Effects and Premiere, the Page Up and Page Down keys also help to speed things up.

By selecting Edit > Keyboard Shortcuts you can add your own custom keyboard shortcuts. The downside is that the Home, End, Page Up, Page Down, and arrow keys can't be used to create shortcuts. The upside is that you can set keyboard shortcuts for any command in a palette menu. To do this, in the Keyboard Shortcuts and Menus dialog (which appears when you select Edit > Keyboard Shortcuts), change the Shortcuts For drop-down list from the default Application Menus to Palette Menus.

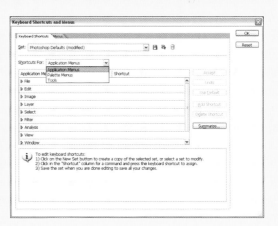

(continued on next page)

Click on Animation (Timeline) to create keyboard shortcuts for all of the options in the Animation (Timeline) palette menu.

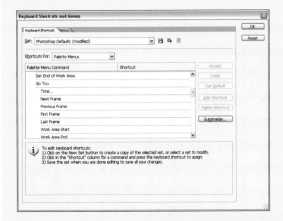

By default, not one option in the entire Animation (Timeline) palette menu has a shortcut.

Notice that two of the commands are Go To > Previous Frame and Go To > Next Frame. I highly recommend creating custom keyboard shortcuts for these options if you will frequently be working with video in Photoshop. They will speed up your navigation in the timeline, and therefore your entire production, in a big way.

To change the keyboard shortcut for a command, click in the blank space to the right of a command and press the keyboard shortcut on your keyboard. If you choose a keyboard shortcut that is already in use, a warning appears. You can accept the changes by clicking the Accept button, which changes the keyboard shortcut to your new command but leaves the old command without a shortcut. Click Undo to cancel the changes that you made to the shortcuts. Click Accept and Go To Conflict to change the keyboard shortcut, and give the old command a new keyboard shortcut.

Allowing Frame Skipping

When previewing video, you might have noticed that the preview plays quite slowly at first. And even then, it might not play back your entire video. Photoshop uses RAM to preview video, and it caches frames into RAM for smoother and faster playback. If Photoshop fills up your available RAM, it will stop caching frames. But what if you have a 20-minute video clip? Chances are you wouldn't be able to load that entire beast into RAM if you wanted to, and you might not want to wait that long to get a general idea of your entire video.

To speed up playback by allowing the playback of uncached frames, you can turn on Frame Skipping. From the Animation (Timeline) palette menu select Allow Frame Skipping. This command allows frames of your video to be skipped over during playback. The result will not be an accurate preview, but it will play all of your timeline whether it is cached or not.

Using Work Areas

Work areas are another great asset when working with video. Let's say you have an excessively long video that you're working on. Most likely you'll only want to work on short pieces at a time. You can designate a piece of video to work on with a work area.

Open the what time of year.mov clip from the Chapter 8 folder (**FIGURE 8.11**). This clip is from another classic movie, *Santa Claus Conquers the Martians*. The old, wise sage expounds great knowledge, but he takes a while to spit it out. So, you can create a work area to focus on just a portion of what he's saying. That way, by the time you're done listening to him, you're not as old as he is.

FIGURE 8.11 The what time of year.mov clip.

You set the work area by using the work area bar, which is camouflaged in the interface. The work area bar is the gray bar with blue ends that is immediately below the red and black numbers in the timeline (**FIGURE 8.12**). Similar to the way you trim video, click on the blue notch at the beginning of the work area

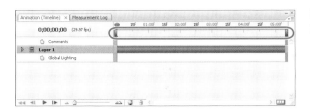

FIGURE 8.12 The work area bar is hard to see.

bar to set the start of the work area, and click on the blue notch at the end of the work area bar to set the end of the work area. Now when you click the Play button or press the spacebar, only that area is previewed and only those frames are loaded into RAM. This saves on RAM *and* on preview time.

> **TIP** To more precisely place the beginning and end of the work area, place your CTI in the desired location, and from the Animation (Timeline) palette menu select either Set Start of Work Area or Set End of Work Area.

> **TIP** You can use the work area to determine the duration of your entire document. From the Animation (Timeline) palette menu select Trim Document Duration to Work Area.

> **NOTE** Work areas are even more useful than they seem at first glance. You can use work areas to do more advanced video editing, as you'll see later in the section "Other Types of Video Edits." Also, when exporting video using the Render Video dialog, the Range area offers an option to export Currently Selected Frames. Frames in the work area are the currently selected frames being referred to, so you can use the work area to specify a section of your video to render.

Adding Timeline Comments

Photoshop allows you to make comments in your timeline, which is helpful when sharing video projects with other users. For example, you might be editing the video, but another person will be adding animations. You can add timeline comments to let others know where key points or problem areas are in the timeline. And even if you are the only user working with the document, it can be a great help to make notes to yourself in the timeline. You can create a comment where a character starts talking, or when a clip should end, or for anything you'd like.

Open the what time of year.mov clip from the Chapter 8 folder now (if you don't already have it open). In the Animation (Timeline) palette, notice that Comments is an animatable property at the top of the palette (**FIGURE 8.13**). Move your CTI to a frame where you want to add a comment, and click the

Time-Vary Stopwatch icon. A dialog pops up for you to type in your comment (**FIGURE 8.14**). This behavior only occurs for the first comment. To make additional comments, move the CTI to a new frame you'd like to add a comment to. Then go to the palette menu and select Edit Timeline Comment (**FIGURE 8.15**).

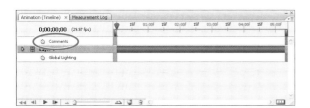

FIGURE 8.13 The Comments property in the Animation (Timeline) palette.

FIGURE 8.14 The Comment dialog. Enter a comment here.

When you create a comment, a Hold keyframe is generated to store your comment. To view a comment for any keyframe, just double-click the square Hold keyframe icon for that frame.

FIGURE 8.15 To add additional comments, select Edit Timeline Comment from the palette menu.

Adjusting Video Projects

In this section, I'll get more specific about setting up video projects and importing footage to get better results.

Adjusting Timeline Duration and Frames Per Second

When you first create a PSD file, Photoshop has no clue how long you want your animation to be. If you import a video clip, Photoshop creates a new document that is as long as your footage. But what if you trim down the video?

You can use the Document Settings to adjust the duration of your entire Photoshop document. To access the Document Settings, select Document Settings (**FIGURE 8.16**) from the palette menu. From here you can manually change the

FIGURE 8.16 Access the Document Settings via the Animation (Timeline) palette

duration of your document (**FIGURE 8.17**). Be careful. It's possible to create a document that is shorter than your footage. If this happens, the footage that extends beyond the duration of the document will not play back or render.

FIGURE 8.17 The Document Timeline Settings dialog.

From the same Document Timeline Settings dialog, you can also adjust the frame rate for the entire project. I'll talk momentarily about adjusting the frame rate for individual clips. But the frame rate in the Document Timeline Settings dialog adjusts the master frame rate for the entire document.

Interpreting Footage

Photoshop allows you to control how imported footage is interpreted. This gives you control over the frame rates of individual clips, as well as how the alpha channel is interpreted, de-interlacing options, and color management. Remember that the Document Timeline Settings you just looked at are for the entire document, whereas Interpret Footage settings are for each clip.

To access the Interpret Footage settings, select a layer and then choose Layer > Video Layers > Interpret Footage (**FIGURE 8.18**). The top of the Interpret Footage dialog contains settings for alpha channel interpretation. For more information, see the sidebar "About Alpha Channels."

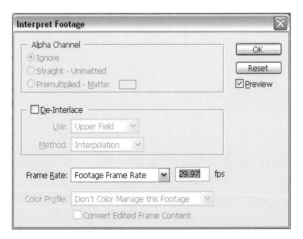

FIGURE 8.18 The Interpret Footage dialog.

About Alpha Channels

An alpha channel is additional data stored in a video or image file that defines the transparency in that file. Let's say you have video of a model dancing in front of a green screen, and you want to put the dancer on top of a background full of colorful graphics to create an iPod-type look. You could remove the green screen so that the dancer is dancing with a transparent background. When you export that video, you would export the video with an alpha channel, which defines the transparent areas in the video. When that video is imported into another video program, the imported video will show just the dancer, not the green screen background. If there is no alpha channel in the video file you create, the video will still contain the dancer with the green screen background.

You can create alpha channels in Photoshop by saving a selection area. To do this, choose Save Selection from the Select menu while you have a selection active.

In the Interpret Footage dialog, you have three options for interpreting alpha channels of imported footage:

- You can ignore the alpha channel. In the preceding example, the green screen background would appear even though an alpha channel was present.

- You can select to interpret the alpha channel as a straight alpha channel. A straight alpha channel has all of the transparency information in the alpha channel. Think of straight as being short for "straightforward."

- The third option is the most complex. That is, you can interpret the alpha channel as a pre-multiplied alpha channel. A pre-multiplied alpha has an edge that is pre-blended with a particular background color. The transparent edge is slightly blurred for a more natural-looking composite. It sounds great, but it sometimes introduces problems. Let's say you are rendering a tree from a 3D program, and you assume the tree will be on a hill, so you pre-multiply it with a blue background. The slightly softer edges feathered with blue will make the tree look more believable on the hill. But what if your clients change their minds and you have to put the tree render in a dark forest? That blue edge will make your composite look fake and the tree will not blend in well. So, you would need to change the Matte color in the Interpret Footage dialog to the original color that your object was pre-multiplied with. In this case, blue.

So which type of alpha channel is better? That's a good question. Straight alpha channels are easier to work with, but pre-multiplied alphas can look better in theory. Pre-multiplied alpha channels are also compatible with more software programs. But if you're not creating an alpha channel, it doesn't matter. You need to direct your video editing program to use the type of alpha channel that your footage has.

The next area contains de-interlacing options. When video is broadcast, it must be interlaced, meaning that it is split into horizontal bars and mixed (or interlaced) with the following frame. On a computer screen, interlaced footage can cause weird artifacts (**FIGURE 8.19** on the next page). Turn on de-interlacing

FIGURE 8.19 These "combing" artifacts are a result of interlaced frames.

to eliminate these artifacts. From the Use menu, specify whether Photoshop should display the Lower Field of video first or the Upper Field. Most types of NTSC and PAL video are lower field first. Consult Chapter 10, "Plug-ins and Resources," for more information on resources for learning video.

The Frame Rate option at the bottom of the Interpret Footage dialog allows you to change the frame rate. If you have a piece of time lapse footage, you may want to increase the frame rate far above the standard 29.97 fps. But most of the time, you'll probably leave this set at Footage Frame Rate, which uses the native frame rate of the video clip.

Below Frame Rate is Color Profile, which allows you to specify color management options; see the section "Color Management and Video" at the end of this chapter for more information.

Previewing Photoshop Video on an External Monitor

Many options are available to you when editing your video, and not setting an option correctly could ruin your entire video. These critical options include frame rate, pixel aspect ratio, pixel dimensions, interlacing options, and more. Sometimes it helps to preview your project on an external monitor before rendering so you know what you're end result will look like when your project is rendered and output to a video monitor.

To do this, you need a video preview device, such as a video monitor, hooked up to your computer via FireWire (or for the mega nerdy, IEEE 1394).

Although this next step is optional, I recommend it. Select File > Export > Video Preview to set up options for your preview. You can choose to preview in full screen or wide screen, and you can also set up scaling options.

Then select File > Export > Send Video Preview to Device to preview your document on your external monitor.

Animation Conversions

Keep in mind that Photoshop was created to be a photo shop, not a video editor, so it only provides two ways to create animation: with frames and in the timeline. Photoshop allows you to go back and forth between these two modes to create video tricks not possible with the options available in the Animation (Timeline) palette alone.

Flattening Frames into Layers

Open the herbie fashion show.psd file from the Chapter 8 folder (**FIGURE 8.20**). Herbie the Robot animates from left to right and also spins around as if he is modeling the latest in metallic finishes.

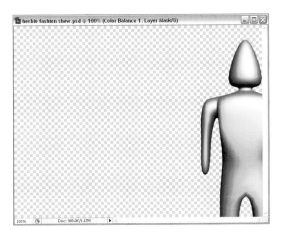

FIGURE 8.20 The herbie fashion show.psd file.

FIGURE 8.21 Choose Flatten Frames into Layers from the Animation (Timeline) palette menu.

Let's flatten Herbie—not by telling him he looks fat in gold, but by creating a separate image out of every frame in the animation. From the Animation (Timeline) palette menu select Flatten Frames into Layers (**FIGURE 8.21**). The result is quite awesome (**FIGURE 8.22**). You see every frame of the entire animation at

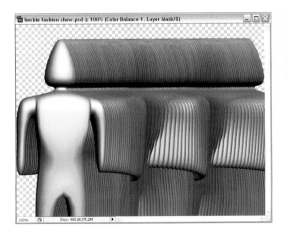

FIGURE 8.22 The results of applying Flatten Frames into Layers. Each frame in the animation is a separate still image in the layer.

once. Each frame is now a separate still image occupying its own layer in this Photoshop document. You can create very dynamic visual patterns with this feature. Imagine you have video footage of a hummingbird, for example. You could flatten that video into layers and have multiple images of the hummingbird at different stages of flight. You could then put those images in a row in a static design. Think of how cool it would look if you blended all of the frames of that animation together using Blend modes.

The downside of this feature is that it creates a lot of layers, depending on how long your animation is. This animation is a relatively brief three seconds (and some change) long. At 30 frames per second, flattening created over 90 frames! Make sure you have enough RAM available on your system before overloading Photoshop with more layers than it can handle.

The upside of this feature, on the other hand, is some cool bonuses. My favorite is that it keeps the original layers intact. Also, it turns off each layer's visibility for you automatically. And if you want to undo this whole procedure, you can do it in just one step. Press Ctrl/Cmd+Z once and you're back to where you started.

Converting Layers into Frames

The ability to convert layers into frames is one of the most significant creative tools in Photoshop. The Convert Layers into Frames feature takes the layers of your Photoshop document and plays them back in order, with each layer appearing for one frame.

Open the gettysburg.psd file from the Chapter 8 folder (**FIGURE 8.23**). This file contains the first six words of the Gettysburg address. Each word is on a separate layer and is in roughly the same spot. When you convert these layers into frames, you'll essentially be creating a video that plays these frames in order. Go to the source of all good video tools, the Animation (Timeline) palette menu, and select Make Frames from Layers. The timeline shows the staggered layers as frames in an animation (**FIGURE 8.24**).

NOTE   To use the Convert Layers into Frames feature, you must have at least two layers in your Photoshop document.

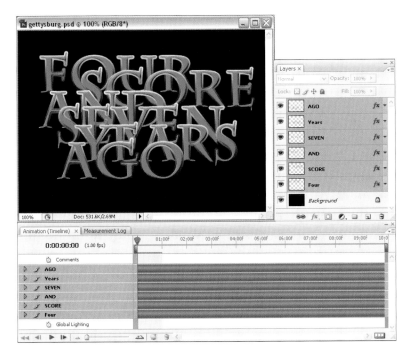

FIGURE 8.23 The gettysburg.psd file.

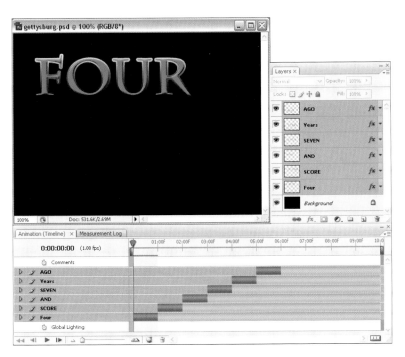

FIGURE 8.24 After using the Make Frames from Layers command, each layer becomes a frame in an animation. Now these words are staggered in time.

NOTE For those of you familiar with Adobe After Effects, the Convert Layers into Frames feature is similar to the Sequence Layers Keyframe Assistant.

The ability to create frames from Photoshop layers doesn't initially seem as impressive as it really is. Think of it: You can make an animation out of anything you can stagger into layers. So, even though you can't animate scale, you can create multiple versions of the same layer and scale up each layer incrementally. When converting these layers to frames, the layer's scale will be animated. To learn about my favorite application of this feature, check out the sidebar "Faking 3D Animation."

NOTE The gettysburg.psd file plays back so slowly because I've set the frame rate to 1 fps.

TIP Even though the Convert Layers to Frames feature makes all layers visible for only one frame, you can manually adjust the In point and Out point for each layer to set the duration to anything you'd like.

Faking 3D Animation

By far the biggest complaint I've heard about Photoshop CS3 Extended is that it doesn't allow you to animate in 3D. While that is true, you can use the Make Frames from Layers feature to fake it.

Here's how to fake the animation of 3D rotation. Duplicate a 3D layer many times. On each layer, double-click the layer thumbnail to enter 3D Object mode and rotate it. Start with the 3D layer that is second from the bottom of the stack. After entering 3D Object mode, make sure that the Rotate the 3D Object tool is selected, and press the right arrow key to nudge the rotation of this object around the Y axis. Press Enter to exit. On the next layer up in the stack, repeat this same procedure, except this time nudge the layer twice with the right arrow. Continue to incrementally add an arrow nudge with each layer. After several layers, you'll have all the frames you need to create a 3D animation. It's not as powerful as animating a regular animation property in Photoshop, but it's certainly easier than learning a 3D program.

Converting Timeline Animation to Frame Animation

Photoshop allows you to convert a timeline animation to a frame animation while you're in the Animation (Timeline) palette. Click the Convert to Frame Animation button at the bottom right of the Animation (Timeline) palette (**FIGURE 8.25**). This converts all of the frames of your timeline animation into individual layers, except that video layers will not convert to frames or play back. I honestly can't think of a reason to use this feature, but I provide this information only to complete the features of Photoshop Extended. If you think of a reason for this, email me and let me know.

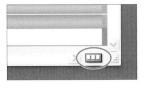

FIGURE 8.25 Click this button to convert timeline animation to frame animation.

From my experience, the Convert to Frame Animation feature is a little like "crossing the streams" in *Ghostbusters*. You lose all the power of keyframes, interpolation, and mask animation by converting animation from timeline to frames. And once you go from timeline animation to frame animation, the control from these features is permanently reduced. So, unless you find a situation where you really need to work with frames, avoid using this feature.

Other Types of Video Edits

Now that you have a more solid foundation of Photoshop's video features, you can return to the concept of editing. These next few edits are much more sophisticated than anything you've seen thus far with video.

Extracting Video

Earlier in this chapter, in the section "Splitting Layers," you cut a piece of video a few times so that you could extract an undesirable chunk of it. However, if you instead performed an extract edit, you could do this in one fell swoop. Now that you know how to use work areas, you can take advantage of this time-saving feature.

Open the army of zombies.mov file from the Chapter 8 folder. You saw this clip earlier when you learned about trimming video clips. You didn't get far enough into this video to see that it contains three parts: the first five frames that you trimmed at the beginning of this chapter, the main section of zombies, and a third section with a female zombie. In this exercise, you'll extract the entire center section.

Extraction depends on the work area. So, first move the beginning of the work area to the last frame of the brief intro, which is about the fourth frame mark (0:00:00:04). You can use the CTI as a guide if it helps you. Next, move the end of the work area to 0:00:03:07, which is the start of the third section with the female zombie. Your work area should now look like **FIGURE 8.26**. From the Animation (Timeline) palette menu select Extract Work Area to extract and ripple delete the area of your video where the work area was (**FIGURE 8.27**). A ripple delete automatically fills the gap created in the footage due to the extraction. Everything to the right of the gap moves to the left to fill it.

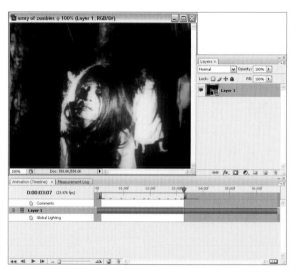

FIGURE 8.26 In preparation for the extract edit, your work area should resemble this. Geez. Did everyone in the 60s get buried in a toga?

FIGURE 8.27 The project after performing the extract edit.

Notice also that Photoshop creates two separate layers for you. Essentially, these are two instances of the same layer, so it's as if you had split them using Split Layers. At any time you can change the In and Out points of these layers and restore the extracted section.

Lifting Video

Lifting video is similar to extracting video, only it leaves the gap created by the removed footage open. Press Ctrl/Cmd+Z to undo the Extract command you just performed. With the work area still ranging from 0:00:00:04 to 0:00:03:07, select Lift Work Area from the Animation (Timeline) palette menu. This command still removes the video where the work area was, but it leaves the space open (**FIGURE 8.28**). If you had another layer underneath this layer, it would show through during the gap.

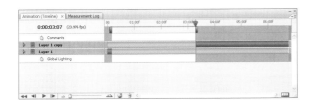

FIGURE 8.28 After performing a lift edit.

Slip Edits

Slip edits are edits that I use often and just can't live without. However, the concept can be difficult to grasp at first.

To help you understand this type of edit, open what is probably my favorite video clip you'll be using in this book, party wizard.mov (**FIGURE 8.29**). This is a video clip of the wizard lady letting off some steam and getting her groove on. Before delving into what a slip edit is, you need to set up this project.

FIGURE 8.29 The party wizard.mov clip. Taken from the movie *How Wizard Lady Got Her Groove Back*.

At 0:00:01:05, she kicks her foot out, so trim the In point of this clip to this point. At 0:00:02:08, she kicks out her other foot, so move the Out point of this clip to that point. Your timeline should now look like the one in **FIGURE 8.30**. The viewable portion of this video shows a kick with her right foot to a kick with her left foot. As mentioned earlier, the parts of this video that you cut are now a faded green in the timeline, which indicates that those parts are still there, just hidden.

FIGURE 8.30 After trimming the In and Out points of the party wizard.mov clip.

Now you're ready to perform a slip edit. Let's say you want this video to start with the left foot kick, but you need to keep the In point at 0:00:01:05 and the Out point at 0:00:02:08. This would be a frustrating and time-consuming task if it weren't for slip edits. Slip edits allow you to keep the In point and Out point of the layer in place but still move the contents of the video. To do this, click on the faded green area to the left of the In point of the video, and drag to the right. Notice how you can now see where the video actually begins (**FIGURE 8.31**). But in this case, you actually want the video to start with the left foot kick. So grab the side of the video on the right of the Out point of the clip and drag to the left until the video starts with the left kick (**FIGURE 8.32**). Slip edits allow you to experiment with the parts of the video you want to be viewable without altering your In and Out points.

FIGURE 8.31 After performing a slip edit by clicking on the clip to the left of its In point and dragging to the right.

FIGURE 8.32 After performing a slip edit by clicking and dragging the clip after the Out point.

Slip edits are useful when video is in sync with audio or when video cuts happen at a specific time, like every second. With slip edits, you can adjust the video content without wrecking your project.

Additional Video Adjustments

In this section, I share a few other bells and whistles that can be virtual lifesavers when editing and working with video.

Replacing Footage

Replacing footage does exactly what it implies: It allows you to swap out footage with another piece of footage. What's not exactly clear off the bat is how important this feature is.

Let's first investigate the utilitarian purpose of this command. You use Replace Footage when you've broken a link from your video to its source clip. This happens when you move, rename, or delete the source video file.

Open the dude wheres my file.psd image from the Chapter 8 folder. A pop-up dialog appears explaining the step you're about to perform, but don't spoil it. Click OK. This video layer is linked to the party wizard.mov clip, but at the time I imported it, it had a different filename. Now Photoshop can't locate it. To remedy this, select Layer > Video Layers > Replace Footage. In the Replace Footage dialog, navigate to the original footage to reconnect the link. In this case, select party wizard.mov. Click OK to restore your project to its original state.

Replace Footage also has another great purpose. Let's say you're working on a video project for a client, but the client only has a low-res version of the video. Or maybe the client only has stock footage with a watermark on it. The good news is that you don't have to wait until the good footage comes in to get to work. You can use the Replace Footage command to swap out video layers while keeping all of the effects and adjustments applied to them. Let's look at how this works.

Open the bad quality.psd file from the Chapter 8 folder (**FIGURE 8.33**). This is a black and white version of the what time of year.mov clip. This clip has been compressed a lot, and the quality is terrible. It also has a Layer Style applied to it. Select Layer 1, and as before, choose Layer > Video Layers > Replace Footage. This time, select the what time of year.mov file. Click OK to swap out the old clip for the higher-res version (**FIGURE 8.34**). Notice that the Layer Style is still applied to the replacement footage, although the Blend mode of the Layer Style creates a different effect on the colors of the footage.

FIGURE 8.33 The bad quality.psd file. Notice the Gradient Overlay Layer Style that has been applied.

FIGURE 8.34 After replacing the low-quality layer with a higher-quality version.

Replace Footage also keeps all adjustments, even after replacing footage, so you're free to work on that video project using low-quality or watermarked video. When the good video arrives, just swap it out using the Replace Footage command, and all edits, trims, effects, and other video adjustments will carry over to the replaced footage.

FIGURE 8.35 At the bottom of the Actions palette menu you can see all of the libraries of actions that come with Photoshop.

FIGURE 8.36 All the actions in the Video Actions set.

Video Actions

Photoshop CS3 Extended ships with an entire library of actions just for video documents. To see these, click the Actions palette menu. At the bottom of the menu are libraries of actions that come with Photoshop (**FIGURE 8.35**). From this menu, select Video Actions to load those that specifically pertain to video.

What Are Actions?

Actions are an automated feature in Photoshop that can perform a series of specified tasks quickly. For example, if you had a digital camera that took pictures that were a little too dark and a little too red, and you often posted your photos to the Internet, you could create an action that would automatically lighten, remove the red color cast, and scale your images to an appropriate size for the Web. You could also use a Batch command to apply this action to an entire folder of images. For more information on how to set up and use actions, consult the Photoshop Help Viewer.

With this set of actions in your Actions palette, click the arrow next to the Video Actions folder to expand it, if it isn't already expanded. You can now see the long list of video actions in this set (**FIGURE 8.36**).

As an example, you'll use the Broadcast Safe action. When creating colors for video, you need to be careful because video is limited to a certain range of colors. Pure black and pure white don't come across in video. Very vibrant colors also do not translate well to video. Photoshop actually includes an action just to bring the luminance values of your video into a range that is safe for broadcast. And it includes another action that will make just your colors' saturation broadcast safe. The Broadcast Safe action performs both actions.

Open unsafe.mov from the Chapter 8 folder (**FIGURE 8.37**). This is a video of extremely saturated reds, greens, and blues—typically the worst offenders for creating broadcast-safe video. These actions work on a per layer basis, so select Layer 1 in the Layers palette. Next, select the Broadcast Safe action in the Actions palette by clicking on it. Then click the Play selection button at the bottom of the Actions palette (**FIGURE 8.38**). After playing this action, the colors and luminance values in the video are now safe for broadcast (**FIGURE 8.39**).

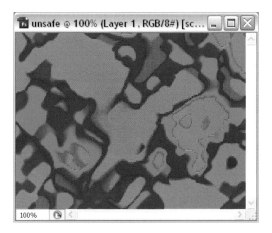

FIGURE 8.37 The unsafe.mov file.

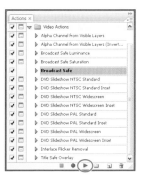

FIGURE 8.38 The Play selection button at the bottom of the Actions palette.

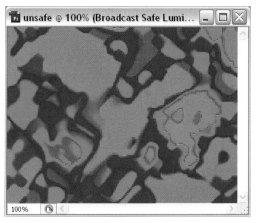

FIGURE 8.39 After playing the Broadcast Safe action with this layer selected, the colors and luminance values are now up to code for broadcast.

This is just one example of all the automated benefits available to you because of these Video Actions. You can also use actions to do everything from creating DVD slide shows to making an alpha channel.

NOTE   With the Broadcast Safe action, you need to make sure that the top layer is selected in order for your entire document to become broadcast safe.

NOTE   Actions can also contain messages and dialogs. As you play the Broadcast Safe action, you will get several pop-up dialogs giving you information about what the action is doing to your image, as well as other helpful tips.

Cleaning Up the Timeline with Favorites

In Chapter 7, "Animating," you worked with the time lapse.psd file. It was a great project, but you only needed to adjust one layer to animate Global Lighting. Most of those other layers just got in your way. Let's revisit this project to clean things up a bit.

Open the time lapse.psd file from the Chapter 8 folder and look at how cluttered the timeline is (**FIGURE 8.40**). Let's say that you only need the rotating hands layer and the hours layer visible in the timeline. You still want the contents of the other layers to be visible in the document window, you just don't want them cluttering your timeline.

FIGURE 8.40 The cluttered timeline of the time lapse.psd file.

Select both the rotating hands layer and the hours layer by clicking on one of them, and then Ctrl/Cmd-clicking on the other. With only these two layers selected, click the Animation (Timeline) palette menu and select Show > Set Favorite Layers. All layers that are not favorites in the timeline are hidden, although they still display in the document window (**FIGURE 8.41**).

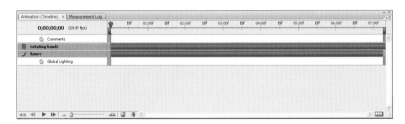

FIGURE 8.41 Layers that are Favorites can be isolated so they are the only layers that appear in the timeline, even though all layers still show in the document window.

To restore the view of all layers, click the Animation (Timeline) palette menu and select Show > All Layers. At any time you can choose to view the Favorites again by selecting Show > Favorite Layers from the Animation (Timeline) palette menu. You can also use the Set Favorite Layers command at any time to create new favorites.

NOTE   Photoshop does not consider any adjustments to Favorites as a command that can be undone using Undo. Use Show Settings from the Animation (Timeline) palette menu to make any changes to Favorites.

Color Management and Video

Color management is the process of achieving consistent color. You can color manage images in a video layer and image sequences so that colors are consistent from application to application and from user to user, no matter the platform. Don't confuse color management with color correction, which is the process of altering colors to achieve better results. The concept of color management in video is relatively recent, although it has been around in the print world for awhile.

Color management is based on the concept of profiles. These profiles define a space, or gamut, of color. I like to think of these spaces as a color "language." Color profiles are embedded in images and travel with the image so that all programs that use that image understand its color language. Without these profiles to define the color space of an image, the image could shift colors as it travels to and from different programs and computers and is forced to adapt to a different color space (language).

9

Creative Video Techniques

Now it is my great privilege to open a fat can of creativity and pour it all over our video. In this chapter, you'll apply all sorts of standard Photoshop adjustments to video footage. Included in this category are Photoshop filters, Layer Styles, painting tools, cloning, healing, Blend modes, and the impressive new feature Image Stacks.

Using Styles and Filters on Video

Up first, you'll look at adding Layer Styles to Video Layers. For more information on Layer Styles, consult Chapter 3, "Even Cooler 3D Tricks."

Adding Layer Styles to Video

You can apply Photoshop Layer Styles to video just as you would any other layer. A few Layer Style effects, however, won't be very beneficial unless your video or image sequence has an alpha channel. Effects such as Outer Glow, Stroke, and Drop Shadow apply to only the boundaries of a layer.

Several Layer Style effects will allow you to channel your inner Ted Turner and add color to video clips. Open the tor from the dead.mov file from the Chapter 9 folder. This clip is from the infamous B-movie *Plan 9 from Outer Space*. In this piece of footage, the actor is rising from the dead, but he takes quite a while to do this. So, drag the CTI to somewhere in the middle of the timeline. The exact location is not important. You just want to be able to see a frame that is more representative of the entire clip (**FIGURE 9.1**).

FIGURE 9.1 The tor from the dead.mov file about midway through the timeline.

The video is in black and white, so you'll colorize it using Layer Styles. Double-click the area to the right of the layer's name to open the Layer Style dialog. On the left side, click the words Color Overlay to turn on Color Overlay. The Color Overlay options appear on the right side of the dialog (**FIGURE 9.2**). At this point, the screen is just filled with red, which isn't that remarkable. But change the Blend Mode setting from Normal to Overlay to blend this red color into the video clip. The result is much more intense (**FIGURE 9.3**). I'll talk more about Blend modes toward the end of this chapter.

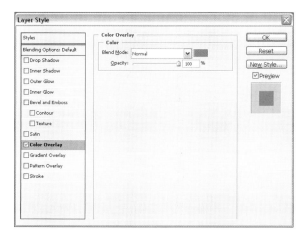

FIGURE 9.2 The options for the Color Overlay effect in the Layer Style dialog.

FIGURE 9.3 The video clip colorized by the Color Overlay effect in the Overlay Blend mode.

You could also apply a Gradient Overlay to add multiple colors to your video. Try applying a Pattern Overlay effect using Blend modes to create some stimulating visuals. You could also simulate a vignette effect by applying an Inner Shadow or an Inner Glow effect and adjusting the settings.

Applying Layer Styles to video is a little different than most of the adjustments you'll be learning about in this chapter. With other adjustments, such as filters and painting, the alterations are only valid for one frame. Layer Styles are applied to the entire duration of the video layer.

Liquifying Video Layers

Liquify is one of the most entertaining components of Photoshop. The purpose of Liquify is to make organic distortions in a layer. It's almost as if the layer is made of liquid, and you can just smear its pixels around. Taking a picture of your grumpy boss into Liquify and going to town will make you feel much better. Trust me here, folks. I'm speaking from experience.

But aside from being digital stress relief of the highest order, the Liquify filter is very useful for production work. For example, if you have an image of a character that needs a bigger nose or more pointy ears, Liquify is the tool for you.

Let's try out this filter:

1. Open the Magic in your face.avi file from the Chapter 9 folder.

2. Drag your CTI to frame 0:00:05:05 (**FIGURE 9.4**).

FIGURE 9.4 Put your CTI at five seconds and five frames into the timeline.

FIGURE 9.5
The Liquify tools.

3. With Layer 1 selected, choose Filter > Liquify.

   The tools in the upper-left area of the Liquify dialog are key to using this filter effectively (**FIGURE 9.5**). The top tool, the Forward Warp Tool, is selected by default.

4. Click and drag on an image or video layer to smear the image. In this case, click and drag on parts of the wizard lady to warp them.

   I chose to warp her helmet to turn it into one of the helmets from the Warner Brothers cartoon interpretation of Wagner's *Flight of the Valkyries* (**FIGURE 9.6**). Maybe that reference is a little obscure.

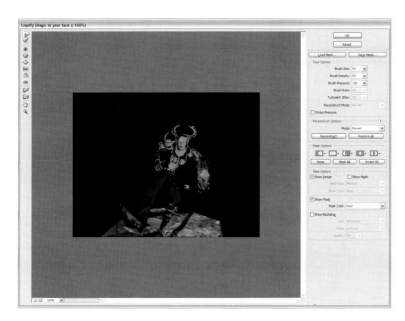

FIGURE 9.6 After warping the character's helmet with the Forward Warp tool.

5. Now, make her face look like Shrek by selecting the fifth tool from the top, which is the Bloat tool. Clicking and holding with the Bloat tool "inflates" a particular region. Click and hold the mouse button over the bottom of her face to bloat it a little (**FIGURE 9.7**).

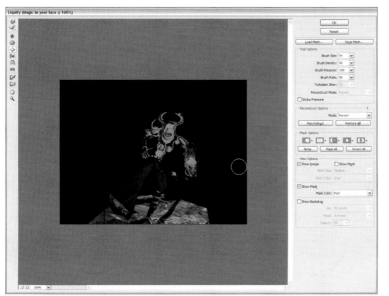

FIGURE 9.7 After using the Bloat tool on the face of the wizard lady.

6. Select the tool above the Bloat tool, the Pucker Tool. It does the opposite of bloat. It sucks things into the area that you click and hold on with the mouse. It's almost like a mini-vortex tool. Pucker the top of the wizard lady's face (**FIGURE 9.8**).

FIGURE 9.8 Use the Pucker tool to scrunch the top of her head.

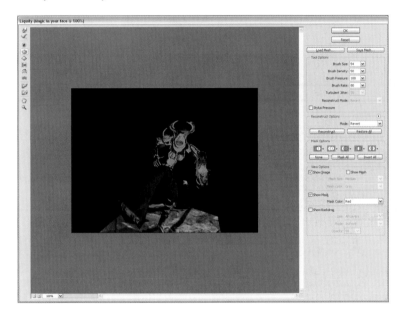

Aside from being great entertainment, the Liquify tool is very helpful in many situations. Honestly, when I submit a photo of myself to a publication, I usually take the image into Liquify first to slim down my neck, reduce the size of my Durante-sized nose, and make other such modifications to present a more pleasing likeness. Liquify can do similar cosmetic miracles for video.

If you find that you've overdone the changes you want to make with the Liquify tools (which happens quite a bit because they're really fun to use), you can use the Reconstruct tool. Click and drag the Reconstruct area to restore areas back to their original state. **FIGURE 9.9** shows how I've used the Reconstruct tool to restore the bottom of the wizard lady's face a little. Click OK to accept the results.

Note that when you applied Liquify, a little notch appeared in the Altered Video bar under the layer properties (**FIGURE 9.10**). This happens every time you apply Liquify or any of the other effects I'm about to talk about. I'll explain Altered Video later in this section. What you need to know now is that this application of Liquify only applied to this particular frame. Even the frames on either side of this frame, at 0:00:05:04 and 0:00:05:06, were unaffected. Also, when you preview such changes, they will go by very quickly, seeming almost like subliminal messages.

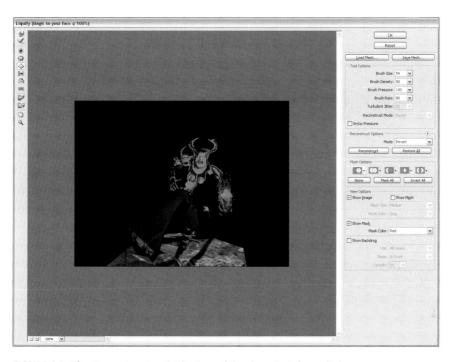

FIGURE 9.9 After Reconstructing the bottom of the character's face a little.

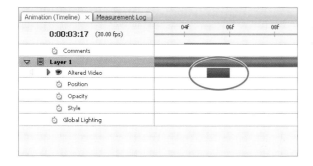

FIGURE 9.10 The Liquify adjustment appears under Altered Video in the timeline.

TIP   As in the regular Photoshop workspace, you can use the left bracket ([) and right bracket (]) keys on your keyboard to reduce and enlarge the size of the Liquify tool brushes.

Lighting Effects and Video

Lighting, luminance, and color adjustments are great features of Photoshop CS3 Extended, because they are Photoshop's specialty anyway. In this section, you'll use Photoshop's standard tools to create a day for night shot, which is a video clip that was shot during the day but needs to look like it was shot at night.

Open the storm.psd file from the Chapter 9 folder (**FIGURE 9.11**). I've already started the luminance adjustment by adding two layers. One is a basic Levels adjustment layer. You can apply adjustment layers, and even image adjustments from the Image menu to video layers. The white blob layer is just a patch of faded white to bring out the brightest area in the clouds. You'll use this white blob layer in a later exercise. Keep its visibility off for now.

FIGURE 9.11 The storm.psd file.

NOTE   If you get a pop-up dialog when opening a file warning you that Pixel Aspect Ratio Correction is for preview purposes only, just click OK to close it. It's just helpful information (that's not very helpful).

In this particular clip, you'll take advantage of the Lighting Effects filter. In a production workflow, you may want to convert this layer for Smart Filters before proceeding so that you can adjust the Lighting Effects settings if you need to. Video layers converted to Smart Objects still play back video and can be animated. In many ways, video layers have advantages that standard Photoshop layers do not. For now, skip the conversion of this layer to a Smart Object.

When applying adjustment layers to video, the adjustment lasts for the duration of the document unless you edit its duration in the timeline. When applying image adjustments from the Image menu, the effect only lasts for the duration of that frame. Adjustments from the Image menu also fall under the category of Altered Video. Therefore, they are nondestructive, unlike the result of applying adjustments from the Image menu to standard image layers.

TIP When applying filters to video layers that have been converted to Smart Objects, the effects last for the duration of the timeline, not just a single frame.

The Lighting Effects filter is used to add high-end lighting with multiple light sources. Select the circling birds layer in the Layers palette, and the choose Filter > Render > Lighting Effects. The Lighting Effects dialog opens, which has several very powerful options (**FIGURE 9.12**). At the top, you can choose from several common presets from the Style drop-down list. After adjusting your own custom lighting settings, you can also click the Save button below this list to add your custom light settings to the list.

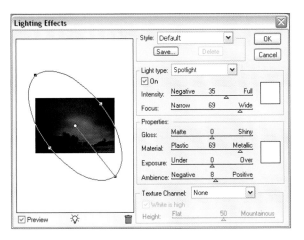

FIGURE 9.12 The Lighting Effects dialog.

From the Light type drop-down list choose Omni. If necessary, click and drag the white circle in the center of the preview area until it is over the spot of light in the sky. You can also click the gray points on the outer circle of the light to resize the light to cover a larger area, or a smaller one. **FIGURE 9.13** shows where I placed my omni light and how large I made it.

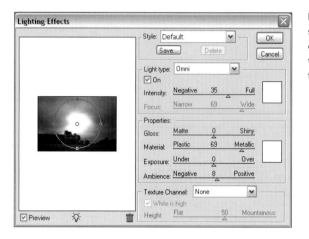

FIGURE 9.13 My light settings. Notice that I haven't changed too much, other than to change the Light type to Omni.

But this is way too bright, so change the Intensity value to 20. The image is starting to look pretty good, but there's still just a little too much overall light in the shot. This kind of light is referred to as ambient light. Lower the ambient light in the shot by setting the Ambience value to 3. Now you're getting somewhere (**FIGURE 9.14**). Click OK to accept these settings. The image looks pretty good, and it's a pretty good fake. Most of the general public would probably accept that this was originally a night shot.

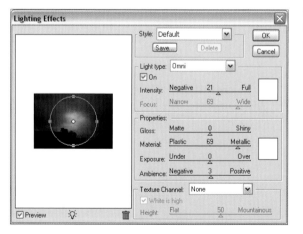

FIGURE 9.14 The Lighting Effects settings before accepting them.

From this point you could add some additional bells and whistles to help sell the shot. You could open the Lighting Effects dialog again and add two tiny orange lights under the streetlights. If this picture was truly taken at night, those streetlights would be on. These are the small modifications that make a big difference when trying to create such digital trickery.

Later in this chapter you'll add some lightning coming from the bright area in the center of the document.

> **TIP** You can create additional lights by clicking and dragging the lightbulb at the bottom of the dialog into the scene. You can throw away lights by dragging them to the trash can icon in the bottom center of the Lighting Effects filter.

> **NOTE** Notice how the Intensity value actually extends into the negative range. The Lighting Effects filter can actually be used to remove light from a scene as well as put light into it.

Lighting Effect Light Types

Here's a list of the light types in the Lighting Effects filter. You'll find similar light types in 3D programs.

- **Directional:** Shines parallel rays of light from a source. If you could see the light rays from a directional light, they would look like a cylinder. Use this light type to re-create the light from large sources, like the sun.

- **Omni:** Creates light in every direction from a single point. Think of this like a lightbulb.

- **Spotlight:** Is the default light setting. Spotlights shoot light outward from a single point, like real-world spotlights. If you could see the light rays from a spotlight, they would look like a cone.

Using Other Photoshop Filters on Video

Filters add special effects to still images or video. You can use filters to add artistic effects, such as a watercolor look or a mosaic. And, you can use practically any Photoshop filter on video, because each frame is treated as a separate still image when applying filters.

Using the Magic in your face.avi file, I've provided you with a random smattering of creative possibilities using filters on video layers.

- Filter > Artistic > Cutout (**FIGURE 9.15A**).
- Filter > Artistic > Watercolor (**FIGURE 9.15B**).
- Filter > Blur > Gaussian Blur (**FIGURE 9.15C**).
- Filter > Blur > Motion Blur (**FIGURE 9.15D**).

FIGURE 9.15A Filter > Artistic > Cutout.

FIGURE 9.15B Filter> Artistic > Watercolor.

FIGURE 9.15C Filter > Blur > Gaussian Blur.

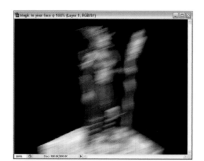

FIGURE 9.15D Filter > Blur > Motion Blur.

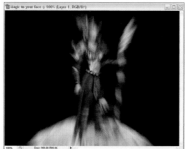

FIGURE 9.15E Filter > Blur > Radial Blur.

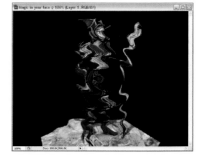

FIGURE 9.15F Filter > Distort > Zig Zag.

- Filter > Blur > Radial Blur (**FIGURE 9.15E**).

- Filter > Distort > Zig Zag (**FIGURE 9.15F**).

- Filter > Pixelate > Color Halftone (**FIGURE 9.15G**).

- Filter > Pixelate > Mosaic (**FIGURE 9.15H**).

- Filter > Sketch > Photocopy (**FIGURE 9.15I**).

- Filter > Stylize > Wind (**FIGURE 9.15J**).

- Filter > Texture > Stained Glass (**FIGURE 9.15K**).

Remember that when you apply filters, they only apply to the frame on which the CTI is located when you apply the filter.

TIP   If you want to apply a filter to every frame of a video, set up an action to go to the next frame and apply a filter. Repeat this action or have the action repeat the steps to apply the filter to the entire video.

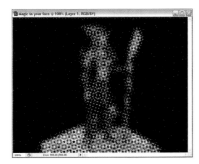

FIGURE 9.15G Filter > Pixelate > Color Halftone.

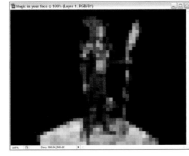

FIGURE 9.15H Filter > Pixelate > Mosaic.

FIGURE 9.15I Filter > Sketch > Photocopy.

FIGURE 9.15J Filter > Stylize > Wind.

FIGURE 9.15K Filter > Texture > Stained Glass.

QuickTime Video Filters at Export

Although it might seem as though I'm starting to sound like a QuickTime spokesman, I'm really not. It's just that Adobe products work so much better when you have the current version of QuickTime installed on your computer.

Having QuickTime also gives you some bonus filters that you can apply when exporting video. To access these filters, open a document that has a video layer in it. Then select File > Export > Render Video. In the File Options area, change the QuickTime Export drop-down list to QuickTime movie and click the Settings button immediately to the right of the drop-down list (**FIGURE 9.16**). In the Movie Settings dialog that pops up, click the Filter button (**FIGURE 9.17**). You are then able to access the QuickTime filters that you can apply to video (**FIGURE 9.18**).

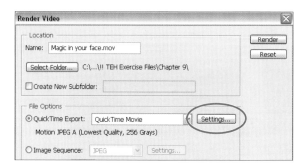

FIGURE 9.16 With QuickTime movie selected as the format, click the Settings button.

FIGURE 9.17 In the Movie Settings dialog, click Filter to access the QuickTime filters for video.

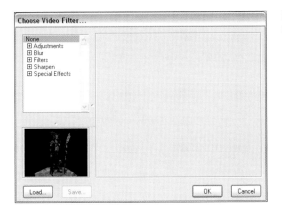

FIGURE 9.18 The available QuickTime filters.

Five categories of filters are available: Adjustments, Blur, Filters, Sharpen, and Special Effects. As an example of what these filters do, click the Special Effects menu. Select the Film Noise filter from the list (**FIGURE 9.19**). The Film Noise effect simulates the damage that old film often has. The thumbnail of the video below the filters immediately begins to play back. You can see that these filters are already animated and apply to the entire video. This behavior is different than the filters in Photoshop that only apply to one layer.

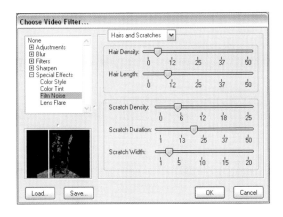

FIGURE 9.19 After selecting the Film Noise QuickTime filter.

Once you have selected a filter from the left side of this dialog, you can adjust the options for the effect on the right side of the dialog.

One detail you need to be aware of is that many color effects are in the Quick-Time filters. I highly recommend that you use Photoshop adjustment layers to do any color or luminance adjusting rather than using QuickTime filters.

Adjustment layers are much more powerful and allow for greater flexibility. But if you need a Blur effect or a Sharpening applied to an entire video clip, QuickTime filters are probably the most time-effective options.

About Altered Video

As discussed earlier, when you apply filters, paint, image adjustments, and other alterations to a video layer, that frame will then have a section of Altered Video underneath it in the timeline (**FIGURE 9.20**). This is Photoshop's way of keeping track of your video changes and keeping them nondestructive. You cannot select or move the Altered Video to apply it to a different frame. Likewise, you can't expand the alteration to apply to additional frames.

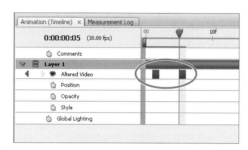

FIGURE 9.20 After applying effects to a frame of video, the frame will be signified by this mark of Altered Video underneath it in the timeline.

Toggling Altered Video visibility

To see your original video footage without the alterations, click the eye icon next to Altered Video on the left side of the Animation (Timeline) palette (**FIGURE 9.21**). Click the spot where the eye used to be to turn the Altered Video back on.

FIGURE 9.21 Use this eye icon to toggle the visibility of Altered Video.

Navigating sections of Altered Video

You can use a neat little navigator to jump between sections of Altered Video. Let's say that you cleaned up a couple of sections of video with Photoshop's painting tools (to be discussed shortly). If you were zoomed out of your timeline, those spots would be hard to see, and even more difficult to precisely land on (**FIGURE 9.22**).

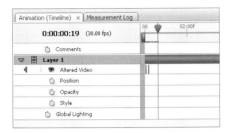

FIGURE 9.22 From this view point, it's difficult to see (and navigate to) these small sections of Altered Video.

Similar to the way you used the keyframe navigator, click the left and right arrows in the Altered Video navigator to jump to sections of your timeline that have alterations made to them.

Restoring frames

As previously mentioned, all filters, painting, and other changes that create Altered Video are completely nondestructive. To remove all alterations applied to a particular frame, move the CTI to that specific frame in the timeline. Select the layer with Altered Video, open the Layer menu, and select Video Layers > Restore Frame. This action removes all Altered Video applied to that layer at that frame. From the same Layer menu, select Restore All Frames to remove all Altered Video from the entire layer.

NOTE Other than using Undo, there is no way to remove one alteration while keeping another. For example, if you applied a filter to a frame and also painted on it, and then you restore the frame, both changes will be deleted.

Using Paint Tools on Video

Photoshop has one of the greatest arsenals of paint tools found in any software program. With Photoshop's family of paint tools, you can paint with all sorts of brushes, duplicate pixels, and even blend paint strokes together. The unbelievable, jaw-dropping good news is that you can use all of these tools on video as well. The following sections provide a sampler of what is possible when using this versatile and complete toolset on video.

Painting on Video

Painting on video layers is identical to painting on regular layers except that the paint strokes only last for one frame. To paint on a video layer, simply select it in the Layers palette, select the Paintbrush tool in the Tools palette, and start painting in the document window.

NOTE   If the idea of painting on one frame at a time seems tedious, I'll show you a helper to make this task easier later on this chapter in the section "Using Onion Skins."

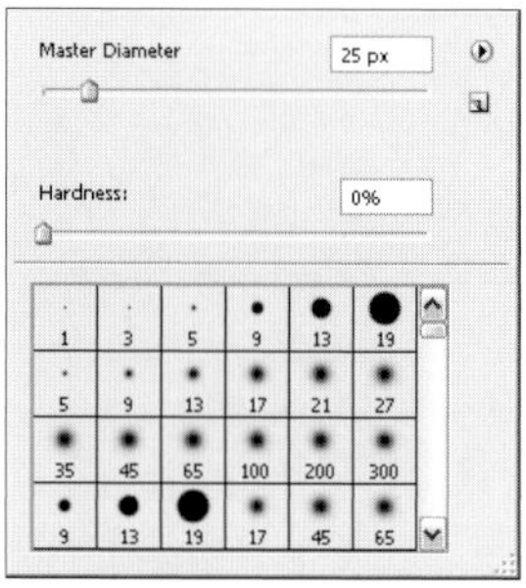

You can right-click in the document window to access a pop-up dialog that allows you to change the Master Diameter (size) of your brush, the brush Hardness (feathered edge), and the shape of your brush (**FIGURE 9.23**). But the real powerhouse of brush customization is the Brushes palette (**FIGURE 9.24**). Not only can you select which brush to use, but also how it functions. The options available in the Brushes palette allow you to add a great deal of variety to the shape and consistency of your paint strokes. For example, you can randomly scatter your paint brush strokes around your cursor as you paint or color blend between the foreground and background colors as you paint. The Brushes palette menu contains many libraries of brushes that ship with Photoshop, which you can choose from, or you can load your own (**FIGURE 9.25**).

FIGURE 9.23 When you right-click in the document window with the Paintbrush tool selected, a pop-up dialog gives you limited options.

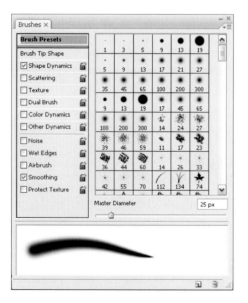

FIGURE 9.24 The Brushes palette provides access to the entire host of paintbrush options and features.

FIGURE 9.25 The Brushes palette menu.

NOTE Fortunately, Adobe has structured its palette menus in similar ways. Using the Brushes palette menu is very similar to using the Actions palette menu that you learned about in Chapter 8, "Editing Video."

NOTE The options and features in the Brushes palette will be grayed out unless you have a tool selected that can use brushes.

The Render Order of Video Layers

It's important to remember the order in which effects are rendered in Photoshop. When you perform edits that fall under the category of Altered Video, those adjustments are rendered, or processed, before Layer Styles. So if you have a layer with an Outer Glow effect, for example, and then you paint on the Outer Glow, your paint would not actually paint on top of the Outer Glow because painting is rendered before Layer Styles. The Outer Glow in this case would actually be recalculated based on the new paint strokes and would glow around the new paint strokes, not just the old ones. It's not the most crucial point in the world, but if you're not aware of it, you could unknowingly create a frustrating digital Three Stooges bit with you playing the role of Curly.

Cloning Video

Other tools that use the standard Photoshop brushes are also very useful for video.

One of the most helpful tools is the Clone Stamp tool. You've worked with cloning a few times in this book, but not when it comes to video. When cloning video, you can actually clone from different places in time (as you'll see shortly), and you can even clone from separate documents!

1. Open the dog on the beach.psd file from the Chapter 9 folder. This clip shows the beach, and then a black dog running along the shore.

2. Make sure your CTI is at the 0:00:01:23 mark (**FIGURE 9.26** on the next page), and select the Clone Stamp tool in the Tools palette.

FIGURE 9.26 At the 0:00:01:23 mark of the dog on the beach.psd file.

Let's make more dogs at this frame.

3. Hold down the Alt/Opt key to sample the dog, and then release the Alt/Opt key and click to paint with the sampled area. **FIGURE 9.27** shows how I did this a few times to fill out some playmates for this dog.

FIGURE 9.27 After cloning to create more dogs.

This is a cool trick, but the fact that the dogs all look exactly the same is a dead giveaway that this shot is a fake. But you can also use the Clone Stamp tool to clone in time. So, with the dog from this frame sampled, go to another frame and paint with the Clone Stamp tool to add dogs from another frame to this frame (**FIGURE 9.28**). As with other paint strokes, remember that this alteration only applies to the current frame, not to the entire timeline.

FIGURE 9.28 After cloning the same dog from other frames to create more randomness.

TIP   The Clone Stamp tool can also be used to eliminate data instead of add it. If you have an element, or a piece of an element, that you'd like to get rid of, sample from the area around the unwanted object, and paint over the unwanted object.

About Rotoscoping

Rotoscoping is a fairly common industry term that has its roots in traditional animation. It used to refer to the process of hand tracing every frame of live action video. This method of animation was used quite a bit in the legendary Disney film *Snow White*. It was probably seen the most in the character of the dashing dude that awoke Snow White from her poison apple nap. It added an extremely organic feel to many of his movements. But as you can imagine, it must have been extremely tedious tracing every frame of animation.

Now, in the digital era, rotoscoping has a more generic application. It is typically used today to refer to almost anything that you have to fix on all frames. The Photoshop family of painting tools has become a great assistant to any rotoscoping job. Let's say you want to create a headless horseman character. You could use the Clone Stamp tool to rotoscope away an actor's head to create that effect. By its very nature, rotoscoping will always be annoying and painstaking. But now that you can use Photoshop's tools to do this type of animating, the job is much easier.

Healing Video

The Healing tools include the Spot Healing Brush tool, the Healing Brush tool, and the Patch tool. You'll use the Spot Healing Brush tool to remove some rocks from the first frame of the beach video you were just working with. If you still have the dog on the beach.psd file open, go to the first frame. If you don't have it open, open it now from the Chapter 9 folder.

The first frame of this video shows only the beach. It's a nice view, but there's a few rocks on the shore that are not attractive in this shot (**FIGURE 9.29**). Select the Spot Healing Brush tool (not the Healing Brush tool) from the Tools palette. Simply click and paint on the rocks to automatically remove these blemishes from your video (**FIGURE 9.30**).

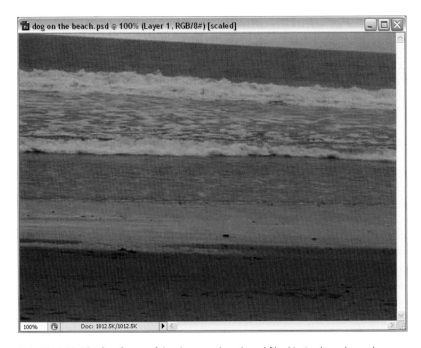

FIGURE 9.29 The first frame of the dog on a beach.psd file. Notice how the rocks along the shoreline are unsightly.

FIGURE 9.30 After getting rid of some of the rocks with the Spot Healing Brush tool.

Rasterizing Video Layers

In some rare instances, you might want to break a link to a video file and use a video layer to create a still image of one of the frames. The Rasterize Video feature allows you to do just that. Select Layer > Video Layers > Rasterize to convert your entire video layer to a standard Photoshop image layer, using the current frame that the CTI is located on as the rasterized frame. Any alterations that you have made to that frame will become part of the still image layer when rasterized.

Again, this probably won't be a feature you use all the time, but it can come in real handy when you need it to. For example, you might want to send a PSD file to a client so the client can review your layout. But maybe the animation is just a small part of the entire document. You can rasterize the video and send a copy of the PSD without the bulky video file for client review. This is much better than just deleting the video layer, because with a rasterized video layer, you get a representative still image at a frame of your choosing.

Cel Animation

Cel animation is basically traditional animation, where every frame is drawn by hand. But what if you want to create a hand-drawn cartoon from scratch, without starting with video? Photoshop has the solution, and a little help to boot.

Creating Cel Animation

If you're going to create cel animation, you need to start with a blank canvas. To this end, Photoshop allows you to create blank video layers. They're just layers that act like video layers but have nothing in them. These are perfect for creating homemade animations because, like regular video layers, the paint strokes you apply are only valid on that particular frame. With standard layers, if you were to paint, that paint stroke would last for the duration of the timeline. That's fine for backgrounds and static objects, but not for animating characters.

To create a new blank video layer in an existing document, select Layer > Video Layers > New Blank Video Layer. You can then paint on each frame, and each frame will be completely independent of the frames around it.

Using Onion Skins

Unfortunately, there is a problem with the cel animation capabilities as described in the preceding section. As you draw your animations, how do you know what you drew on the previous frame? Let's say you were drawing a character dancing. It would be important to use the prior frame for reference when drawing the current frame. The ability to see previous (and even future) adjacent frames is provided by the Onion Skin feature.

Open the file dancing.psd from the Chapter 9 folder (**FIGURE 9.31**). In this file, I've created a new blank video layer, and I've drawn the first frame of a stick figure about to dance. Advance to the next frame and turn on the Onion Skin feature by clicking the Toggle Onion Skins button (**FIGURE 9.32**). The Onion Skin feature allows you to see a faded version of the Altered Video on the previous frame (**FIGURE 9.33**). You can use this frame as a basis for drawing future frames. The frame is locked and unselectable, and it appears only as a guide to help you create adjacent frames.

FIGURE 9.31 The dancing.psd file.

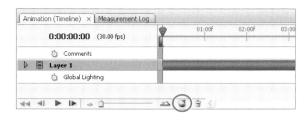

FIGURE 9.32 The Toggle Onion Skins button.

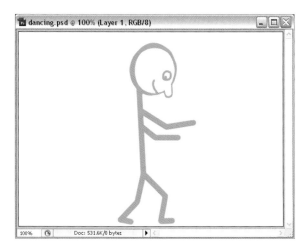

FIGURE 9.33 After turning on onion skins, you can easily paint the next frame of your cel animation.

NOTE To adjust settings for onion skins, (such as how many frames are displayed by the skins and the opacity of the onion skins), select Onion Skin Settings from the Animation (Timeline) palette menu.

Compositing

Compositing is the process of combining elements, which is a huge topic, and there's quite a bit to it. Photoshop gives you several great ways to combine imported objects. You'll spend the remainder of this chapter looking at two of my favorites: Blend modes and the brand new Stack modes.

Compositing Using Blend Modes

Opacity is a somewhat simple method to composite layers. It's not very intelligent, and it just performs a basic fade. Blend modes allow layers to interact with each other in more complex ways. For example, if I put a layer in Overlay mode, it removes 50% gray and uses colors brighter than 50% gray to lighten the layers underneath it; colors darker than 50% gray darken the layers beneath it. This is remarkably useful for blending layers together.

Let's look at a practical example. Reopen the file storm.psd from the Chapter 9 folder. Turn on the visibility of the white blob layer (**FIGURE 9.34**). Next, you'll bring in a video clip of some lightning. You could select File > Open and drag and drop the lightning video into your existing document, but there's a better way. Select Layer > Video Layers > New Video Layer from File. In the Add Video Layer dialog, navigate to the Chapter 9 folder and select the lightning.mov file. The lightning clip is added on top of your existing layers. Because of its black

FIGURE 9.34 The storm.psd file with the white blob layer's visibility turned on.

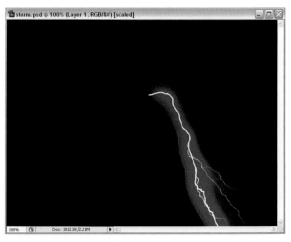

FIGURE 9.35 After importing the lightning.mov clip, it takes up the entire document. This obscures the view of the layers beneath it.

background, it obscures the view of all layers beneath it (**FIGURE 9.35**). That's not good. If you simply faded the Opacity value of the layer with the lightning, it would also fade the intensity of the lightning and the blue glow around it. And if you applied black uniformly to the layers beneath, even at a very low Opacity value, it would darken every pixel of the layers below. Your highlights are too important to do that.

So instead, you can change the Blend mode of Layer 1 (the layer with lightning). The Blend modes are found at the top of the Layers palette (**FIGURE 9.36**). From this drop-down list, choose Screen. Screen removes black and brightens highlights, which gives you exactly the results you're looking for (**FIGURE 9.37**).

FIGURE 9.36 Access the Blend modes from the drop-down list at the top of the Layers palette.

FIGURE 9.37 The Screen Blend mode not only knocks out black, but it intensifies the light colors of the lightning.

Even though compositing is a hefty subject, Blend modes can do an otherwise tedious task instantly. I highly recommend perusing the Help system to become familiar with the various Blend modes available to you.

Compositing Using Stack Modes

Before proceeding, I have to provide a small disclaimer. Most likely, Stack modes will be the coolest feature you've seen all year, but the final result is only an image. If similar tools could be applied to video and then output to video, that would be amazing. But unfortunately, such is not the case quite yet.

Stack modes combine images in a stack and process them. The best way to explain Stack modes is to just let you see them in action. Open the curvy road.psd file from the Chapter 9 folder (**FIGURE 9.38**). To use Stack modes, you first need to set up an image stack. When doing this from video, it can be a little tedious, so I've done it for you. For this setup, I imported a video clip, flattened the frames into layers, and then made frames from the layers to create a series of still images.

FIGURE 9.38 The curvy road.psd file.

To understand what Stack modes do, you need to understand the contents of this footage. The clip is taken from a video of a road, with cars driving on the road and in front of the camera. It's extremely important to note that in all of the frames there is never a good shot of the road. But that's okay. You'll isolate the road by using Stack modes.

In the Layers palette, select the bottom layer, Frame 0, and then scroll to the top of the layer stack and Shift-click Frame 113 to select all of the layers in this document. Right-click on the name of any of the layers and choose Convert to Smart Object. All of the layers condense to become a single Smart Object. This step is crucial. If you're not working with a Smart Object, you won't be able to use Stack modes.

Press the spacebar to preview this document. Even though this one layer is a Smart Object, it can still play back the image sequence it contains.

With the image sequence converted to a Smart Object, you're ready to use Stack modes to combine the images that make up the Smart Object. Select Layer > Smart Objects > Stack Mode > Median to average all of the images and keep only what is constant throughout the frames. In this case, all of the cars are eliminated from the resulting image (**FIGURE 9.39**). The result is pretty impressive, especially when considering that there wasn't a single frame of this animation that didn't have a car in it. You can also try experimenting with the Mean mode to help remove noise from an image sequence.

FIGURE 9.39 The Median Stack mode averages all frames and completely eliminates unwanted objects that are not consistent from frame to frame.

NOTE Stack modes are completely nondestructive. You can change modes at any time because they are not cumulative. You can also select None to remove any applied Stack modes.

The Stack modes feature is really intended for technical imaging, not video. From my experiments, most of the other Stack modes return useless results, although some of them create visually odd and interesting patterns. Try exploring what the modes do to your image stacks. But be aware that the Help system isn't very helpful to most people when searching for information about Stack modes. For example, if you search on the Kurtosis mode to find out what it does, the Help system provides you with this answer:

"kurtosis = (sum((value – mean)^4) over non-transparent pixels) / ((number of non-transparent pixels – 1) * (standard deviation)^4)."

And because I'm more of a graphics/movies/video games nerd than a science/math nerd, this explanation doesn't help me at all.

NOTE   You can still access your original frames by double-clicking on the Smart Object's layer thumbnail.

10

Plug-ins and Resources

No software program stands alone—not even Photoshop. In this chapter, I'll briefly describe other plug-ins and software applications to help you get the most from Photoshop CS3 Extended, or to take Photoshop to the next level. After all, it's the debut appearance of these new Extended features, so there's a lot of room to grow in the future.

The worlds of Photoshop, 3D, and video are all vast, and each offers its own set of challenges to master. It's beyond the scope of this book to train you to be experts in all of these areas. So, I'll share with you some extra resources if you're interested in furthering your study in any of these domains.

Third-party Plug-in Solutions

A third-party plug-in is a software program that adds additional functionality to an application and is created by another vendor. Photoshop CS3 Extended benefits greatly from some of the plug-ins created by other companies.

Strata

If I created a digital arts award show, the hands-down winner of best Photoshop CS3 Extended plug-ins would go to Strata. This company has created not just one amazing plug-in for Photoshop CS3 Extended, but an entire suite of amazing plug-ins that you just can't live without. You can purchase the Strata 3D[in] plug-ins for Photoshop Extended as three separate plug-ins: Design 3D[in], Live 3D[in], and Foto 3D[in]. For more information on these plug-ins, including free video training podcasts, go to the Strata Web site at www.strata.com.

Strata Design 3D[in]

The Design 3D[in] plug-in includes many components and is probably my favorite of all Strata products. Design 3D[in] includes the following tools:

- **Match[in].** Works with Vanishing Point to allow the placement of 3D objects in perspective.

- **Model[in].** Adds the much needed functionality of 3D modeling inside Photoshop. This plug-in allows you to either adjust existing models or create 3D models from scratch. Strata is known for creating easy-to-use 3D software, so this is a very important plug-in. Model[in] also allows you to import paths from Adobe Illustrator to use to create 3D models.

- **Render[in].** Allows you to create a high-end, photorealistic render from Photoshop. As I mentioned in Chapter 2, "Playing with Lighting and Appearance Settings," Photoshop CS3 Extended does not provide a high-end rendering solution. That means you'll probably never achieve a photorealistic scene with an imported 3D model. But Render[in] includes a render with advanced reflections and other such features. This plug-in also allows you to render a high-end image to a series of layers that you can further edit in Photoshop.

Strata Live 3D[in]

Strata Live 3D[in] allows you to export 3D content from Photoshop in a form that can be seen by others. It can be embedded in your 3D file, in a PDF file, or in an HTML document. And through the magic of Live 3D[in], the 3D file embedded in these documents can still be posed in 3D space. And since practically every computer user can read PDF and HTML files, you can share your 3D objects with almost everyone.

Strata Foto 3D[in]

Strata Foto 3D[in] gives you the power to create 3D textured objects from objects you've photographed. There's a little bit of a set up to it, but it's a godsend if you are new to 3D modeling. Let's say you have a new product that you are trying to display in 3D so that clients can see all dimensions of it. You could photograph it from all angles and then use Foto 3D[in] to make a textured 3D object from the photos.

Format Plug-ins

Many 3D software makers want to be a part of Photoshop CS3 Extended as well. If you are using a 3D program that is not supported by Photoshop, do a Web search to see if there is a format plug-in that allows you to import your 3D models into Photoshop. The Web site www.e-frontier.com for example, offers a free plug-in that allows you to import models from Poser 7.

NOTE If you are new to the world of 3D, Poser is a fantastic application that is tailor-made to customize, pose, and animate human figures. These models are already made for you in Poser, and all you have to do is adjust them.

Google Warehouse

Google Warehouse is an online collection of 3D models. You can search through, share, and download 3D models from Google Warehouse. Check out its Web site at sketchup.google.com/3dwarehouse.

Adobe has also created a plug-in for Photoshop CS3 Extended that allows you to browse the 3D content on Google Warehouse from Photoshop. The plug-in is available at labs.adobe.com.

LightWave Rendition

Another big player in the world of 3D is NewTek. It is the force behind Light-Wave, another professional-level 3D application. At the time of this writing, NewTek was developing a plug-in for Photoshop Extended called Rendition that allows you to use LightWave's sophisticated rendering engine to render 3D models in Photoshop. I received no response from requests to NewTek for a release date or further information. For more details check out the NewTek Web site at www.newtek.com.

Other Plug-ins

For the ultimate up-to-date list of plug-ins for Photoshop (Extended or otherwise), go to www.adobe.com/products/plugins/photoshop. The site provides a long list of the plug-ins available for Photoshop Extended, as well as contact information for the various companies that produce them.

Resources

To pursue further study in Photoshop, 3D, or video, check out the following resources that I have personally found useful. Resources are grouped by media type and are in order of helpfulness.

Photoshop Help

The Help documentation that ships with Photoshop is actually a very valuable resource. That may be hard for you to swallow if you have used the Help documents that ship with other programs, or even the Help that was in older versions of Photoshop. Adobe is changing the way that help documentation works, and kudos to the powers that be for it. On several occasions I have seen a concept better demonstrated and explained in the program's Help than in all the best books and Web sites on the subject.

To get to the Photoshop Help, click the Help menu, and select Photoshop Help. Contrary to other experiences with Help, this will not launch a simple PDF or HTML document. Instead, it launches an application called the Adobe Help

Viewer (**FIGURE 10.1**). From here, you can click on What's new? to learn about the new features in the CS3 release of Photoshop. You can also do a search for a topic from the search field in the upper-right area of the Help Viewer.

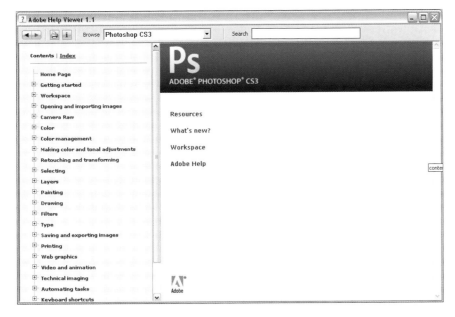

FIGURE 10.1 The Adobe Help Viewer.

The search results are very impressive. In times past, the answer to a question (assuming you could even find it) would be rhetorical and not at all helpful. For example, when looking up information on pixel aspect ratios, the Help of the past might have offered something like "to use pixel aspect ratios, click the use Pixel Aspect Ratios button." Of course, this is a fictional example, but it sounds all too familiar to those who have tried to get answers using older Help systems.

Now the Help system is much more useful because it offers real-world concepts and background instead of just describing Photoshop features. For example, look at the entry on Aspect ratio (**FIGURE 10.2** on the next page). It doesn't describe any buttons or features in Photoshop. This Help entry simply offers real-world information and background to bring you up to speed, which is why the Help Viewer is your best resource for most questions, in my opinion.

FIGURE 10.2 The Help Viewer entry on Aspect ratio.

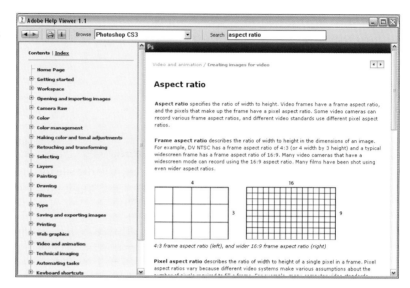

From the Browse drop-down list at the top of the interface, you can also change the Adobe program you are searching in. Let's say you want to start a video project, and you're not sure where you should start. You could open the Help Viewer, and from the Browse drop-down list select the Photoshop Help, the Premiere Pro Help, and the After Effects Help to compare their features (**FIGURE 10.3**).

FIGURE 10.3 From the Browse drop-down list in the Help Viewer, you can access the help documentation of all current and installed Adobe applications.

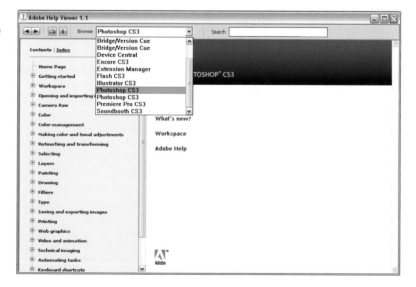

NOTE You can only browse through the Help documentation of current Adobe programs that you have installed.

Online

A multitude of online sites offer free training, whether your interest is Photoshop, 3D, or video.

If you'd like to take your Photoshop texturing skills to the next level, you can access free tutorials from sites all over the Web. However, my favorite site for free texture tutorials is without a doubt www.good-tutorials.com. The tutorials are free, concise, and well done. Also currently available on this site are free 3DS Max tutorials.

For 3D, sites like www.3dbuzz.com, www.3dcafe.com, and www.3d-tutorial.com are tremendous resources. 3D Buzz offers free training videos, great forums, and even some high-quality online classes for a small fee. If you have a question about which 3D program to invest your money and time in, this is a great place to start.

Creative Cow, at www.creativecow.net, is another standard resource for increasing your knowledge of video and video-related issues and programs.

To master any of these disciplines, I highly recommend the training at lynda.com. Lynda.com offers high-quality video-based software training from some of the best authors in the business. Here you can find video training on Photoshop, 3D programs, video programs and issues, as well as everything from Microsoft Office to Web design and coding. I've authored a number of training courses for lynda.com, including training on 3DS Max 9 and Photoshop Extended. Video-based training is often a really enjoyable way to learn. Although lynda.com is a great resource, the cost for a monthly subscription is ridiculously inexpensive for all the training it allows you to access. My favorite training on lynda.com is the standout Photoshop training from the legendary Deke McClelland. If you truly want to become a Photoshop master, I would whole-heartedly recommend his courses.

Podcasts

Podcasts are audio and video files that are typically free. They can be viewed through iTunes or other free players. Many times, they are iPod ready, so you can download them to your iPod or other portable media player and watch or listen to them on the go.

My brother Todd and I have created an entertaining and informative video podcast. Between the two of us, we train on every major Adobe application. Our podcast is called the All Things Adobe podcast, which you can download for free on iTunes or directly from our Web site at www.chadandtoddcast.com.

Podcasts are a great way to learn Photoshop. Dozens of very high-quality, free podcasts offer all sorts of great Photoshop tips and tricks. To find them, simply do a Google or iTunes search for Photoshop podcasts.

From my experience, I've found a great deal of free training podcasts for Photoshop, but not nearly as many for 3D or video.

Books

Books are also a great way to learn technical concepts, such as those you've learned about in this book. But I'm very picky about my books. The one book that I can heartily recommend to you is Ben Willmore's *Photoshop CS3 Studio Techniques* (Peachpit, 2008). I've read each edition of this *Studio Techniques* series since Photoshop version 6. Ben Willmore is a master at explaining hard to grasp concepts, and he gives each edition of his book a complete overhaul. I've purchased every edition of this book and will continue to do so for as long as Ben writes them.

Index